Child Sexual Assault

Also by Sheila Kershaw

CONFRONTING PREJUDICE: Lesbian and Gay Issues in Social Work Education
(*co-author*)

Also by Joy Trotter

NO-ONE'S LISTENING: Mothers, Fathers and Child Sexual Abuse

CONFRONTING PREJUDICE: Lesbian and Gay Issues in Social Work Education
(*co-author*)

Child Sexual Assault

Feminist Perspectives

Edited by

Pat Cox
Senior Lecturer
University of Central Lancashire

Sheila Kershaw
Senior Lecturer in Social Work
Leeds Metropolitan University

Joy Trotter
Senior Lecturer
University of Teesside

Foreword by Liz Kelly

Consultant Editor: Jo Campling

palgrave
macmillan

Published by
PALGRAVE MACMILLAN
Houndmills, Basingstoke, Hampshire RG21 6XS and
175 Fifth Avenue, New York, N. Y. 10010
Companies and representatives throughout the world

PALGRAVE MACMILLAN is the global academic imprint of the Palgrave
Macmillan division of St. Martin's Press, LLC and of Palgrave Macmillan Ltd.
Macmillan® is a registered trademark in the United States, United Kingdom
and other countries. Palgrave is a registered trademark in the European
Union and other countries.

ISBN-13: 978–0–333–77153–2
ISBN-10: 0–333–77153–2

This book is printed on paper suitable for recycling and made from fully
managed and sustained forest sources. Logging, pulping and manufacturing
processes are expected to conform to the environmental regulations of the
country of origin.

A catalogue record for this book is available from the British Library.

Library of Congress Catalog Card Number: 00–042077

Printed and bound in Great Britain by
CPI Antony Rowe, Chippenham and Eastbourne

Pat would like to dedicate this book to Jenni, Sheila, John and Tom Taylor, for their support, love and belief in her; to Robert Hepworth for happiness; and to Jo Campling, who many years ago encouraged her to think about a book.

Sheila would like to dedicate this book to her mother and to her late father, 'who'd be oh so proud'.

Contents

Part III: Into the Future   161

Foreword

Disconnection or Connections: or Will We Ever Learn?

Liz Kelly

The story of writing this foreword is one which speaks to the best of feminist process – a lengthy dialogue, involving thinking deeply about the lives of women and children, how we make sense of them, the implications of the language we use, and the connections between theory and practice. It has been an example of feminist praxis. I read and commented on each chapter in draft form and have been deeply moved by how seriously each of the authors responded to these engagements of the mind. Feminists have long recognized that our collective endeavours are invariably more powerful and effective than our individual efforts, and this book is yet one more example of this truism.

By the time this book is in print it will be over twenty years since the first of my friends told me about being sexually abused by her father. The next year I began work on the research, which would seven years later be published as *Surviving Sexual Violence* (Kelly, 1988). In listening to women's accounts of violence and abuse I remembered my own smaller encounters as a girl and young woman with abusive men outside the family. The reflections in this foreword draw on my involvement with the development of feminist perspectives on sexual abuse in childhood, the issues raised in this book, and those which pre-occupy current discussions and debates between feminists.

It is remarkable (and perhaps also revealing) that most of the key texts which sparked this wave of feminist work on sexual abuse are now out of print (for example, Armstrong, 1978; Driver and Droisen, 1989; Herman, 1981; Kelly, 1988; MacLeod and Saraga, 1988; Nelson, 1982; Rush, 1980; Ward, 1984). Acknowledging the profound challenges these texts issued to the prevailing orthodoxies of the day, in terms of both explanation and intervention, is necessary and important. The significance of 'memory bearing women' and 'memory bearing texts' cannot be overestimated, since they remind us not just of the origins of certain ideas, but also the contexts in which they were first voiced. The necessity of writing our own history accurately has become all the more important in these days when accounts of the history of second wave feminism do an injustice to the complex history and impact of a diverse and ever changing movement (Cameron, 1993; Kelly, Burton and Regan, 1996; Radford, 1994; Richardson, 1996).

It is appropriate that the central focus of this book is feminist practice, since this is where we would hope to find, and indeed ought to be looking for, the legacies of the early challenges. Unlike the earlier literature which drew primarily on the testimonies of adult survivors, the emphasis here is very definitely on children and young people. I welcome this, while at the same time having a slight regret that the needs and experiences of adult survivors are not addressed. Thoughtful reflections on the contribution of survivors groups, practice in rape crisis centres and feminist work in mental health are stories which still need to be told.

The title of the foreword draws on the ideas of Robin Morgan, specifically two quotes from *'The Demon Lover': On the Sexuality of Terrorism* (1989):

> If I had to name one quality as the genius of patriarchy it would be compartmentalism, the capacity for institutionalising disconnection.... The past parted from the present, disjoined from the future. Law detached from justice. Vision dissociated from reality.
>
> (Morgan, 1989, p.51)

> If I had to characterise one quality as the genius of feminist thought, culture and action it would be connectivity, and this involves noticing. In its rejection of the static this capacity is witty and protean.... It is therefore a volatile capacity – dangerous to every imaginable status quo, because of its insistence on noticing. Such noticing involves both attentiveness and recognition, and is in fact a philosophical and activist technique for being in the world, as well as for changing the world.
>
> (Morgan, 1989, p.53)

The themes of connection and disconnection thread through each of the sections that follow, and can also be found in many of the chapters.

Which story is told

We have become accustomed to representations of the 1980s as the decade in which sexual abuse in childhood was 'discovered': unearthed from layers of historical disbelief and denial. Adults of all ages began to speak of the pain of their childhood; professionals and institutions acknowledged their failure to notice, hear or suspect; societies began to face the implications of this disturbing knowledge.

But this is the story of late twentieth century policy and media recognition, it is not the history of child abuse. Both child welfare organisations and feminists were aware of sexual abuse and sexual exploitation in the nineteenth century, of physical abuse of children and women in families, and first wave feminists made connections between woman and child abuse (Gordon, 1989). What we have witnessed is a process of *re-discovery,* in which feminists have again made connections. What is different is the extent of research and media attention given to the issues: both have contributed to a context in which distinctions rather than connections, novelty rather than historical accuracy, have been the order of the day. Ignorance of history has fostered the fiction that sexual abuse in childhood was discovered and defined by social workers/researchers, rather than being the outcome of women and children seeking belief, justice and change.

Sexual abuse in childhood has ceased to be unspeakable – this euphemistic unease, which has been justly named a 'silence', was decisively broken early in the second wave of the feminist movement, where one of the earliest forms of activism were 'speakouts' on sexual violence. Sexual abuse has been named, and children and adults have graphically described their experiences. What it is possible to tell, however, depends crucially upon what others are able and willing to hear. As women and children spoke the unspeakable, our vocabulary and emotions were continually stretched, as was our credulity. Both the extent and forms of abuse that children and adults revealed, alongside the findings of paediatricians in babies as young as a few months have merged in a catalogue of horror which has been difficult to contemplate let alone comprehend. And it should come as no surprise that it has been feminists who have been among those who have listened and tried to make sense of accounts of the sadistic physical and sexual torture which comprises ritual abuse (see Nelson, this volume) and the emerging evidence that some women are involved in this and other forms of sexual abuse (Kelly, 1991; 1996b). It was feminists in South East Asia and in the west who exposed prostitution tourism in the late 1980s – (Haruhi, Ymi and Naoko, 1987; O'Connell Davidson,1995) and provided trenchant critiques of the sex industry's exploitation of women and children (Barry 1979; Dworkin, 1981; Jeffreys, 1998) – issues which were only recognized on the international child welfare agendas in the 1990s.

From listening and believing to 'statement validity analysis'

As recognition of sexual abuse grew two new principles emerged – that adults should listen to and believe children. Books were published and read which reported direct experience, and television programmes gave space to the pain, rage and anger of adult survivors. But as several chapters note, in the last few years the voices and experiences of children, adult survivors and protective parents have got smaller and smaller. The voices and perspectives that dominate public discourse today are those of professional 'experts'. Survivors are only required by the media to speak their pain, to – in the all too revealing language of journalism – make features 'sexier'. What the media want in the late 1990s are not survivors, but victims – young people and adults who will tell their stories of hurt and damage, and preferably cry on camera (see Armstrong, 1994 for an incisive feminist account of this shift). Carers and parents are invited to tell their stories only when they fit the preferred themes of insensitive and unjust agency intervention or of false accusations.

The complex issues involved for carers in making sense of confusing knowledge/experience/information, of daring to name what is happening as abuse, of struggling with what to do and what the consequences might be of doing or not doing it are seldom addressed, let alone understood. Several chapters attest to the fact that too often mothers who act as protective parents are still treated appallingly by agencies charged with child protection. Neither the feminist critiques of the 1980s, nor the more recent connections made between child abuse and domestic violence (Humphreys, 1997; Mullender and Morley, 1994; Mullender and Humphreys, 1999) have taken root in child protection practice. Yet the principle of woman protection often being the most effective form of child protection would undoubtedly result in better outcomes for many children.

Both children and adult survivors have heard a consistent message throughout the 1990s, that they should tell, and if they do they will be listened to, protected and have access to justice. But the promises have not been kept: hardly any reported sexual abuse cases result in criminal prosecutions; civil child protection findings of sexual abuse are not considered sufficient to remove rights of abusive fathers to contact with the children they have abused; those children who are taken into care for their own protection all too frequently are re-victimized; and long-term support services for children and adult survivors are so scarce as to be virtually non-existent.

The policy rhetoric of 'the best interests of the child' conceals a contradiction: that children (and adults abused as children) have become 'objects of concern', their painful histories a terrain on which adults vie for authority and position (Armstrong, 1994). In the desire to protect institutions rather than children, intervention is now directed not at discovering the truth but formulated around legalistic and forensic concerns about evidence. We have moved rapidly from the position of believing children to one where their story is frequently only considered valid if a high status adult will vouch for it. The scale of this shift can be seen in the development of so-called scientific methods such as 'statement validity analysis'; the only purpose of such techniques is to provide adults with tools through which they 'assess' the credibility of children's accounts. It is worth noting at this point, that no similar methods have even been mooted, let alone developed, to assess the validity of the denials of those accused of abuse.

From survival to damage

The choice of the word survivor by the first self-help group in London in the early 1980s was intended to move away from the negative meanings which attach to the word 'victim', to recognize the strengths that coping with abuse at the time and later, requires. It was part of a move to view sexual abuse and its aftermaths as complex realities which children and adults struggle to make sense of, which have legacies which have to be lived with. It also signified recognition that survivors were everywhere, in every gathering of significant numbers of people – in churches, work teams, women's groups, sports clubs, universities. Abuse was normalized; it involved 'people like us', whoever 'us' was.

The preferred story now is one of damage – of survivors who populate prisons, mental health services, who have problems with alcohol and drugs. One consequence of this disconnection has been a 're-silencing' – with professionals becoming increasingly reluctant to name themselves as survivors. Silence has once again become a form of survival – since one's own experience is no longer understood as a resource to be drawn on, enabling an informed advocacy, but viewed as dangerous partiality, which will interfere with professional judgement. Claiming a public 'identity' as a survivor has always been a troubled decision, but there is no doubt that the 'damage discourse' has increased the costs of 'coming out'. While everyone makes their own decisions about revealing aspects of personal history, part of what must be taken into account here is the increased vulnerability of those whose public visibility means they cannot go back into the 'safety' of secrecy, and the decrease of adult role models for children and young people who are beginning their search for meaning.

From sexual abuse to commercial exploitation

During the 1990s awareness of the ways in which adults organize abuse networks, and the connections with child pornography and child prostitution, increased. At first in Europe this official recognition was focused on 'elsewhere' – sexual exploitation of children in developing countries by white western men. But in the last few years attention has shifted 'closer to home'. While feminist analysis has had a profound influence on how sexual abuse in the family is understood, it has had less influence with regard to sexual exploitation. And this is despite the fact that in South East Asia and other areas of the world, feminists have been at the forefront of struggles against sexual exploitation of women and children.

This was very clear to me at several European seminars and at the International Congress on Sexual Exploitation in Stockholm. Very few of the delegates were willing to recognize that child pornography is sometimes produced in familial contexts, and child prostitution may be organized by fathers, brothers or boyfriends. Many wanted to resist including anything in sexual exploitation which did not involve a 'commercial' monetary element. Too many in the international children's rights movement know next to nothing about sexual abuse in any context, but they do know about child labour. For them shifting the focus from 'sex' to 'exploitation' is much more comfortable. What gets lost are the connections feminist analysis involves:

* the use of sex as a form of power
* the fact that children and women are victimized in many relationships and contexts

- that pornography and prostitution are not separate from, but intimately connected to, other forms of male violence, including the abuse of adult women by/in the sex industry
- that much child pornography and child prostitution is not 'commercially' driven, but produced and organized for personal consumption and satisfaction by individuals or small networks of abusers.

From child abusers to paedophiles

Part of this shifting of attention has involved what I call 'the return of the paedophile' (Kelly, 1996a). This change in language has been so rapid in Britain that many in the child protection field have begun using 'paedophile' as either a collective term for all abusers or to refer to what is presumed to be a particular type of abuser (usually those who abuse outside the family).

Immediately the word 'paedophile' is used, we move away from recognition of abusers as 'ordinary men' – fathers, brothers, uncles, colleagues, neighbours – and are returned to the more comfortable view of them as 'other', a small minority who are fundamentally different from most men. That they have lives, kinship links and jobs, disappears from view in the desire to focus on their difference. Attention shifts from the centrality of power and control to notions of sexual deviance, obsession and 'addiction'. 'Paedophilia' returns us to the medical and individualized explanations which we have spent so much time and energy attempting to replace. Rather than sexual abuse demanding that we look critically at the social construction of 'normal' masculinity and male sexuality, the safer terrain of 'abnormality' beckons.

The disconnection of 'paedophiles' in much of the clinical literature on sex offenders not just from men in general, but also from men who sexually abuse children in familial contexts, means important connections are ignored. Connections in the forms of abuse, in the strategies abusers use to entrap, control and silence children are lost. This means that investigations of 'familial sexual abuse' seldom involve either searches for child pornography or suspicions about possible abuse by other men. This contrasts with what we know from adult survivors who tell of relatives showing them pornography, expecting them to imitate it and being required to pose for it. Some also tell of being prostituted by relatives. A significant proportion of organized networks are based within families.

Few of the men who abuse children in prostitution fit clinical definitions of 'paedophile': men whose sexual interest is confined to children. Sarah Swann (1998) who founded a Barnardo's project supporting young women trapped in prostitution asks: 'What is a paedophile anyway? As far as we can see on this project, he's over 30, drives a nice car and has a wife and kids.' Julia O'Connell Davidson (1995) has documented how many men involved in prostitution tourism are 'opportunistic' child abusers – if young women are available they will pay for sex with them, as well as with adult women.

Information given to me by an Australian woman visiting the UK to look at work on sexual assault of older women, revealed the danger of this particular form of disconnection. She noted recent reports that as protective policies get stronger, 'paedophiles' are shifting from seeking work in children's homes and children's organisations and are moving into services for the elderly. Just what does the term 'paedophile' mean in this context? What this example demonstrates vividly is that the issue here is power and control and the desire not to get caught. It also highlights the continuing importance of feminists noticing and making connections.

From abuse of power to cycles of abuse

But analyses which make power a central feature have also lost ground: within the media, parliament, and most professional groups the preferred explanation has become 'cycle of abuse'. 'Cycle of abuse' is based on a psychic determinism: experience 'A' leads to behaviour 'B' with minimal choice/agency in between. It is also an explanation which, through its gender neutrality, disconnects theory from evidence: in particular that girls are more likely to be abused, and that men have a virtual monopoly on perpetration. If cycles of abuse are so inevitable where are the thousands of female abusers?

Apart from offering abusers carte blanche to avoid responsibility, this explanation makes the thousands of survivors who, as result of their own experiences, choose to never treat children in similar ways invisible, even logically impossible. This pernicious idea does an outrageous injustice to countless women and men whose courageous and passionate testimony made sexual abuse in childhood a social issue. It also subverts support for children, since the aim becomes preventing them 'repeating the cycle' rather than enabling them to cope with having been victimized. A recent twist is the shift from talking about the sexualized behaviour some children who have been abused display as 'acting out' to defining children as young as 3 and 4 as 'abusers'. But 'breaking cycles' is a much easier and safer goal to explore than changing the structure of relations between genders and generations.

From denial to resistance of knowledge

One of the words I remember being used most in discussions and conferences about sexual abuse in the 1980s was 'denial', that there was individual and collective denial of the extent and realities of abuse. Today (and perhaps this was always the case) it is more accurate to talk about resistance – the knowledge is there, but both it and its implications are resisted.

There remains huge resistance to the basic message of who or what the main problems are: male abuse; systems ill-suited to children's needs and competencies; structures which are founded on preventing 'disasters' rather than enabling staff, and delivering justice and restitution for children.

From child-centred practice to children's rights and children's perspectives

This shift can be traced through the emergence of sexual abuse as an issue in the late twentieth century. While not wishing to detract from the importance of children's rights or of taking account of children's perspectives, child-centred practice placed the actions and responsibilities of adults at the centre of the discussion. At the same time, there is a danger of forgetting the ways in which children's understandings and perspectives have been controlled and manipulated by abusers. Most professionals are familiar with the concept of 'grooming', but this is only seen as relevant to initial access, rather than also being an ongoing process of controlling the child and environment, to maintain access and secrecy. Children's sense of self and what things mean is deliberately distorted through this element of abuse.

Our task is not simply to listen to children, to take account of their perspectives, but to enable them to unpick the lies and distortions which are invariably an integral element of sexual abuse. For example, should we just accept it as 'children's perspectives' when children say they do not want their abuser to go to prison, or do we think to ask them 'why?' And if in asking why we discover that they have been told that if they tell this is what will happen and it will be their fault, what do we do? Do we dare explore underneath the perspectives of children and adult survivors that their mother knew – can we (and they) bear to know that fathers groom the environment just like other abusers, that they deliberately abuse children in contexts intended to make the child believe that the mother knows (Laing, 1999)? How do we create a balance between children being consulted, listened to and respected, and a feminist praxis which engages critically with ways perceptions have been distorted and responsibility inappropriately assigned?

Making connections

Many of the accounts of how abuse in children's homes was ignored and covered up highlight the ways in which whistle blowers are isolated and discredited. But aren't all survivors who tell whistle blowers – naming fathers biological, fathers theological, and fathers sociological as abusers is not a route to popularity. When feminists name men as the group most culpable for the prevalence of sexual abuse the response is all too similar. When any of us chooses to blow the whistle we are taking on the powerful – the person who chooses to use 'power over' a child for their own needs and gratification, who is all too frequently also a person who has forms of structural power, and a location in powerful systems and institutions. Blowing the whistle is a declaration of intent, a challenge to forms of power which have been presumed to be secure. It is no wonder whistle blowers are seen as a threat, and why such efforts are made to discredit them. Here again we need to keep our eyes on connections – the similarities in the ways whistle blowers, be they survivors, colleagues, feminists (and possibly all three) are discounted.

Reflecting on what a feminist agenda for action should be in the late 1990s, my attention is drawn to those children and adults we are failing the most: girls in care where re-victimisation is commonplace, and who are also targeted by pimps; adult survivors who reach the point where they can no longer cope with the unresolved legacies of abuse and for whom services are virtually non-existent; mothers, especially those who are also being abused, who endeavour valiantly to protect their own children, yet are ordered by the courts to send their children on contact visits; and women who reveal that it is their own history of childhood abuse which made them suspicious or able to believe their child, only to find that this makes agencies either suspicious of their belief or doubtful of their ability to protect the child.

I live in hope that some time soon, a child or group of children will make contact with a lawyer with enough vision and awareness to enable them to take agencies to court for 'failure to protect'. If we are honest we have all 'failed to protect' in so far as sometimes we have not heard what children have been trying to tell us, or been unable to craft an intervention which kept them safe – but it is only mothers who are targeted for culpability in theory, law and practice.

I sometimes despair about what it will take to create a residential care system which protects children. We have had scandals, enquiries and media coverage, all pointing to a series of key areas which need addressing. The results have been national and local policies replete with fine sounding words, but on the ground the system continues to fail children and workers alike. Policies on planned admission and appropriate placements are broken every day through reactive crisis management: the multiple placements which are the inevitable consequence mean we compound the damage and have even more resentful children. Disaffected and exhausted workers have more time off work, with the outcome that their colleagues are working shifts of 27 hours on their own; how can they aspire to anything more than damage limitation? Addressing these material realities as part of what contributes to negative cultures within children's homes is as important as all the recent emphasis on screening for abusers.

Noticing what has happened in service provision over the last decade brings not only statutory services into the frame but also the large children's charities. Many of them, like our current government, seem to be driven by media agendas and 'flavours of the month', rather than what we know about what children need and what makes a difference. Being a 'dedicated follower of fashion' means that mundane everyday sexual abuse is less worthy of interest and investment, and projects which have been vital local resources for children and protective parents are scaled down or de-funded in order to develop something 'new'. We need some form of accountability for children's charities in terms of the services they offer. We also need to notice the ways in which some of the children's charities have colonized feminist work, taking on aspects which are less threatening and eschewing the deeper challenges to current orthodoxies. The most obvious current example of this is the NSPCC 'Full Stop' campaign. While no-one could criticize the ambition of ending child cruelty, the philosophical underpinning of the campaign seems vague to say the least – as one friend put it: 'it's a full stop and no sentence'. Compare this, and the resources that have been invested in it, with the thoroughness and clarity of feminist prevention work (such as the Zero Tolerance campaigns, the Respect pack developed in Hackney and the developmental work undertaken in a primary school in Cottingley, Leeds).

Through the teaching and training I do, it is also evident that many of the most strategic workers in children and young people's lives are still not being given the skills, information and framework they need in order to be an effective resource. For example, how many residential staff, nursery workers, teachers and youth workers get adequate training (at qualification and in-service levels)? And we might want to ask the question also about social workers, the police service and others. Can one lecture on domestic violence in a social work diploma course be enough to equip workers to work with the overlaps between woman and child protection? And this is before we even think about access to feminist ideas and perspectives. Feminist ideas are no longer as fashionable as they were, and it has become *de rigeur* in many academic and vocational courses to critique feminist ideas. This is increasingly replacing any engagement with the fundamental questions feminist analysis raised about the family, childhood and adulthood.

I am acutely aware of the tenacity of ideas which justify aggressive masculinity and blame women for their own and their children's experiences of victimization. We need to explore in more depth than we have why such ideological beliefs are so impervious to change: is it that people really believe them, or are these ways of thinking simply excuses for non-intervention, or for not having to question one's own implication in systems of power and control?

My hope is that this book will be both a support to all those who still use feminist ideas to inform their work and be an introduction to the continued relevance of feminist perspectives to those who have had limited access to them, thus far. We need to continue noticing, making connections between forms of abuse, and between ourselves and the women and children whose voices and needs must not be allowed to disappear again.

References

Armstrong, L. (1978) *Kiss Daddy Goodnight*, New York, Pocket Books.
Armstrong, L. (1994) *Rocking the Cradle of Sexual Politics: What Happened When Women Said Incest*, New York, Addison Wesley.

Barry, K. (1979) *Female Sexual Slavery*, New York, Prentice Hall.

Cameron, D. (1993) 'Telling it like it wasn't: how radical feminism became history' *Trouble and Strife*, 27, pp.11–15.

Driver, E. and A. Droisen (eds) (1989) *Child Sexual Abuse: Feminist Perspectives*, London, Macmillan.

Dworkin, A. (1981) *Pornography: Men Possessing Women*, London, The Women's Press.

Gordon, L. (1989) *Heroes of their Own Lives: The Politics and History of Family Violence*, London, Virago.

Haruhi, T., T. Ymi and L. Naoko (1987) 'For a song: female sexual slavery in Asia' *Trouble and Strife*, 12, pp.10–15.

Herman, J. L. (1981) *Father–Daughter Incest*, Cambridge MA, Harvard University Press.

Humphreys, C. (1997) *Case Planning Issues where Domestic Violence Occurs in the Context of Child Protection. Report to Coventry Social Services Child Protection Unit*, Coventry, Coventry City Council Social Services Department.

Jeffreys, S. (1998) *The Idea of Prostitution*, Melbourne, Spinifex Press.

Kelly, L. (1988) *Surviving Sexual Violence*, Cambridge, Polity Press.

Kelly, L. (1991) 'Unspeakable acts: women who abuse' *Trouble and Strife*, 21, pp.13–20.

Kelly, L. (1996a) 'Weasel words: paedophiles and cycles of abuse', *Trouble and Strife*, 33, pp.44–9.

Kelly, L. (1996b) 'When does the speaking profit us?: reflections on the challenges of developing feminist perspectives on abuse and violence by women', in M. Hester, L. Kelly and J. Radford (eds) *Women, Violence and Male Power*, Buckingham, Open University Press.

Kelly, L., S. Burton and L. Regan (1996) 'Beyond victim or survivor: sexual violence, identity and feminist theory and practice' in L. Adkins and V. Merchant (eds) *Sexualizing the Social: Power and the Organization of Sexuality*, London, Macmillan.

Laing, L. (1999) 'A different balance altogether? Incest offenders in treatment', in J. Breckenridge and L. Laing (eds) *Challenging Silence: Innovative Responses to Sexual and Domestic Violence*, London, Allen and Unwin.

MacLeod, M. and E. Saraga (1988) 'Challenging the orthodoxy; towards a feminist theory and practice' *Feminist Review Special Issue on Child Sexual Abuse*, 28, pp.16–55.

Morgan, R. (1989) *'The Demon Lover': On the Sexuality of Terrorism*, London, Methuen.

Mullender, A. and R. Morley (eds) (1994) *Children Living with Domestic Violence: Putting Men's Abuse of Women on the Child Care Agenda*, London, Whiting and Birch.

Mullender, A. and C. Humphreys (1999) *Domestic Violence and Child Abuse: Policy and Practice Issues for Local authorities and Other Agencies*, London, LGA Publications.

Nelson, S. (1982) *Incest: Fact and Myth*, Edinburgh, Stramullion Press.

O' Connell Davidson, J. (1995) 'British sex tourists in Thailand' in M. Maynard and J. Purvis (eds) *(Hetero) Sexual Politics*, London, Taylor and Francis.

Radford, J. (1994) 'History of the Women's Liberation Movement in Britain: a reflective personal account' in G. Griffin, M. Hester, S. Rai and S. Roseneil (eds) *Stirring It: Challenges for Feminism*, London, Taylor and Francis.

Richardson, D. (1996) '"Misguided, dangerous and wrong": on the maligning of radical feminism', in R. Klein and D. Bell (eds) *Radically Speaking: Feminism Reclaimed*, London, Zed Books.

Rush, F. (1980) *The Best Kept Secret: Sexual Abuse of Children*, New York, McGraw Hill.

Swann, S. (1998) 'Barnardo's Streets and Lanes Project' in *Whose Daughter Next? Children Abused through Prostitution*, Ilford, Barnardo's.

Ward, E. (1984) *Father–Daughter Rape*, London, Women's Press.

Acknowledgements

Pat, Sheila and Joy would like to thank Liz Kelly, who generously agreed to act as our reader, who read and gave constructive feedback through a number of drafts, who encouraged the three of us and our contributors, and wrote the foreword.

Notes on Contributors

Pat Cox is a white woman of English–Irish heritage who was a social work practitioner in child care and child protection for thirteen years and who is now a Senior Lecturer based at the Faculty of Health, University of Central Lancashire, where she researches, writes and teaches. Her previous publications reflect her particular interest of keeping the issue of child sexual assault alive, and her research interests are in the areas of child protection, feminist theory, research and practice, and working with women.

Dr Lorraine Green is a research fellow in the Centre for Applied Childhood Studies and a lecturer in Sociology and Social Work at the University of Huddersfield. The material used in her chapter is drawn from her PhD thesis which dealt with issues of institutionalisation, sexuality and sexual assault in relation to children's homes. She is currently engaged in a cross-comparative European research project, examining the balance between legal intervention and therapeutic support systems in relation to child sexual assault.

Gillian Hirst is a white woman who works as a Senior Probation Officer. She began work for the Probation Service in 1980 and from 1991 to 1994 acted as Probation Tutor for the University of Liverpool Diploma in Social Work course. She has taken an active role in responding to the Effective Practice Initiative and in managing the changes this requires.

Chris Horrocks is currently lecturing in psychology at the University of Huddersfield. Her main teaching contributions are in the areas of psychology, child abuse and developmental psychology. She has recently completed a three-year study of young people leaving care. Her research interests are qualitative research methods, feminist research methods and adolescence.

Kate Karban is Senior Lecturer in Social Work and Mental Health at Leeds Metropolitan University. She has worked as a social worker in children and family and mental health settings and was involved in the Residential Child Care Initiative. Her research interests include residential child care, gender and sexuality and mental health.

Sheila Kershaw is a Senior Lecturer in Social Work at Leeds Metropolitan University. Before moving into academia, she worked for many years as a children and family social worker for Bradford NSPCC and Bradford Social Services. Sheila first became aware of feminist issues in the early 1980s, through her early involvement with Women's Aid refuges and Rape Crisis Centres. Her research interests and publications focus on women's issues and gender and sexuality.

Sarah Nelson is author of *Incest: Fact and Myth* (1987), a pioneering British feminist analysis of sexual violence in the family. As a professional journalist she has written extensively on sexual abuse, including the 'Orkney affair' and subsequent Inquiry of 1991–92. She is currently a research fellow at Edinburgh University in the Department of Sociology, where her work includes the physical health consequences of child sexual assault, the role of social work, and the experience of psychiatric services by adult women survivors. She is a white feminist, and comes from Aberdeen.

Varsha Nighoskar worked as a social worker, then as an Assistant Psychologist for a Community and Mental Health Trust in the North East of England, before becoming a full-time mother.

Juliette Oko is a Senior Lecturer at the University of Teesside. Prior to this she worked as a training officer in Children and Families, as well as working in the north of England as a Children and Families social worker. She qualified in social work in 1988 and worked in London as an Adults and Approved Social Worker. Currently she teaches undergraduates and students undertaking the Diploma in Social Work and is researching issues around anti-discriminatory practice theories.

Ann Potter currently works for Barnardo's, managing a project which provides a range of therapeutic services to children and families, and which is developing services to work with children who have been sexually abused and with their safe carers. She has worked for fifteen years in local authority settings, eight of those in the capacity of Chair of Child Protection Conferences. In a personal capacity, throughout her adult life, she has been involved in a range of community activities seeking to develop mutual support networks and 'listening' services for women who have experienced abuse. Her contribution to this book is made in a personal capacity and does not necessarily reflect the views of her current employer.

Joy Trotter has been a Senior Lecturer at the University of Teesside since leaving social work practice in Cleveland in 1987. Her research areas are around child sexual assault, feminist practice and lesbian and gay issues, and she has published in these areas. She is currently completing her PhD on sexuality in secondary schools.

Introduction

Pat Cox, Sheila Kershaw and Joy Trotter

Feminist analyses, which paved the way in the 1970s and 1980s for advancing understanding of the sexual assault of Black and white children, young women and young men, have been marginalized and overlooked. This book is therefore intended to provide a much needed addition to two neglected areas of child protection theory and practice: child sexual assault and feminisms.

As long ago as 1971, Kate Millett was acknowledging men's power in families over women and children: Shulamith Firestone (1971) considered that the oppression of women and children was the prototype of all other forms of oppression. Phyllis Chesler, writing in 1972 identified the sexual abuse of female children as possibly one of the major factors conditioning female children into submissiveness (Chesler 1972). Other pioneering North American feminists such as Robin Morgan (1978) also began to consider the issue of personal and sexual politics within families. Louise Armstrong (1978) and Florence Rush (1980) focused specifically on the sexual assault of female children and established the importance of survivors accounts.

Much of the awareness about child sexual assault in Britain surfaced within women-only settings (London Rape Crisis Centre, 1984; Feminist Review Collective, 1988) and both Liz Kelly and Sarah Nelson (in this volume) were among the earliest writers to develop this knowledge and bring it to a wider audience (Kelly, 1988; Nelson, 1982). Various initiatives ensued, often independently of each other: for example, conferences at both Teesside and North London Polytechnics in 1984 and 1985; special interest groups in Liverpool, Leeds and other Social Services and allied departments. Pressure was put on managers in these and other local authorities to develop policies and practices that incorporated feminist understandings about the causes and effects of child sexual assault (see also Boushel and Noakes, 1988).

Despite this apparent wealth of information and activity, it has been interesting for us three editors (who were all practitioners in child protection throughout the 1980s) to look back over our in-service training and course materials and compare how much (or sometimes how little) feminist material was included. We now struggle to remember how and where our consciousness raising in women-only groups overlapped with the special interest groups described above, in which we listened to survivor accounts, educated ourselves and each other about new developments and attempted to influence practice. Each of us can remember racing round town in our lunch hours to acquire books as they were published (for example, Sarah Nelson's *Incest: Fact and Myth* in 1982). However, if it is difficult for those of us who lived through these times to recall details about how we developed our own awareness, how much more difficult is it now for practitioners who don't have the same access to feminist texts (many are out of print) and who work (for the most part) in settings where social work and probation practice in child sexual assault has become an issue of management, rather than one of personal and political commitment. It is perhaps significant that, although a number of us are survivors of sexual assault, no-one has chosen to discuss personal experiences in their chapter – this may also be an indirect comment on the present 'culture' in which survivors live, work and practice. It is our hope that for all of us, as well as for our readers, this book may be the beginning of reclaiming that commitment to child sexual assault as being both personal and political, as well as professional.

Attitudes towards children, young women, young men and their rights (including their right to be protected) have rarely been so complex. There are three major strands to be considered. The first strand provides a broad background where masculinity (and its acceptable face of 'new laddism') is the subject of many news items and articles. Secondly, in the field of child sexual assault and twelve years after the events in Cleveland, we have seen the publication of the government sponsored *Messages from Research* (1995) and the investigations into the abuse of children in public care in North Wales, Merseyside and Cheshire. Finally, children are attributed adult status with responsibilities as well as rights and blamed for being prostitutes and murderers: conversely, children's rights are also said to have 'gone too far' (Stephen Dorrell, speaking on Radio 4, 12 March 1997). The reality for many children, young women and young men is that their rights are only permitted as long as they do not impinge on adults in any significant way (John, 1997). While these appear to be three separate issues, it is our contention that they are not inseparable, rather they are interdependent and it is feminist analyses which clearly reveal the connections.

The genesis of this book arises from our sharing views and experiences of practice and theory in child sexual assault. We contend that, in relation to child sexual assault, all is not as it appears. While recent publications have focused on policy issues and on other child protection concerns (Dartington Social Research Unit, 1995; Utting, 1997), few have focused on practice (Parton, 1996). More importantly, of the few that do address practice, even fewer locate it in feminist contexts. More recently – struggling against the tide of interest in masculinity – other authors have revisited feminisms and women's movements (Rowbotham, 1999) but generally speaking feminist perspectives do not evoke positive responses unless formulated in ways acceptable to the 'malestream' (Carter, Everitt and Hudson, 1992).

This book, therefore, mirrors the struggle of sexually assaulted children, young women and young men to be heard. In the predominantly male worlds of academia and publishing we have struggled individually to create space for and interest in, feminist analyses. Now, because of shared beliefs, we write to reclaim the words and the language which make so many people uncomfortable. The voices of women writers and practitioners will be heard, creating another 'moment', another 'wave' (Gordon, 1989) and providing another link in the chain of historical understanding about child sexual assault. In 1997, when women workers were prevented by their employers from participating in a television documentary about the ten year anniversary of Cleveland, one of them, Sue Richardson, was only able to take part by resigning from her job. The power of the prevailing culture to determine *what* is said about child sexual assault and *who* is to say it has never seemed stronger (Richardson, 1998). The need for a counterbalance in the form of this book has never been greater.

The investigations into abuse in various parts of the North West of England and North Wales allow the notion of 'individual men as abusers' to continue. Television documentaries about abusers confirm this, as does media coverage about the exposure of individual offenders. Again, links are rarely made (Davies, 1998) between the actions of these men and the privileges enjoyed by most men in relation to the women with whom they live and work and in relation to children, young women and young men. There is confusion and inconsistency about how 'childhood' is constructed (usually as white, male, able-bodied and middle class) and about whether or not children, young women and young men are the subjects of their own lives or objects in the lives of adults (Cox and Hirst, 1996). Feminist analyses recognize the similarities between the confused messages children receive about 'agency' (Williams, 1997) and the abuses meted out to them. Also, most feminist analyses recognize differences and diversities within and between groups of children (Logan *et al*, 1996; Wilson, 1993). A starting point for all the women contributors to this book is that the rights of children, young women and young men include the right to be protected from sexual assault, in any of its myriad forms.

In writing this book we aim to introduce a new generation of practitioners, educators and students to these influential perspectives and to encourage others to revisit valuable insights into the sexual violation of children by adults, emphasizing the importance of feminist analyses within this particular social work context. We also aim to develop a greater sense of the complex interconnections between rights and responsibilities and through raising such awareness among workers and students, to provide a better understanding of the manifestations of child sexual assault.

All the contributors to the book are women, coming from different feminist positions, combining theory, practice and research. Each contributor writes from her own perspective and using her own definition of feminisms and feminist practice, rather than the book offering overarching theoretical definitions. All the women have different styles of writing and we have taken an editorial decision not to impose a false homogeneity on this publication.

Pat Cox's chapter begins with a brief overview of historical developments in the knowledge base of child sexual assault, including how feminist perspectives have been marginalised and how the language used to describe and analyse abuse has become gender-free. She considers the significant contributions of feminist perspectives and language in establishing the prevalence and extent of child sexual assault and in addressing how (predominantly) masculine cultures and constructions of masculinity contribute to the widespread occurrence of sexual assault. She analyses the influence of some of these historical developments on the present and future for social work practice and education, emphasizing that feminist aetiologies and language are vital both for understanding and for responding sensitively to child sexual assault. She concludes by suggesting that knowledge brings with it responsibilities and that 'knowing about it now' requires more of feminist practitioners and academics than is currently supposed.

Kate Karban and Chris Horrocks' chapter provides a brief review of inquiry reports relating to children who have been sexually assaulted in out-of-home settings: reports which have consistently emphasized the necessity to listen to children and young people. From a feminist perspective this seemingly uncomplicated notion may be problematic in practice. However, the chapter provides a more complex analysis. It argues that systems of corporate parenting and child protection incorporate a specific discourse within which children and young people's voices might not be heard. In order to alleviate their distress it is essential to acknowledge and challenge the objectification of children and young people which pervades the prevailing discourse of childcare and child protection. Different ways of listening are explored so that a more diverse understanding of children and young people's experiences can be presented and their voices can be heard in ways which actively engage them. While there are many commonalties among young people who have experienced sexual assault, individual life histories are complex: it is necessary to know the unique story of each individual, and to respond accordingly. The chapter concludes by considering how to create environments so that such stories can be heard.

Sarah Nelson's chapter explores the personal impact of learning about satanist ritual abuse; the process of coming to terms with this knowledge and the conflicts involved in communicating it to others. It considers the meanings of 'gullibility' and 'evidence' in a debate where 'unbelievers' have accepted uncritically the claims and distortions of accused adults. Satanist ritual abuse presents unique challenges for all who work with sexual assault and especially for feminists. The routine involvement of women in intergenerational satanist ritual abuse, especially in the socialization of children, profoundly challenges feminist assumptions about the behaviour of mothers and their assumptions about the role of women in child sexual assault. The chapter also discusses the responsibilities of feminists and explores the gendered power dynamics in the satanist ritual abuse debate.

Sheila Kershaw's chapter contributes to increased understandings about prostitution and the sex industry by considering prostitution of young people as an aspect of child sexual assault. She highlights the relevance of feminist analyses of male violence in relation to prostitution and examines the similarities and differences in the causality, structure, operation, and the effects of prostitution, upon young women and young men. Following this, she considers the implications and meanings of these similarities and differences, making particular reference to male sexuality and power. She notes that significant numbers of young people are forced into this risky and dangerous way of life and that legislative changes have increased some young people's vulnerability in terms of their health, welfare and personal safety. Fearful of having to disclose information about their lifestyle to the authorities, many prostituted young people are inadvertently denied easy access to health education and protection. Criminal and civil legislation is used against young people as punishment for their involvement, rather than being used to pursue actively the adult clients who use, exploit and assault them. Finally, in the light of her argument, Sheila considers the need for changes in thinking and practice to ensure better protection of young women and men engaged in street prostitution.

Joy Trotter's chapter presents an analysis of child protection work in relation to sexuality. Over the last two decades social workers have increased their knowledge and experience of child sexual assault yet despite considerable contributions from feminist researchers and commentators, issues around sexuality have been disregarded. The implications of this for workers and for parents of sexually assaulted children are great, and research findings illustrate a number of these. Of major importance for both workers and parents is the privacy and confidential nature of what is often profoundly personal information: the process by which some of this information becomes public is often arbitrary, the information is frequently inaccurate and the resulting responses can be damaging and dangerous. Although it is not surprising that social workers are uncertain about their practice in relation to sexuality (it is a subject that remains virtually taboo in their training, official guidelines and textbooks), this oversight, neglect or avoidance must be challenged.

Varsha Nighoskar's chapter provides a practice-based perspective on a complex area of social work: work with learning disabled parents of sexually assaulted children. It presents a case study and discussion of how many professionals struggle with crucial practice issues around managing information, communicating effectively, enhancing dialogue and empowering clients. She also demonstrates how workers contribute to the perpetuation of women's alleged responsibility and vulnerability and the chapter goes on to outline how this deters clients from communicating about child sexual assault. Drawing on her own experience of work in India and Britain, the chapter concludes by suggesting guidelines for effective communication around child sexual assault and learning disability.

Gillian Hirst's chapter explores the extent to which work with sex offenders is based on feminist understandings by analysing articles written between 1982 and 1996 from the most widely read professional journal for probation officers. Evidently, Probation Service work with men who commit sex offences has attracted a degree of attention from practitioners, managers, researchers and the Home Office, which is in excess of that given to other types of offending. The pieces examined reveal a shift in the descriptions of practice and practitioners: the former become increasingly concerned with the demonstration of effectiveness with particular individuals rather than an expression of values; and the latter being depicted less as generic professionals and more as skilled technicians. Feminist politics are rooted in personal experiences and the chapter makes clear the author's personal understanding of the factors that contribute to the incidence of sex offending.

Lorraine Green's chapter is based on research which analyses how children in residential care experience sexuality and their corresponding sexual behaviour, and how residential workers, social work organisations and society in general respond to the sexuality of young people in residential care. Despite numerous scandals and inquiries into sexual assaults against young people in residential settings, there is very little research or attention given to studying the phenomena: exploitation, prostitution and sexual assaults continue to occur. The chapter concludes that, as a result of the disempowering acceptance of the validity of rigid gender stereotypes, the majority of young women are extremely vulnerable to and often experience continued sexual exploitation from both within and outside the residential settings.

Ann Potter's chapter analyses the form, content and process of the child protection conference and reflects on how the conference (originally designed to assist professional workers and non-abusing family members to protect children effectively) is often an arena in which abusive behaviour is reproduced and repeated. She considers the consequences of this for children, non-abusing parents (usually mothers) and for the professional workers who participate, and concludes that in this, as in so many other aspects of practice in child sexual assault, it is feminist analyses which reveal the reality underlying the rhetoric.

Juliette Oko's chapter begins by discussing feminisms' loss of popular appeal. Within social work, feminisms have been taken over by the principles of antidiscriminatory practice which, as a professional ideology, is now considered central to good practice. She argues that social work needs to be more rigorous in its application of theory to practice and any praxis will have to be meaningful to the client. The chapter concludes with the proposal of a new model of intervention, one that overcomes some of the theoretical problems of antidiscriminatory practice and which can still be seen as feminist-inspired: a postmodern feminist approach combined with a strengths-based model, defined initially by the client.

References

Armstrong, L. (1978) *Kiss Daddy Goodnight*, New York, Pocket Books.

Boushel, M. and S. Noakes. (1988) 'Islington Social Services: developing a policy on child sexual abuse' *Feminist Review Special Issue on Child Sexual Abuse*, 28, pp.150–7.

Carter, P., A. Everitt and A. Hudson (1992) '"Malestream" training? Women, feminism and social work education', in M. Langan and L. Day (eds) *Women, Oppression and Social Work: Issues in Anti-Discriminatory Practice*, London, Routledge.

Chesler, P. (1972) *Women and Madness*, New York, Doubleday.

Cox, P. and G. Hirst (1996) 'Putting young heads onto older shoulders: social work education for work with children, young women and young men', in S. Jackson and M. Preston-Shoot (eds) *Educating Social Workers in a Changing Policy Context*, London, Whiting and Birch.

Dartington Social Research Unit (1995) *Child Protection: Messages from Research*, London, HMSO.

Davies, N. (1998) 'The most secret crime', *The Guardian*, 2–5 June 1998.

Feminist Review Collective (1988) *Feminist Review Special Issue on Child Sexual Abuse*, 28.

Firestone, S. (1971) *The Dialectic of Sex: A Case for Feminist Revolution*, London, Jonathan Cape.

Gordon, L. (1989) *Heroes Of Their Own Lives: The Politics and History of Family Violence*, London, Virago.

John, M. (ed.) (1997) *A Charge Against Society: The Child's Right to Protection*, London, Jessica Kingsley.

Kelly, L. (1988) *Surviving Sexual Violence*, Cambridge, Polity Press.

Logan, J., S. Kershaw, K. Karban, S. Mills, J. Trotter and M. Sinclair (1996) *Confronting Prejudice: Lesbian and Gay Issues in Social Work Education*, Aldershot, Arena.

London Rape Crisis Centre (1984) *Sexual Violence: The Reality for Women*, London, The Women's Press.

Millett, K. (1971) *Sexual Politics*, London, Hart-Davis.

Morgan, R. (1978) *Going Too Far: The Personal Chronicle of a Feminist*, New York, Vintage Books.

Nelson, S. (1982) *Incest: Fact and Myth*, Edinburgh, Stramullion Press.

Parton, N. (1996) 'Child protection, family support and social work: a critical appraisal of the Department of Health research studies in child protection', *Child and Family Social Work*, 1(i), pp.3–11.

Richardson, S. (1998) *Maintaining Awareness of Unspeakable Truths: Responses to Child Abuse in the Longer-Term*, paper presented at 'Trade in People, Abductions and Abuse of Children in the European Union: Problems and Solutions' Conference, European Parliament, Brussels, 15–16 October 1998.

Rowbotham, S. (1999) *A Century of Women: The History of Women in Britain and the United States*, London, Penguin Books.

Rush, F. (1980) *The Best Kept Secret: Sexual Abuse of Children*, New York, McGraw Hill.

Utting, W. (1997) *People Like Us, The Report of the Review of the Safeguards for Children Living Away from Home*, London, HMSO.

Williams, F. (1997) 'Presentation of "Work in Progress"', *Seminar Series*, University of Liverpool, 11 June 1997.

Wilson, M. (1993) *Crossing The Boundary: Black Women Survive Incest*, London, Virago.

Part I
Debates and Issues

1
Knowledge and Resistances in Child Sexual Assault

Pat Cox

Introduction

It might appear that there is a much greater knowledge about and, correspondingly, improved public awareness of, the issue of child sexual assault compared with previous decades. Professional and volunteer workers in this field, survivors, non-abusing parents and their supporters might disagree. (Markham, 1997; Spencer, 1997; Taylor-Browne, 1997) In this chapter I want to argue that while there is a reasonably extensive professional knowledge about the existence and forms/manifestations of sexual assault, there is not yet general public acceptance that the range of contact and non-contact activities which constitute the sexual assault of children, young women and young men are usually of a 'gendered' nature: nor is there widespread acceptance of its prevalence. Inevitably, I am talking about the complexities of knowledge: what we know; what we can let ourselves know; about how some forms of knowledge are privileged over others: men's knowledge is usually privileged over women's; white people's over that of Black people; adults' over children; printed or written over spoken (see Kelly in this volume). In England during the sixteen months (1997–98) that the Tribunal of Inquiry into Abuse in Children's Homes in North Wales was hearing evidence, almost all media coverage focused on the notion of individual men as abusers (usually referred to as 'paedophiles'), ignoring the knowledge from feminists' writings, research studies and personal accounts (see below: sections History and Knowledge). Consequently, there are fears that: '... the already fragile public and political will to protect children will be concentrated into an emphasis on policing and on punitive action.' (Balen, Cox and Preston-Shoot, 1997, p.3).

A messenger's position affects not only the message delivered, but also how that message is received (Phoenix, 1994; Walkerdine, 1997). I am a white woman, a feminist in that in any situation gender is always my primary analysis, with a long-standing personal and professional commitment to making some difference in the complex and uncertain area that is child sexual assault.

I have given careful consideration to the language used in this chapter. A problem in writing about any socially constructed group(s) is that use of generic terms such as 'children' and 'young people' blurs the range of experiences of childhood and adolescence and does not demonstrate effectively the commonalities and differences within these groupings. 'Children' are not an homogeneous mass, but are differentiated by 'race', by gender, by class background, by whether or not they are children with physical or learning disabilities, by differing sexual preferences, by age and by religion. It is difficult to find ways of continually acknowledging divisions, without prefacing each mention of children, young women and young men with a full list of all these differences. Because of space constraints, I ask readers to trust that when the abbreviated phrase 'children, young women and young men' is used, diversities within this grouping are encompassed: readers are asked to do so also. The word 'survivor' is also used throughout, being both positive and respectful and acknowledging the harsh realities survived by so many.

History

Sexual assault of children, young women and young men is not a recent phenomenon: its recurrence throughout the centuries and across different countries and cultures has been established through examination of myth, legend and song, and through reclaiming the historical accounts of abused children, young women and young men (Agger, 1994; hooks, 1982; Miles, 1989). More recent history in the nineteenth and twentieth centuries in Europe and North America demonstrates the fact that sexual assaults on children, young women and young men are committed primarily by men (Armstrong, 1996; Masson, 1984; Moran-Ellis, 1996). Summaries of key historical developments are found in Driver and Droisen, 1989; Gordon, 1989; Masson, 1984; MacLeod and Saraga, 1988; Summit, 1988.

Although a detailed history of child sexual assault is beyond the scope of this chapter, it is important to note that there have been previous periods of awareness of child sexual assault: re-discovery comes in 'waves' and then is lost: (Gordon, 1989; Hooper, 1992; Masson, 1984; Summit, 1988). As Olafson, Corwin and Summit write (1993, p.8), the reality of child sexual assault: '... has repeatedly surfaced into public and professional awareness in the past century and a half, only to be suppressed by the negative reaction it elicits'.

Gordon's history of intervention in child abuse in North America draws attention to the connection between the development of strong feminist movements and heightened awareness of how children, young women and young men are abused in families. She writes (1989, p.4):

> For most of the 110 years of this history, it was the *women's rights movement* that was most influential in confronting, publicizing and demanding action against family violence. Concern with family violence usually *grew when feminism was strong and ebbed when feminism was weak*. (Pat Cox's emphasis.)

Thus the circle of developing awareness and knowledge followed by avoidance has been the pattern of many previous decades. I argue that we are once again in danger of not building on the tremendous gains in understanding and knowledge developed by Black and white women (Kelly, 1989; McNaron and Morgan, 1982; Wilson, 1993). Not building will lead not only to losing understanding and knowledge, but also possibly to protection strategies that are at best, increasingly adult centred and apolitical, at worst, perfunctory and dismissive.

The 1970s and early 1980s can be characterized as a period of 'public and professional awareness' (Olafson *et al.*, 1993). Credit for raising consciousness about sexual abuse at this time goes to many unnamed Black and white women working in women's refuges and rape crisis centres, who listened to women's accounts of sexually abusive experiences in childhood. Some social workers, psychologists, doctors and others recognized child sexual assault as the root cause of much childhood disturbance and adult pain. Women survivors began to speak out in increasing numbers, developing personal definitions of their experiences and providing self help and support systems. In England, a BBC programme *Childwatch* brought the issue of child sexual assault to a wider public and ChildLine (anonymous counselling and advice service for children, young women and young men) was set up. Well known figures spoke out about being sexually assaulted as children, including Black writer Maya Angelou (1984), white comedian Marti Caine and restauranteur John Tovey. At least two English soap operas

(*Eastenders* and *Brookside*) ran storylines depicting the causes and consequences of sexual assault.

By the middle of the next decade, a discernible 'ebb' (Gordon, 1989) was in progress. Peter Lilley (then minister for social security) interviewed in 1993 about the Child Support Act, seemed unaware of the fact that women would not want to disclose the whereabouts of a partner who had previously sexually assaulted their children. When the minister for Wales, John Redwood, initiated debates (July 1995) about single parent families headed by women, there was little acknowledgement that some women choose to live without partners rather than live in a two parent family with an abuser (Hester and Radford, 1996). The majority media response to the Department of Health Overview Report of research studies (Dartington Social Research Unit, 1995), focused more on the implications for social work practice than on what the report said about abuse. The feasibility study (Ghate and Spencer, 1995) for a national survey to ascertain the prevalence of child sexual abuse did not feature in any news reports.

Knowledge: 'formal' and 'public'

There exist a number of definitions of what constitutes child sexual assault. For example, in England and Wales the 'formal' definition of child sexual abuse (as it is often referred to) derives from Department of Health *et al.* (1999) guidelines, with legal definitions in Section 31 of the Children Act (1989). In addition to the 'Working Together Guidelines' (as they are referred to by professional and volunteer workers), many survivors, supporters and workers are also aware of definitions produced by the Standing Committee on Sexually Abused Children (S.C.O.S.A.C., 1984) and by the Incest Survivors Campaign during the 1980s.

Different definitions have been used in England and Wales and in North America when gathering official data based on practice decisions, when undertaking clinical research and when devising self-report surveys. Such differences in definition might be considered to have consequences for 'knowledge' and its application. However, as Joan Sangster (1998) reminds us it is important not to over-privilege the contested nature of, and multiple explanations for, child sexual assault at the expense of the causes, the reality and the effects. And in fact, any reading of a number of surveys and studies (or studies of studies) shows that clear themes emerge.

Regional and national statistics on child sexual assault in England and Wales and in North America are gathered regularly. Incidence and prevalence studies are based on surveys using questionnaires and interviews. There have been a number of studies in England and Wales since 1978: all have used differing definitions (some of which are linked to legal codes, some not), various sample selections, sundry methods (for example, survey, interview, self report) and have phrased the questions in different ways: this leads to variations in findings. Mrazek, Lynch and Ben-Tovim (1983) took information from professional workers at a time when awareness was not as extensive as it was to become: their figure of 0.3 per cent prevalence is now regarded as a gross under-estimate. Nash and West (1985) found that 48 per cent of their sample had experienced some form of abuse: the extrapolation from this study is that half of all women have had sexually abusive childhood experiences. Baker and Duncan (1985: MORI poll survey) took a nationwide representative sample and used a definition which included non-contact activities. Extrapolation from their findings is that 12 per cent of women and 8 per cent of men had been abused. The study of 16–21-year-olds by Kelly, Regan and Burton (1991), also using an inclusive definition, produced a figure of 1 in 2 young women and 1 in 4 young men. Birchall (1989) in her review of incidence studies (excluding Kelly, Regan and Burton) writes (p.25):

> On comparing some cardinal details of the available data, however, the indications of prevalence of the most serious forms of abuse appear to be more convergent.

In relation to official statistics on child sexual assault, direct comparisons between England and North America are difficult, as American figures reflect cases which have been reported, not those which have been confirmed. There have been more prevalence studies and incidence surveys undertaken in North America: however, many of them have used broad, pre-determined definitions (Chandy, 1998). Again, while use of sundry definitions, variety in sample selections and differing forms of data collection mean that the results are difficult to standardise, there are clear themes here also.

Finkelhor's 'study of studies' (1986) found that prevalence of child sexual abuse ranged from between 6 per cent and 62 per cent for women and between 3 per cent and 31 per cent for men. One of the most comprehensive studies was undertaken by Russell (1983) whose subjects were interviewed by specially trained women. Using a comprehensive definition, including non-contact abuse, she arrived at a prevalence figure of 54 per cent. Sixty-two per cent was achieved by

Wyatt (1985), who in her research also used trained interviewers. Reviewing the studies by Wyatt and by Russell, Finkelhor (1986) noted that use of interviewers trained to ask questions sensitively had affected responses. Fromuth and Burkhart (1987) and Haugaard and Emery (1989) found that using different definitions affected prevalence results. La Fontaine (1990), in her review of English and North American studies, estimated a 10 per cent prevalence rate which includes contact abuse only. (If non-contact abuse were included, this rate would be much higher.) La Fontaine comments on the methodological limitations of earlier studies but concludes (p.68):

> There has been enough research to show that the sexual abuse of children is not a negligible issue or a question of public hysteria but a serious social problem. Even the lowest estimate of its prevalence indicates a large number of children are involved.

'Other forms' of knowledge

These numbers and estimates concern only that which has been collected and measured – official knowledge – which is important, but not the whole truth. The true number of survivors is not known and may never be known (see also Nelson, and Potter this volume). Information from studies and first-person accounts shows that many adults have had periods of time when they are unable to recall sexual assaults experienced in childhood. Briere and Runtz's study (1987) showed that only 39 per cent of the survivors interviewed named their experiences of abuse prior to specific and direct questions about their sexual history. Maltz and Holman (1987) posited that 50 per cent of all survivors of child sexual assault have periods of time when they are do not remember their experiences. Herman and Schatzow (1984) found that 62 per cent of adults in an Incest Survivors Group had previously 'not remembered' all or most of such childhood experiences. Work by Briere and Conte (1993) and Banyard and Williams (1999) explores the complexities of this phenomenon. First-person accounts from Black women (Angelou, 1984; Wilson, 1993) and white women (Darlington, 1996; Fraser, 1987; Spring 1987) also testify to the frequency of 'not remembering' as one particular coping technique.

A review of English and American studies ranging from the 1920s to the 1990s (Pilkington and Kremer, 1995), concluded that 'significant numbers' of children, young women and young men have been sexually assaulted:

Thus, it can be assumed that there is a 'dark figure' of sexual crimes on children that is absent from the official statistics published by government agencies (Browne and Lynch, 1995, p.80)

There are a number of additional reasons why we cannot say with confidence that we know the true numbers of those who are sexually assaulted in childhood. Bogle (1988), enumerates the potential diffi-culties for Black communities when the police are involved in investigations of sexual assault and how, for some survivors, these difficulties may act as a deterrent against reporting sexual assaults. Due to heterosexist oppressions experienced by young lesbian women and gay men (Logan *et al.*, 1996) it is doubly difficult for many of them to speak out about being assaulted. Disabled children, young women and young men often are unable to communicate their experiences of assault, due to the impact of our 'disabling society' (Kennedy and Kelly, 1992). Professional and public knowledge of the extent of sex abuser rings, the scale of the world wide child pornography industry (Davies and O'Connor, 1997) and of international sex tourism (Cook, 1998) is at an early stage. The numbers of young women and young men who are sexually assaulted and then forced into prostitution cannot be estimated (Sparks, 1997). Torture and abuse that takes place within the context of war is often unrecorded (Agger, 1994; Pecnik and Miskulin, 1996). Jehu's work (1994) on sexual assaults in counselling and therapeutic encounters is sobering reading, as are the accounts by adult women and men of their treatment at the hands of priests and nuns who supposedly cared for them as children (Bunting 1997; Gould, 1998). Finally, perpetrators of sexual assault rarely disclose everything: survivors are not always able to and sometimes simply do not wish to (Sorensen and Snow, 1991; Summit, 1983).

All of the above 'public', 'formal' and 'other' (non-privileged) knowl-edge, reveals a social issue of huge proportions which: '... raises fundamental questions for policy, practice and prevention.' (Kelly, Regan and Burton, 1991, p.8)

Having demonstrated the established and widespread nature of child sexual assault, I will discuss issues of gender which permeate current forms of knowledge. The majority of studies include issues of gender and, in spite of variations in findings between studies, (see above) the finding that is consistent, from the 1980s onwards, is that the over-whelming number of perpetrators are men. The figures are supported by first-person accounts of Black and white women survivors (Angelou, 1984; Spring 1987) and also by accounts in texts on self help and healing (McNaron and Morgan, 1982; Sanford, 1991). Another consistent factor, apparent in those studies which include the gender of perpetrators, is that the numbers of women abusers have remained far lower than those of men. Finkelhor, Meyer Williams and Burns in their 1988 study of abuse in day care found that 40 per cent of the abusers were women. However, they are careful to emphasize:

> It should not be surprising that many of the abusers in day care were women, because women comprised the vast majority of day care staff. In fact it is more surprising that men, who constitute a small proportion of day care workers, should commit such a disproportionate amount of abuse. (Finkelhor *et al.*, 1988, pp.40–1)

Experts in the field of child protection point out that women abusers should not distract attention from the large numbers of men who abuse (Kelly, 1996b). The NSPCC state that the figures in their 1990 Report do not support the 'tip of the iceberg' view of women as abusers (Kelly, 1991). The first published study of women abusers is qualitative (focusing on a limited number of subjects) rather than quantitative (Saradjian, 1996). And Finkelhor asserts:

> To take the appearance of some forms of sexual abuse by women to mean that sexual abuse is not primarily committed by men is also wrong and has no support in any of the data. (Finkelhor, 1984, p.184)

Resistances

Questions remain as to why, in spite of overwhelming evidence from research, theoretical knowledge, autobiographies and practice experience, the cumulative effects of different forms of knowledge of child sexual assault that have been amassed has not had greater impact on our collective consciousness. What happens to this knowledge and what explanations are there for its absence from policy debates?

As stated earlier, knowledge about child sexual assault was initiated by women working with women. Writings from Black and white feminists – Agana, 1990; Campbell, 1988, 1997; Driver and Droisen, 1989; Kelly, 1989; MacLeod and Saraga 1988; Nelson, 1982; Wilson, 1993 – have provided explanations of, and analyses for, the prevalence of child sexual assault and the gender of most perpetrators. Many of these writers point out that exposing the issue of child sexual assault has not changed either the power structures or the relationships which are responsible for its existence (Moran-Ellis, 1996). Like many survivors and supporters, non-abusing parents and professional and volunteer workers, I believe that there is both personal and institutional reluctance to engage with the gendered and heterosexist nature of child sexual assault and that this is the reason why sexual assault is mentioned so rarely when family policy or 'family life' are discussed. Resistance to this knowledge is found among members of the public (Markham, 1997) and among social work students and practitioners (Hirst and Cox, 1996; Spencer, 1997). As has been pointed out elsewhere (Kelly, 1997/8) many abusers are apparently 'family men'. For many women, irrespective of sexual preference, this means a fundamental re-thinking of close relationships with men, whether as partners (Moran-Ellis, 1996) sons, brothers and other relatives, and of relationships with neighbours and with colleagues. For many men it seems easier to think of individual abusers – see reportage of the Tribunal of Inquiry into Abuse in Children's Homes (Cox, Kershaw and Trotter: Introduction) – than to examine the power structures which make sexual assault possible (see Potter this volume). Some men express their discomfort in either disagreement with, or outright attack on, the definitions and studies cited earlier (Radford, Kelly and Hester, 1996). Resistance to this knowledge is a major issue in child sexual assault and until this resistance is addressed, there are implications for how well children, young women and young men can be protected (Cox, 1997).

'Public secrets' that are known, and not known, is a description used by Taussig, an anthropologist cited in Williams (1997), and Summit (1988) describes child sexual assault in this way. Julie Taylor-Browne (1997) asserts that it is the messengers who are (generally) blamed, rather than the perpetrators: the messengers (survivors, supporters, workers) are bringing unpalatable facts to light while perpetrators' deeds are secret: 'public secrets'. That we are right to do so, does not mean that forces will not be mobilised against us. We face this resistance – 'avoidance' – in many different forms and at many different levels. This is clearly demonstrated in the amount of media coverage given to False Memory Syndrome (Kitzinger, 1996) as opposed to that given to the studies and accounts outlined above (Orr, 1997).

Myers, (1994) examining the 'backlash' in North America, echoes Gordon (1989) and Olafson, Corwin and Summit (1993):

... the problem (child sexual assault) is periodically pushed below the surface of recognition, where it is ignored.... The critical issue today is whether society will once again shut its eyes. (Myers, 1994, p.23)

Williams (1997), speaking about 'scientific' studies which propagate racism, says:

> Like clockwork, black people must put aside the activities of every-day life and subject ourselves to the cyclical inspection point of proving our worth, justifying our existence and teaching our history, over and over again. (Williams, 1997, p.49)

In like manner, it seems to many supporters and workers that much of the time that should be spent working with survivors, non-abusing parents or perpetrators of sexual offences, is spent explaining why child sexual assault occurs and justifying what is being done and why (Moran-Ellis, 1996). As Louise Armstrong notes:

> In speaking out we hoped to raise hell. Instead, we have raised for the issue a certain normalcy. We hoped to raise a passion for change. Instead, what we raised was discourse, and a sizeable problem-management industry (Armstrong, 1996, p.274).

Strategies

Julie Taylor-Browne (1997) advocates involving survivors and support-ers in developing services, and practice and policy responses. In this she follows many feminist writers and practitioners who are critical of the taking over of child sexual assault by male 'experts' (Kelly, 1989; Armstrong, 1996). This undoubtedly requires planning and prepara-tion to attain true involvement, rather than tokenistic participation and may seem easier to achieve in voluntary rather than in statutory settings. Nevertheless, as pointed out by Oko (this volume), Taylor-Browne's work merits serious consideration of what could be done to facilitate such involvement.

Rebuttal is particularly important in relation to any reportage which misrepresents or impugns protection practice on the part of those working to protect children, young women and young men from sexual assault. Finkelhor (1994) writes of the need constantly to refute damaging statements. His recommendations are developed by Markham (1997) and Spencer (1997). They each share their experi-ences of working with journalists and other media personnel in order to educate wider public and professional audiences. Spencer (1997) gives practical advice to skill and empower workers. Finkelhor (1994) also recommends that in relation to developing greater public support for children to be protected from sexual assault, it is better to put effort and energy into convincing those who are neutral or undecided, rather than those who disagree with policies and practice.

Having accepted feminist analyses of child sexual assault, Crompton (1992) and Pringle (1997, 1998) argue that these analyses and the research which highlights the gendered nature of most abusive acts must be shared with others; serious debate must be stimulated. They propose that men must together critically examine social constructions of masculinity and begin to address male socialization and behaviours. It is likely that for many men, their recommendations tread new ground. But then, strategies for protection require an openness and willingness to consider what might not have been previously contemplated.

Hirst and Cox (1996) believe that qualifying training for social workers in all fields should integrate not only theory and practice in protecting children, young women and young men from sexual assault, but also theory and practice in working with those who commit sex offences, so that qualifying workers will integrate survivor perspectives *and* knowledge of the 'denial, distortion and deceit' (Roberts, 1995, p.3) which form the behaviour patterns of those who commit sex offences. Integration of these two strands of protection practice raises students' awareness and knowledge of the inherently gendered nature of so many sexual assaults.

Kitzinger (1997), points out that many preventative programmes aimed at empowering children, young women and young men to resist assault do not address either 'sex' or 'power', thus undermining the programmes by not confronting the underlying issues. (The groupwork programme with young women described in Trowell's recent study (1998) appears to be an exception to this.) Kitzinger sees this as being avoidance on the part of the adults concerned and of wider society: the way to make such programmes effective is, therefore, to face what the real issues are and address them. In developing programmes and services, it is vital not only to centralise feminist analyses and explanations (see Oko, this volume), but also to be aware of differences of class, sexuality, disability and 'race'. Kelly and Scott (1986) point out:

> Many of us (workers in the field) have a tendency to treat all cases of child sexual abuse as though every person came from the same

socioeconomic and cultural background ... failure to acknowledge ... diversity impedes the development of group-specific prevention and treatment programmes. (Kelly and Scott, 1986, quoted in Wilson, 1993, p.170).

Conclusion

Discussing racism, Williams (1997) says 'The solution to racism lies in our ability to see its ubiquity but not concede its inevitability' (p.66).

For the sake of survivors, non-abusing parents and supporters, personal and institutional resistances to the forms of knowledge outlined above need to be transcended by all who are concerned with the protection of children, young women and young men. The body of awareness and knowledge of the prevalence and the gendered nature of the causes, manifestations and consequences of child sexual assault should not only not disappear, but should become firmly established in public, professional and political consciousness. The difficulties are many, but 'societal avoidance' (Summit, 1988) is also a high price to pay. In not turning away from knowledge, we retain our awareness of the ubiquity of child sexual assault, and are enabled to do more than we believe we can.

References

Agana, P. (1990) 'Training for life' in M. Sulter (ed.) *Passion: Discourses on Black Women's Creativity*, Hebden Bridge, West Yorkshire, Urban Fox Press.

Agger, I. (1994) *The Blue Room: Trauma and Testimony Among Refugee Women*, London, Zed Press.

Angelou, M. (1984) *I Know Why the Caged Bird Sings*, London, Virago.

Armstrong, L. (1996) *Rocking the Cradle of Sexual Politics – What Happened When Women Said Incest*, London, The Women's Press.

Baker, A. and S. Duncan (1985) 'Child sexual abuse: a study of prevalence in Great Britain', *Child Abuse and Neglect*, 9, pp.457– 67.

Balen, R., P. Cox and M. Preston-Shoot (eds) (1997) 'Editorial Comment', *Social Work Education: Special Issue on Child Protection*, 16(2), pp.3–5.

Banyard, V. L. and L. M. Williams (1999) 'Memories for child sexual abuse and mental health functioning: findings on a sample of women and implications for future research' in L. M. Williams and V. L. Banyard (eds) (1999) *Trauma and Memory*, California, Sage.

Birchall, E. (1989) 'The frequency of child abuse: what do we really know?' in O. Stevenson (ed.) *Child Abuse: Public Policy and Professional Practice*, Hemel Hempstead, Harvester Wheatsheaf.

Bogle, M. (1988) 'Brixton black women's centre: organising on child sexual abuse'. *Feminist Review Special Issue on Child Sexual Abuse*, 28, pp.132–5.

Briere, J. and M. Runtz (1987) 'Post sexual abuse trauma: data and implications for clinical practice *Journal of Interpersonal Violence*, 2(4), pp.367–79.

Briere, J. and J. Conte (1993) 'Self-reported amnesia for abuse in adults molested as children', *Journal of Traumatic Stress*, 6 (1), pp.21–31.

Browne, K. and M. Lynch (1995) 'Guessing at the extent of child sexual abuse', *Child Abuse Review*, 4(2), pp.79–82.

Bunting, M. (1997) 'Abuse claims shake church', *The Guardian*, 8 November 1997.

Campbell, B. (1988) *Unofficial Secrets – Child Sexual Abuse: The Cleveland Case*, London, Virago.

Campbell, B. (1997) *Unofficial Secrets – Child Sexual Abuse: The Cleveland Case*, London, Virago.

Chandy, J. M. (1998) *Victims of Sexual Abuse: Outcomes and Resilience*, paper presented at the second 'International Conference on Social Work in Health and Mental Health', Melbourne, Australia.

Cook, R. (1998) 'The net closes', *The Guardian*, 1 April 1998.

Cox, P. (1993) '"Professional survival": a double jeopardy. Some implications for training, education and practice' in H. Ferguson, R. Gilligan and R. Torode (eds) (1993) *Surviving Childhood Adversity: Issues for Policy and Practice*, Dublin, Social Studies Press.

Cox, P. (1997) *Challenges and Opportunities: Protecting Children, Young Women and Young Men in a Changing Europe*, paper presented at 'Culture and Identity – Social Work in a Changing Europe' Conference, Dublin, August 1997.

Crompton, I. (1992) *Child Sexual Abuse; Politics, Ideology and Social Work Practice*, Warwick, University of Warwick.

Darlington, Y. (1996) *Moving On: Women's Experiences of Childhood Sexual Abuse and Beyond*, Sydney, The Federation Press Pty Ltd.

Dartington Social Research Unit (1995) *Child Protection: Messages From Research*, London, H.M.S.O.

Davies, N. and E. O'Connor (1997) 'Special Investigation' *The Guardian*, 5 April 1997.

Department of Health, Home Office, Department for Education and Employment (1999) *Working Together to Safeguard Children: A Guide to Inter-Agency Working to Safeguard and Promote the Welfare of Children*, London, HMSO.

Driver, E. and A. Droisen (eds) (1989) *Child Sexual Abuse: Feminist Perspectives*, London, Macmillan.

Finkelhor, D. (1984) *Child Sexual Abuse: New Theory and Research*, New York, Free Press.

Finkelhor, D. (1986) *A Sourcebook on Child Sexual Abuse*, California, Sage.

Finkelhor, D. (1994) 'The "Backlash" and the future of child protection advocacy – insights from the study of social issues' in J. Myers (ed.) (1994) *The Backlash: Child Protection Under Fire*, California, Sage.

Finkelhor, D., G. Hotaling, I. Lewis and C. Smith (1990) Sexual abuse in a national survey of adult men and women: prevalence characteristics and risk factors, *Child Abuse and Neglect*, 14, pp.19–28.

Finkelhor, D., L. Meyer Williams and N. Burns (1988) *Nursery Crimes: Sexual Abuse in Day Care*, California, Sage.

Fraser, S. (1987) *My Father's House*, London, Virago.

Fromuth, M. and B. Burkhart (1987) 'Childhood sexual victimisation among college men: definitional and methodological issues', *Violence and Victims* 2(4), pp.241–53.

Ghate, D. and L. Spencer (1995) *The Prevalence of Child Sexual Abuse in Britain*, London, H.M.S.O.

Gordon, L. (1989) *Heroes of Their Own Lives: The History and Politics of Family Violence*, London, Virago.

Gould, M. (1998) 'Order apologises for school abuse', *The Observer*, 29 March 1998.

Haugaard, J. and R. Emery (1989) 'Methodological issues in child sexual abuse research', *Child Abuse and Neglect*, 13, pp.89–100.

Herman, J. and E. Schatzow (1984) 'Time limited group therapy for women with a history of incest', *International Journal of Group Psychotherapy*, 34, pp.605–16.

Hester, M. and L. Radford (1996) 'Contradictions and compromises: the impact of the Children Act on women and children's safety' in M. Hester, L. Kelly and J. Radford (eds) (1996) *Women, Violence and Male Power*, Buckingham, Open University Press.

Hirst, G. and P. Cox (1996) 'Hearing all sides of the story: the challenge of integrating teaching on sexual aggression into social work qualifying training', *Journal Of Sexual Aggression*, 2(1), 33–48.

hooks, b. (1982) *Ain't I a Woman? Black Women and Feminism*, London, Pluto Press.

Hooper, C. A. (1992) *Mothers Surviving Child Sexual Abuse*, London, Routledge.

Jehu, D. (1994) *Patients as Victims: Sexual Abuse in Psychotherapy and Counselling*, West Sussex, John Wiley.

Kelly, L. (1989) 'Bitter ironies', *Trouble and Strife*, 16, pp.14–21.

Kelly, L. (1991) 'Unspeakable acts: women who abuse', *Trouble and Strife*, 21, pp.13–20.

Kelly, L. (1996b) 'When does the speaking profit us? reflections on the challenges of developing feminist perspectives on abuse and violence by women' in M. Hester, L. Kelly and J. Radford (eds) *Women, Violence and Male Power*, Buckingham, Open University Press.

Kelly, L. (1997/8) 'Confronting an atrocity', *Trouble and Strife*, 36, pp.16–22.

Kelly, L., L. Regan and S. Burton (1991) *An Exploratory Study of the Prevalence of Sexual Abuse in a Sample of 16 to 21 year-olds*, London, Child and Woman Abuse Studies Unit, University of North London.

Kelly, R. and M. Scott (1986) in M. Wilson, *Crossing The Boundary: Black Women Survive Incest*, London, Virago.

Kennedy, M. and L. Kelly (eds) (1992) 'Special Issue on Abuse and Children with Disabilities', *Child Abuse Review*, 1(3).

Kitzinger, J. (1996) 'Media representations of sexual abuse risks', *Child Abuse Review*, 5(5), pp.319–333.

Kitzinger, J. (1997) 'Who are you kidding? Children, power and the struggle against sexual abuse' in A. James and A. Prout (eds) (1997) *Constructing and Reconstructing Childhood: Contemporary Issues in the Sociological Study of Childhood*, London, Falmer Press.

La Fontaine, J. (1990) *Child Sexual Abuse*, Cambridge, Polity Press.

Logan, J., S. Kershaw, K. Karban, S. Mills, J. Trotter and M. Sinclair. (1996)

Confronting Prejudice: Lesbian and Gay Issues in Social Work Education, Aldershot, Arena.

Maltz, W. and B. Holman (1987) *Incest and Sexuality: a Guide to Understanding and Healing*, Lexington MA, Lexington Books.

Markham, L. (1997) 'Media Issues', *Notanews*, 22, pp.6–8.

Masson, J. (1984) *The Assault on Truth: Freud's Suppression of the Seduction Theory*, London, Penguin.

MacLeod, M. and E. Saraga (1988) 'Challenging the orthodoxy: towards a feminist theory and practice, *Feminist Review Special Issue on Child Sexual Abuse*, 28, pp.16–55.

McNaron, T. and Y. Morgan (1982) *Voices in the Night*, New York, Cleis Press.

Miles, R. (1989) *The Women's History of the World*, London, Paladin.

Moran-Ellis, J. (1996) 'Close to home: the experience of researching child sexual abuse' in M. Hester, L. Kelly and J. Radford (eds) (1996) *Women, Violence and Male Power*, Buckingham, Open University Press.

Mrazek, P., M. Lynch and A. Ben-Tovim (1983) 'Sexual abuse of children in the United Kingdom', *Child Abuse and Neglect*, 7, pp.147–153.

Myers, J. (1994) *The Backlash: Child Protection Under Fire*. California, Sage.

Nash, C. and D. West (1985) 'Sexual molestation of young girls' in D. West (ed.) (1985) *Sexual Victimisation*, London, Gower.

Nelson, S. (1982) *Incest: Fact and Myth*, Edinburgh, Stramullion Press.

Olafson, E., D. L. Corwin and R. Summit (1993) 'Modern history of child sexual abuse awareness: cycles of discovery and suppression', *Child Abuse and Neglect*, 17, pp.7–24.

Orr, M. (1997) 'Response to the Royal College of Psychiatrists' report on recovered memory', *Action Against Child Sexual Abuse*, 27/28, pp.3–4.

Pecnik, N. and M. Miskulin (1996) 'Psychosocial assistance to refugee and displaced women in Croatia', *Groupwork*, 9 (3), pp.328–51.

Phoenix, A. (1994) 'Research: Positioned Differently? Issues of "Race", Difference and Commonality', *Changes*, 12, (4) pp.299–305.

Pilkington, B. and J. Kremer (1995) 'A review of the epidemiological research on child sexual abuse', *Child Abuse Review*, 4, (2), pp.84–98.

Pringle, K. (1997) *Men as Workers in Professional Child Care Settings: An Anti-Oppressive Practice Framework*, paper presented at an international seminar, 'Men as Workers in Services for Young Children: Issues of a Mixed Gender Workforce', Thomas Coram Research Institute, London, May 1997.

Pringle, K. (1998) 'Men and childcare: policy and practice' in J. Popay, J. Hearn and J. Edwards (eds) *Men, Gender Divisions and Welfare*, London, Routledge.

Radford, J., L. Kelly and M. Hester (1996) 'Introduction' in M. Hester, L. Kelly and J. Radford (1996) *Women, Violence and Male Power*, Buckingham, Open University Press.

Roberts, J. (1995) 'Caught up in the whirlpool', *The Guardian*, 11 January 1995, 3.

Russell, D. (1983) 'The incidence and prevalence of intrafamilial and extra-familial sexual abuse of female children', *Child Abuse and Neglect*, 7, pp.133–146.

Sanford, L. T. (1991) *Strong At The Broken Places*, London, Virago.

Sangster, J. (1998) *Representing and Understanding Violence Against Children in Ontario, 1916–1926'* paper presented at 'Child Welfare and Social Action

Conference', University of Liverpool, July 1998.

Saradjian, J. (1996) *Women Who Sexually Abuse*, West Sussex, John Wiley.

Sorensen, T. and B. Snow (1991) 'How children tell: the process of disclosure in child sexual abuse', *Child Welfare*. 70(1), pp.3–15.

Sparks, I. (1997) 'Brutal game of life', *The Guardian*, 8 October 1997.

Spencer, A. (1997) 'Putting one's head above the parapet: professionally speaking', *Notanews*, 24, pp.10–18.

Spring, J. (1987) *Cry Hard and Swim*, London, Virago.

Summit, R. (1983) 'The child sexual abuse accommodation syndrome', *Child Abuse and Neglect*, 17, pp.177–193.

Summit, R. C. (1988) 'Hidden victims, hidden pain; societal avoidance of child sexual abuse' in G. E. Wyatt and G. J. Powell (eds) *Lasting Efffects of Child Sexual Abuse*, California, Sage.

Taylor-Browne, J. (1997) 'Obfuscating child sexual abuse 1: the identification of social problems', *Child Abuse Review*, 6(1), pp.4–10.

Trowell, J., I. Kolvin, M. Berelowitz, T.Weeramanthri, H. Sadowski, A. Rushton, G. Miles, D. Glaser, A. Elton, M. Rustin and M. Hunter (1998) 'Psychotherapy Outcome Study for Sexually Abused Girls' in Jones, D. and P. Ramchandani (eds) *Child Sexual Abuse: Informing Practice from Research*, Abingdon, Radcliffe Medical Press.

Walkerdine, V. (1997) *Daddy's Girl: Young Girls and Popular Culture*, Basingstoke, Macmillan.

Williams, P. J. (1997) *Seeing a Colour-Blind Future: The Paradox of Race*, London, Virago.

Wilson, M. (1993) *Crossing the Boundary: Black Women Survive Incest,*. London, Virago.

Wyatt, G. E. (1985) ' The sexual abuse of Afro-American and white women in childhood' in D. Finkelhor (1986) *A Sourcebook on Child Sexual Abuse*, California, Sage.

2
Children, Young People and 'Protection'

Kate Karban and Chris Horrocks

Introduction

Children and young people who are 'looked after' exist within what is broadly termed the child protection system, a significant number having been sexually assaulted. While the concept of child protection is one that includes notions of rescue and safety, some children have been and continue to be, abused within the looked after system. This chapter will utilize two theoretical positions to scrutinize the concept of protecting children and consider how successfully the child protection system can ensure the well-being of those in its care. Focusing on residential child care services, the discursive practices which surround children and young people both in a wider context and within the looked after system will be examined. Children and young people will then be located within a feminist discourse and the nature of this location will be used to realize an understanding of the 'positioning' of children and young people. Such an analysis will assume a broadly social constructionist perspective, taking a 'top-down' discursive approach which has as its focus issues of power, ideological practice and social process. Blagg *et al.* (1989) make the compelling point that:

> the sexual abuse of children is not a series of isolated acts but is situated within a complex of social and cultural arrangements and understandings rooted within the very fundamentals of our society. (p.5)

Therefore the concept of 'positioning' (Davies and Harre, 1990) is especially important to this analysis and relates to the way in which particular discourses locate individuals, offering different sets of rights and obligations.

Locating children

The history of child welfare services over the last century suggests that there is a continuing concern for those children and young people who are deemed to be in need of care and protection from a variety of social and family ills or misfortunes. The nature and definition of these concerns may have altered over time, but the construction of 'childhood' as a developmental stage requiring the intervention of adults to ensure healthy growth and development is one which, with a few notable exceptions, has held sway. The principal expectation of adults' 'role' within this construction is one of responsible behaviour to safeguard children's interests: there is a clear demarcation between those who do not live up to this expectation and those who are deemed able to protect either their own or other people's children. To some extent the notion of 'governing the family' has been represented as a means of clarifying and enforcing this demarcation through a range of different mechanisms, including family and social policy and gendered expectations of women and men. Within this ideology, children and young people are 'positioned' as being in need of care or protection, the responsibility of their families, powerless and vulnerable; rather than active subjects determining their own lives. The social process of positioning is progressive: people are not fully aware of being socially positioned as subjects with the consequence that they: 'standardly see their own subjective identities as somehow standing outside and prior to society.' (Fairclough, 1989, p.104). For children this has particular resonance in relation to the concept of child protection, which, if they are to be 'protected' affords them a subjective identity which is inactive, making very little (if any) contribution to ensuring their own safety.

The Children Act (1989) has been the focus of considerable discussion elsewhere and need not be repeated. It can however be seen as presenting a particular set of interests *vis-à-vis* the 'family', the state, and those of children and young people themselves. The Introduction to the Act refers to the belief that: '… children are generally best looked after within the family with both parents playing a full part' (Department of Health, 1989, p.1).

Children are therefore firmly placed within the family, establishing specific rights and obligations for parents. Reading the quote from a different location, that of children, it is difficult to find an alternative interpretation that affords children the same level of active participation, rather they are presented as passive possessions of adults in an adult world.

The discourse of 'parental responsibility' describes the duties, rights and authority which a parent has in respect of their child and the 'welfare balance' refers to the aim of the Act in seeking:

> to protect children both from the harm which can arise from failures or abuse within the family and from the harm which can be caused by unwarranted intervention in their family life. (Department of Health, 1989, p.5)

Again the discourse is one which positions children firmly within families, not one that endows them with their own identity and unique location. For those children who are seen to require care outside of their family of origin, the Act incorporates regulations and guidance for the provision of alternative care and, for those children placed outside the local authority, clear responsibility for ensuring the child's welfare in private and voluntary homes, educational establishments and hospitals. Children are clearly positioned within the protectionist domain as passive recipients of interventions which will safeguard their interests. Yet are there consequences to this prevailing discourse? Discourses are not value free: they are inexorably connected to the structures and practices of daily life:

> An individual emerges through the processes of social interaction, not as a relatively fixed end product but as one who is constituted and reconstituted through the various discursive practices in which they participate (Davies and Harre, 1990).

The term discursive practice refers to the way in which we actively participate in, and produce, particular versions of 'reality'. Within the structures and practices of the 'looked after' system, are children and young people subjectively positioned within a discourse of powerlessness which does little to improve their outcomes and may indeed render them unprotected? Do we, by adopting a 'storyline' which depicts children and young people as defenceless and passive, existing more generally within families, thus create a stereotype to which they are 'invited', or have no choice but to comply with? The term 'looked after' is itself not value free: it upholds the ideology of paternalism and adopts a rather diffident and patronizing stance which again places children and young people in an accepting position, making scant contribution to their own lives. In order to consider such issues further, we will take a closer look at prevailing practices.

Policy and practice

It would not be unreasonable to expect that the experience of 'care' should offer opportunities firstly to intervene and respond to the particular reason(s) why a child or young person needed substitute care and secondly to counteract previously identified disadvantageous life experiences. At the very least 'care' should not create further disadvantage. As a result of this intervention, the longer term outlook for children and young people should include improved life chances and overall positive outcomes, ameliorating previous distress and disadvantage. The expectation is that there will be an appreciation and understanding of the effects of separation and change, with the ultimate aim of improving the experiences of children and young people in both the short and longer term.

Policy and practice in providing accommodation for children and young people who have need of a substitute home is based on the notion that family placement is the preferred choice in the majority of situations, especially in the case of younger children. The large children's homes and observation and assessment centres have disappeared to be replaced by less extensive resources based around smaller residential units or 'family group homes' with some specialist provision for remand and respite care (Utting, 1991). These developments have been further encouraged by the cuts in welfare spending and need for local authorities to reduce direct provision of services in favour of commissioning and contracting-out. Critics of child care policy have highlighted the ideological preference for family rather than residential care, despite differential evidence for the success or otherwise of fostering and family placement services. Evidence suggests that the provision of high quality care for children and young people who are unable to live with their families of origin, requires a broad mix of services and a range of options, which are rarely available when planning to meet the needs of any individual child (Berridge and Brodie, 1996).

A further factor in considering the status of services for children and young people is the changing profile of the 'care' population. Many children in need of residential care have had troubled and traumatic lives prior to care: they need specialized help and resources. Many are also likely to be older, that is, aged 12 years or over. Examining residential care, the Warner Report (1992) found that almost one-third of children had been sexually abused. Stone's (1990) study of short-term fostering in Newcastle reported that three-fifths of the children of all ages in her sample were considered by social workers to have experienced abuse or neglect at some time. Within this population children and young people from disadvantaged backgrounds are also found to be over-represented. (Bebbington and Miles, 1989; Gibbons *et al.*, 1995) There is no way of ensuring the accuracy of such figures; what can be relied on is that there will be children and young people 'looked after' who, for various reasons, have decided to conceal the severity of their past experiences. Do children and young people who have faced such difficulties need the kind of intervention that the term 'looked after' might suggest, or do they require more specialized responses to their own unique stories?

The situation is, however, often one of services inadequately resourced to provide the care which is needed, and staff who are insufficiently trained or supported for the complex task with which they are faced (Utting, 1991). The experiences of many children and young people are a testimony to the fact that far from improving their life chances, the experience of being 'looked after' creates further difficulties and compounds prior disadvantage (see also Green, this volume). Health, education, and employment are among the areas in which objective measures confirm this assessment (Biehal *et al.*, 1995; Jackson, 1994; Strathdee and Johnson, 1994). Less tangible outcomes in terms of family and social relationships, and emotional health and well-being, also contribute to the overall picture (Buchanan and Ten Brinke, 1998). Therefore, although the discourse implies an escape from disadvantage and children and young people are positioned within a discourse which makes them the recipients of a protected environment, research evidence suggests otherwise. For some children and young people, abuse within and by the care system harms their lives seriously and sometimes fatally.

Abuse in out-of-home settings

In 1945 Denis O'Neill died at the hands of his foster parents. Doubtless this was not the first death of a child entrusted to the care of the state, but it marked the beginning of a slow move to public consciousness about child abuse in general and about the risks to children removed from their families, ostensibly for their own protection. The former gained pace with acceptance of the concept of the 'battered child'; the belief that parents could physically harm their own children, and the publicity which surrounded the deaths of Maria Colwell and other children in the 1970s and 1980s. The furore surrounding events in Cleveland and concern about sexual assault of children within families, marked a further stage in the development of public consciousness (Campbell, 1988; Richardson and Bacon, 1991). Awareness and concern about children and young people who had already been identified as being at risk and removed from the care of their families into public care was a later, but related development, initiated by disclosures of abuse within residential homes and foster placements, as well as the publicity concerning the historical practice of voluntary child care organizations in sending children and young people to uncertain futures overseas in the 'colonial' empire.

The Children Act acknowledges the risk to children and young people in public care and stipulates various checks and safeguards which are intended to increase protection and safety for children placed away from their families. With regard to residential care the Guidance and Regulations (Vol. 4) state that:

> All those concerned with children's homes must be aware of the possibility that a child may be abused during the period *he* is in a home. (Department of Health, 1991, p.32).

It then sets out a range of procedural and policy devices to dovetail any allegations of abuse occurring within the home with the local child protection services. The guidance also refers to staff handling of any disclosure which may be made within the home, including the recognition that children may be abused by a member of staff within the home. Within the procedures and policies which have since proliferated, there is a noticeable absence of children and young people as key players in shaping their lives, and a continuing discourse which conveys an obligation to protect, rather than encourage children and young people to take social action. There is a clear sense that what is required is the removal or non-entry of 'dangerous' staff or carers to child care services – albeit a desirable aim – and a continuing reliance on safety mechanisms which have already failed to address the imbalance of power experienced by children and young people in general, as well the specific experiences of those who are in the public care.

A brief consideration of some of the Inquiries into abuse within residential care will assist an assessment of the likely effectiveness of the measures contained within the recommendations, recognizing the absence of any significant shift in the positioning of children and young people within the system and the different levels of power relationships within it. The Hughes Report (1986) examined the allegations of abuse between 1960 and 1980 in children's homes and hostels in Belfast and refers to a child or young person being most likely to complain:

> to a person with whom he has a close and trusting relationship. The existence of such a relationship however, does not automatically result in such a disclosure if the child or young person is under threat, ashamed, or ignorant of the implications of what is happening. He may be prepared to put up with the offences because he feels he has no status or rights or because material or social benefits could be thereby obtained. (Hughes, 1986, p.26)

The recommendations included the need for a formal complaints procedure which would go some way towards improving things for those in residential care and helping them to overcome inhibitions about *even* well-founded complaints.

However, although a complaints procedure might be an effective mechanism to ensure the safety of some children and young people, this cannot be guaranteed. Lyon (1997), identifies a number of issues that might undermine the effective functioning of complaints procedures, including a potential lack of confidence in the system where the perception is that such procedures are not truly independent and a recognition that they are not separately funded. The more salutary point she makes is that children and young people felt that it was 'expecting too much' of them to feel confident when making complaints about a system they were living within. To feel able to use the complaints procedure, children and young people needed to feel more secure in their subjective position, they require an identity which does not locate them as vulnerable beneficiaries of services.

The Leicestershire Inquiry (Kirkwood, 1992) addressed the abuse of young people by Frank Beck. A striking feature of the accounts by young people is their concern that they would not be listened to or believed:

> It appeared to me that neither my social worker nor the police believed me, so I gave up telling people. He (Beck) also said that I

was a very disturbed child and said to her (social worker) 'who would you rather believe?' (Kirkwood, 1992, p.68).

The particular issues for children with a learning disability are high-lighted in the report into allegations of abuse at Meadowdale Children's Home (Kilgallon, 1995). Specific details of the offences and the voices of the children and young people concerned are not included in the report, which describes how 'Special attention to these children was seen as a caring positive response to the most needy children, but provided ideal cover for an abuser.' (Kilgallon, 1995, p.12). The fact that children with disabilities are more likely to be living away from their families also increases their vulnerability (Morris, 1995; Utting, 1997). It is also important to comment on the situation of black children who are also over-represented among children in local authority care and residential schools. Here the

> Failure to understand and cater for specific health and personal care needs may further undermine their self esteem and identify them as disregarded children whom it is relatively safe to abuse. (Utting, 1997, p.113)

These issues of identity need to be addressed within the wider context of institutional and personal racism and abuse. Young people themselves have spoken out independently about abuse, including sexual assault within the care system. They have been brought together by organizations such as the National Association of Young People in Care (NAYPIC) and the Safe and Sound Advice Group (NSPCC, 1995). Their comments suggest that far-reaching changes in the systems for protecting children in care need to be introduced: 'I didn't feel safe at all during that investigation' (Vicky, p.1). 'I got no information or explanation about the investigation.... Nobody ever said I believe you're telling the truth' (Marie, p.2). 'I got no support during the investigation – nor did my family' (Andy, p.4). 'I felt that I only got support when it would help them to get more evidence' (Rhiannon, p.5). (NSPCC, 1995)

The young people making these comments are clearly located within a discourse of powerlessness, which affords them very little room to manoeuvre. If they are constructed as passive recipients of interventions, it is not surprising that they feel unable to impact upon the social practices they are living through. Overall, the evidence suggests that the concept of 'listening to children' is limited at every step of the process: children and young people who are already disadvantaged by virtue of their circumstances are disempowered both in terms of reporting abuse and also in terms of how they fare in any subsequent investigations. Any significant improvement which may impact on children and young people's lives must rely on a re-worked and more far-reaching project which will endeavour to locate children and young people more fundamentally within the social relations of power.

What we intend to do here is to foreground 'children' both female and male in relation to child sexual assault and to consider that the prevailing strategies for child 'protection' for looked after children fall short of being based on a clear understanding of the positioning of children within these discourses. Strategies for protecting children appear to be based upon two separate arguments. First, that stricter controls on the selection of carers would effectively 'weed out' actual and potential abusers; second, that given sufficient structures for reporting abuse and making complaints, children and young people will be able to protect themselves by reporting incidents. While we are not advocating abandoning either of these strategies, it is our contention that they are not sufficient means of guaranteeing 'protection', and are not based on explicit understandings of childhood and the needs of children. In particular, strategies such as these frame children *either* as victims needing protection *or* as autonomous and independent beings, highlighting the tensions and contradictions which permeate child care policy and practice.

This portrayal of children also neglects the more complex shadings of power and inequality, based on age, race, disability and class as well as gender. It also fails to take account of the ways in which power is 'exercised and enacted in discourse' (Fairclough, 1989). Given the negative stereotypical portrayal of children and young people who are 'looked after', there is also the possibility that they will be seen as having already 'lost their innocence' as Kitzinger (1997) suggests:

> If the violation of innocence is the criterion against which the act of sexual abuse is judged, then violating a 'knowing' child becomes a lesser offence than violating an 'innocent' child. (p.161)

Before considering the nature of a radical shift in placing children and young people at the centre of any debate concerning their care and well-being, it is pertinent to explore the location of children and 'childhood' in feminist theory.

The location of children and childhood in feminist theory

It is our contention that a feminist perspective on childhood requires further development as, in general, particular issues have been looked at from a specific position each carrying its own discourse. For example, the subject of child sexual assault has been highlighted with a recognition of the gender issues involved and the imbalance of power between women and men. Concepts of 'family' and pathological models of family functioning which fail to acknowledge gender inequality have also been challenged (Driver and Droisen, 1989; Parton, 1990) and questions of masculinity have been explored in relation to the (mainly) male perpetrators of child sexual assault (Hearn, 1990; Pringle, 1998). Discussing welfare policy in relation to the care of children and young people away from their families, Makrinioti argues that:

> the welfare state plays a significant role in perpetuating the notion of childhood as a minority status and in concealing its social visibility by supporting, and in fact re-enforcing children's familialization. (1994, p.268)

In many instances the discourse of childhood has been subjected to the processes of familialization and 'feminisation'. 'Children' have been allied with 'women', which, while understandable in terms of the construction of 'motherhood' and the structural positioning of women with children within the family, has meant that childhood has often been subsumed within the discourse of 'womanhood'. The link between the two has been explored by feminists. Firestone (1979) refers to the fact that 'women and children are always mentioned in the same breath' and that:

> This oppression is intertwined and mutually re-enforcing in such complex ways that we will be unable to speak of the liberation of women without also discussing the liberation of children and vice versa. (p.73)

She also asserts that:

> We must include the oppression of children in any feminist revolution or we will be subject to the same failing of which we have often accused men: of not having gone deep enough in our analysis, of

having missed an important substratum of oppression merely because it didn't directly concern *us*. (p.101)

Rowbotham (1983), describes the efforts to achieve liberation for children and women in Britain, which were inherent in the 1970s' campaigns to secure nurseries and child care, challenging capitalism and asserting the requirement for a society based on 'co-operation and free association' (p.134).

It is crucial that children are seen as more than part of the trappings of a patriarchal nuclear family. Burman *et al.* (1996) points out that: 'adult–child relations are relational: each structures and constitutes the other'. She warns against moving too far from this position, but acknowledges a diversity of interests. Another appreciation of the complexity of the 'feminization' of children is proposed by Alanen (1994), who suggests that while women and children share some social locations and experiences, they may also occupy oppositional points in relation to each other. One consequence of this is that: 'social relations, (including power relations) can be made visible also from the standpoint of the experience of children' (p.40).

It is important, however, to recognize that childhood, unlike gender, is a temporary not a permanent position: the developmental demands of children for care and protection cannot be argued away when convenient. In the same way that Harding (1987) argues for a 'feminist standpoint' which struggles to see women's social experiences from their point of view rather than a distorted version from the perspective of men, the experiences of children must also be recognized. Within this approach, the 'gender agenda' of feminism is paralleled by a 'generation agenda', described as:

a particular social order that organises children's relations to the world in a systematic way, allocates them a position from which to act and a view and knowledge about themselves and their social relations. (Alanen, 1994, p.37).

Such a 'generational agenda', resulting in the representation of a children's standpoint, would enable more diverse and detailed subjective positions to be defined, and would initiate a more identifiable and (we would hope) more powerful set of rights and obligations. However, there are few examples of reference to generational power and inequality, outside of a distinctive approach which emphasizes children's rights within which there are many different variants and not inconsiderable tensions. Stein argues:

> it is very difficult to make sense of the experiences of children and young people without recognising the construction of childhood as a period of dependency and powerlessness and perceiving children and young people as an identifiable social group with their own set of interests. (1992, p.8)

This is in marked contrast to models of childhood which are constructed strictly within both a deficit and a developmental model: that is, children are in the process of becoming adults and as such are inherently inferior. It also offers a direct challenge to a protectionist approach which (with very few exceptions) views children's interests as inherently part of the family's interests. Within this model children are marginalized, but also subject to paternalistic and protective intervention, often undertaken in 'the best interests of the child' (Alanen, 1994; Qvortrup *et al.*, 1994). As Fox Harding (1991) states:

> with an emphasis on the child's viewpoint, the attribution by adults of what is best for the child ... the very existence of a child care 'system', with the function of making decisions about children, is called into question. (p.155)

A feminist analysis must therefore take account of the need to see children as key players in determining their futures and influential in shaping interventions and outcomes with regard to sexual assault. Such a perspective must be infused with a clear view about the positioning of children and an analysis which takes account of generational inequality. Simultaneously, the interconnections with the oppression of women and the 'gender agenda' need to be acknowledged and explored. Thus far we have attempted to argue that feminist theory must continue to develop the notion of generational inequality, rather as it has already (with varying degrees of success) incorporated the related, but not necessarily parallel, issues of difference relating to ethnicity, ability and sexuality. This includes challenging the notion that children are passive victims and recognizing the many strategies of survival and resistance which they may employ. The abuse of female and male children in residential settings needs to be located within a feminist framework which takes account of all forms of interpersonal violence, and along a continuum which incorporates both public and private locations:

> The way violence is used and acted out in relationships, encounters and institutions is specifically gendered and constructed by, as well as a reflection of, the power relations which constitute hetero-patriarchy. (Hester, Kelly and Radford, 1996, p.4)

There is also a need to identify the broader framework within which power and inequality operate. This includes exploring the issue of power within organizations especially as this is mediated by gender and sexuality, and specifically the dynamics within residential child care and other children's establishments (Green, this volume; Jones, 1993).

Stein (1992) distinguishes different forms of abuse including sanctioned, institutional, systematic and individual abuse and locates these within a wider framework of inequality, particularly highlighting the location of gender and generational power. Waldby, Clancy, Emetchi and Summerfield (1989) propose a model which comprises two concepts of power; structural power and personal power. The former offers opportunities for the misuse of power by the powerful. In terms of institutions, we can see the legitimized power over children and over other marginalized people, and the various ways in which this may be manifest in residential settings such as children's homes and residential schools. The latter – personal power – may be exercised in positive or negative ways. Work must be undertaken to empower individuals and groups, to ensure that victimization and persecution cannot occur and that personal power is not exercised to the detriment of others. This requires consideration of real ways to bring about the empowerment of *all* children and young people, while recognizing the enormity of the responsibility placed upon staff in institutional settings to exert power positively towards those in their care.

Another consideration concerns the abuse of boys within the looked after system: this is problematic for several reasons. Often the inherent issues of gender and of sexuality are not fully explored: there may be a reluctance to address such issues which may be constructed within notions of homosexuality rather than abuse. Hence they could – we would argue, incorrectly – be viewed as fuelling homophobia and stereotypical images of gay men as predatory, despite the fact that many known and convicted abusers are married and seemingly heterosexual. The abuse of boys also raises complex issues regarding masculinity and concerns that this is fundamentally undermined when male children are sexually assaulted by men (see Kershaw, this volume). The dynamics of power and inequality within some residential settings may be understood in part as contributing to the 'feminisation' of male children in such a way as to enhance the masculinity of those in charge. Burman *et al.*, (1996) describes how women and children are expected to function together as the 'other' of men:

> The child, like the woman, is an object to be known, the boundaries of whose personal privacy are violated without apology, whose actions are surveyed, regulated, measured, and constructed by the omnipotent viewer, who is positioned as 'caring'. (p.54)

Thus the child is viewed as passive and inferior, dependent on the competent (male) adult.

Gillespie, in exploring the meaning and impact of rape on both women and men, suggests that the similarities and differences are: '... both a product and a reproduction of gendered power relations' (1996, p.163). And Florence Rush states 'Men rape other men because they feminize their victims within heterosexual patterns of dominance and subordination'. (1990, p.169)

Such analyses are supported by accounts of regimes in which sexual assault has taken place: for example, Castle Hill, Meadowdale. A more serious problem concerns the sub-text of the debate concerning the horror of male rape. Notwithstanding the apparent numbers of boys affected *vis-à-vis* girls – which in itself may be a reflection of 'public' concern and the limited ability to hear the voices of girls – there is also the implication that abuse is more traumatic for boys than girls and that (hetero)sexual assault involving girls is somehow less serious and 'normalised' (Warner, 1996). This is to some extent borne out by the fact that, unlike young women, who may be described as 'seductive' or 'sexually provocative', young men are portrayed almost entirely as victims (Mills and Karban, 1996). A similar point is made by Kelly *et al.* (1995) in relation to abuse outside the family where there is a risk that: 'The abuse of girls and young women (becomes) invisible, alongside a differential attention being paid to the abuse of boys and young men.' (p.33)

In this section we hope to have achieved a location of children and young people within a feminist discourse. The positioning of children 'within' a discourse rather than affording them their own children's standpoint is questioned. A major challenge for feminism is reconciling the diversity and difference of interests which prevail, and so it is with children. Like women, children are not a monolithic category, yet they have been 'familiarized' or 'feminized' within a wide social context. Changes in welfare practices must be made if children and young people's voices truly are to be heard in order to improve their safety and well-being. Thus will the potential for a revised understanding of 'childhood' and a consequent re-appraisal of children and young people's positioning be increased. The conclusion of this chapter returns to those children and young people who are 'looked after' and addresses possibilities for change.

A vision for the future

While a Utopian scenario might render the notion of 'substitute care' redundant, with children and young people staying secure within their families and communities (however these might be conceived) it is important to consider some of the aspects of the real world and how these might be altered now. The concept of a 'safe environment' offers an overarching approach for residential care, as one

> ... which values young people and staff alike; it respects the contribution of young people and encourages their own self-determination, diversity, independence and self-esteem within an overall anti-oppressive framework. (Mills 1995, p.59)

Within such an environment it is possible to ensure that young people are offered everyday choices, leading to a strong sense of their own value and efficacy in the world. Without this, safety mechanisms such as complaints procedures, offer only basic first order change, rather than any fundamental shift in power and relationships. This extends to participation in most matters of everyday organization within the establishment, including staff selection, the introduction of new residents, as well as choice of menus and decor. Only when young people have experienced being able to influence their day-to-day lives, will they begin to believe that they can influence other matters of importance. In order to implement this, staff too must feel that they are empowered to take decisions and involve themselves with young people in the running of the home – clear support and supervision structures must be in place for this to be achieved. However, it is necessary to recognize that policies of empowerment for children and young people cannot be achieved in isolation, but must permeate all the everyday practices of care. This is not a small scale project. '... what change can be made to children's position within society *without* subverting existing hierarchies, *without* challenging "society" as we know it?' (Kitzinger 1997, p.172)

Young people must also be listened to genuinely if they are to access support and make sense of their experiences. In interviewing children and young people from a range of family and care backgrounds, Butler and Williamson (1994) found that a quarter of their sample held strong convictions that they would talk to no-one, indicating a lack of trust and belief that no one could help. Other young people felt that their experiences were trivialized, or that judgements were made. It will clearly take more than even a well-thought out complaints procedure to persuade such young people to report instances of abuse within a care setting (see also Green, this volume). If implemented, the principles proposed by Butler and Williamson would go some way to challenge the victim role offered by the child care system, and enable young people to take a more active part in keeping safe, without leaving them vulnerable in the guise of autonomy and independence. This point is reiterated by Utting in his report of the Review of the Safeguards for Children Living away from Home where he comments that 'Looking after them would be easier and much more effective if we really heard and understood what they have to tell us.' (1997, p.7) Finally, it may be useful to reconsider the three aspects of 'care' described earlier in this chapter. These are: the need to respond to the particular reason(s) why a child or young person needs substitute care; to counteract previously identified disadvantageous life experiences; and ensure that further disadvantage is not caused by the provision of 'care'.

Care and protection under the legislation and child care system in and of itself is not sufficient to create a safe and secure environment for children and young people. The provision of accommodation within a custodial model of care fails to meet the very specialized needs of young people disadvantaged by abuse, neglect and family trauma. Their needs may include counselling and therapeutic intervention to help them move forward positively in their lives. At the same time every effort must be made to ensure that positive educational opportunities are available, and that wider social opportunities are within their reach: to avoid the spiral of poor or non-existent qualifications, unemployment and homelessness. Crucially, the experience of care should be one which enhances life chances and possibilities: the damage caused by further abuse and neglect must not continue.

Listening to children and young people, positioned from a standpoint which recognizes generational power and oppressions as well as other dimensions of inequality, can only contribute to this process. Recognition of children's strategies of resistance and survival, and a willingness to listen and learn from these, is central to this endeavour. Do we want to hear?

References

Alanen, L. (1994) 'Gender and generation: feminism and the "child question"' in J. Qvortrup, M. Bardy, G. Sgritta and H. Wintersburger (eds) *Childhood Matters: Social Theory, Practice and Politics*, European Centre, Aldershot, Avebury.

Bebbington, A. and J. Miles (1989) 'The background of children who enter Local Authority Care' in *British Journal of Social Work*, 19 (5), pp.349–68.

Berridge, D. and I. Brodie (1996) 'Residential child care in England and Wales' in M. Hill and J. Aldgate (eds) *Child Welfare Services, Developments in Law, Policy, Practice and Research*, London, Jessica Kingsley.

Biehal, N., J. Clayden, M. Stein and J. Wade (1995) *Moving On, Young People and Leaving Care Schemes*, London, HMSO.

Blagg, H., J. A. Hughes and C. Wattam (eds) (1989) *Child Sexual Abuse: Listening, Hearing and Validating the Experiences of Children*, Harlow, Longman.

Buchanan, A. and J. Ten Brinke (1998) *What Happened When they Were Grown Up?* York, York Publishing Service

Burman, E., P. Aldred, K. Bewley, B. Goldberg, C. Heenan, D. Marks, J. Marshall, K. Taylor, R. Ullah and S. Warner (1996) *Challenging Women: Psychology's Exclusions, Feminist Possibilities*, Buckingham, Open University Press.

Butler, I. and H. Williamson (1994) *Children Speak – Children, Trauma and Social Work*, Brighton, Pennant Professional Books.

Butler, I. with H. Williamson (1996) '"Safe?" Involving children in child protection' in I. Butler and I. Shaw (eds) *A Case of Neglect: Children's Experiences and the Sociology of Childhood*, Aldershot, Avebury.

Campbell, B. (1988) *Unofficial Secrets: Child Sexual Abuse – The Cleveland Case.* London, Virago.

Davies, B and R. Harre (1990) 'Positioning: the discursive production of selves', *Journal for the Theory of Social Behaviour*, 20(1), pp.43–63.

Department of Health (1989) *An Introduction to the Children Act*, London, HMSO.

Department of Health (1991) *The Children Act 1989: Guidance and Regulations Volume 4: Residental Care*, London, HMSO.

Driver, E. and A. Droisen (eds) (1989) *Child Sexual Abuse, Feminist Perspectives*, London, Macmillan.

Fairclough, N. (1989) *Language and Power*, London, Longman.

Firestone, S. (1979) *The Dialectic of Sex: A Case for Feminist Revolution* (2nd edn), London, The Women's Press.

Fox Harding, L. (1991) *Perspectives in Child Care Policy*, London, Longman.

Gibbons, J., S. Conroy and C. Bell (1995) *Operating the child protection system, a study of child protection practice in English local authorities*, London, HMSO.

Gillespie, T. (1996)'Rape crisis centres and "male rape": a face of the backlash' in M. Hester, L. Kelly and J. Radford (1996) (eds) *Women, Violence and Male Power*, Buckingham, Open University Press.

Harding, S. (ed) (1987) *Feminism and Methodology: Social Science Issues*, Milton Keynes, Open University Press.

Hearn, J. (1990) '"Child abuse" and men's violence' in Violence Against Children Study Group, *Taking Child Abuse Seriously*, London, Unwin Hyman.

Hester, M., L. Kelly and J. Radford (eds) (1996) *Women, Violence and Male Power*, Buckingham, Open University Press.

Hughes, W. (1986) *Report of the Committee of Inquiry into Children's Homes and Hostels*, Belfast, HMSO.

Jackson, S. (1994) 'Educating children in residential and foster care' *Oxford Review of Education*, 20, (3) pp.267–79.

Jones, J. (1993) 'Child abuse: developing a framework for understanding power relationships in practice' in H. Ferguson, R. Gilligan and R. Torode (eds) *Surviving Childhood Adversity: Issues for Policy and Practice*, Dublin, Social Studies Press.

Kelly, L., R. Wingfield, S. Burton and L. Regan (1995) *Splintered Lives: Sexual Exploitation of Children in the Context of Children's Rights and Child Protection*, London, Barnardo's.

Kilgallon, W. (1995) *Report of the Independent Review into Allegations of Abuse at Meadowdale Children's Home*, Northumberland, Northumberland Council.

Kirkwood, A.. (1992) *The Leicestershire Inquiry: the report of an inquiry into aspects of the management of children's homes in Leicestershire between 1973 and 1986.* Leicester, Leicestershire County Council.

Kitzinger, J. (1997) 'Who are you kidding? Children, power and the struggle against sexual abuse' in A. James and A. Prout (eds) *Constructing and Reconstructing Childhood: Contemporary Issues in the Sociological Study of Childhood*, London, Falmer Press.

Lyon, C. (1997) 'Children abused within the care system' in N Parton. (ed.) *Child Protection and Family Support: Tensions, Contradictions and Possibilities*, London, Routledge.

Makrinioti, D. (1994) 'Conceptualization of childhood in a welfare state: a critical reappraisal' in J. Qvortrup, M. Bardy, G. Sgritta and H. Wintersburger (eds) *Childhood Matters: Social Theory, Practice and Politics*, European Centre, Aldershot, Avebury.

Mills, S. (1995) 'Creating a safe environment in residential child care' in K. Stone and I. Vallender (eds.) *Spinning Plates – Practice Teaching and Learning for the Residential Child Care Initiative*, London, CCETSW.

Mills, S. and K. Karban (1996) *Developing Feminist Practice in Residential Child Care: Swimming Against the Tide?* Paper presented at 'Feminism and Social Work in the Year 2000, Conflicts and Controversies' Conference, University of Bradford, October 1996.

Morris, J. (1995) *Gone Missing?: A Research and Policy Review of Disabled Children Living Away from their Families.* London, Who Cares? Trust.

NSPCC (1995) *So Who Are We Meant to Trust Now?* London, NSPCC.

Parton, C. (1990) 'Women, gender oppression and child abuse' in The Violence Against Children Study Group, *Taking Child Abuse Seriously*, London, Unwin Hyman.

Pringle, K. (1998) 'Men and childcare: policy and practice' in J. Popay, J. Hearn and J. Edwards (eds) *Men, Gender Divisions and Welfare*, London, Routledge.

Qvortrup, J., M. Bardy, G. Sgritta and H. Wintersburger (1994) (eds) *Childhood Matters: Social Theory, Practice and Politics*, European Centre, Aldershot, Avebury.

Richardson, S. and H. Bacon (eds) (1991) *Child Sexual Abuse: Whose Problem?* Birmingham, Venture Press.

Rowbotham, S. (1983) *Dreams and Dilemmas*, London, Virago.

Rush, F. (1990) 'The many faces of backlash' in D. Leidholdt and J. G. Raymond (eds.) *The Sexual Liberals and the Attack on Feminism*, Oxford, Pergamon Press.

Stein, M. (1992) *The Abuses and Uses of Residential Child Care'*, paper presented at 'Surviving Childhood Adversity' Conference, Dublin, 2–5 July, 1992.

Stone, M. (1990) *Young People Leaving Care*, Redhill, The Royal Philanthropic Society.

Strathdee, R. and M. Johnson (1994) *Out of Care and On the Streets: Young People, Care Leavers and Homelessness*, London, Centrepoint.

Utting, W. (1991) *Children in the Public Care, A Review of Residential Child Care* London, HMSO.

Utting, W. (1997) *People Like Us, The Report Of The Review Of The Safeguards For Children Living Away From Home*, London, HMSO.

Waldby, C., A. Clancy, J. Emetchi and C. Summerfield 'Theoretical perspectives on father–daughter incest' in E. Driver and A. Droisen (eds) (1989) *Child Sexual Abuse, Feminist Perspectives*, London, Macmillan.

Warner, N. (1992) *Choosing with Care – The Report of the Committee of Inquiry into the Selection, Development and Management of Staff in Children's Homes*, London, HMSO.

Warner, S. (1996) 'Constructing femininity: models of child sexual abuse and the production of "women"' in E. Burman, P. Aldred, K. Bewley, B. Goldberg, C. Heenan, D. Marks, J. Marshall, K. Taylor, R. Ullah and S. Warner (eds) *Challenging Women, Psychology's Exclusions, Feminist Possibilities*, Buckingham, Open University Press.

3
Satanist Ritual Abuse – the Challenge for Feminists

Sarah Nelson

Confronting satanist ritual abuse and its characteristics

Over the past decade, very many people working with sexual abuse have confronted disturbing evidence of a form of organized abuse which is particularly shocking, disorienting and different – however experienced they may be in working with sexual violence against women and children. They have included workers in rape crisis centres or women's refuges, social workers, children's home care staff, paediatricians or police working with disturbed, distressed children, mental health professionals or lay counsellors working with adult survivors, lawyers involved in high-profile court cases, journalists covering those cases, academics writing about modern child protection practice, and protective mothers traumatized by information from their own children.

Satanist ritual abuse (hereinafter referred to as SRA) is the major, and best-documented, form of ritual abuse (RA), and is also a form of sadistic organized abuse. It is characterized by special rituals and ceremonies, practised by a variety of cults dedicated to the worship of Satan. There is widespread debate on definitions (Finkelhor *et al.* 1988; Goodwin 1994; McFadyen *et al.* 1993). One of the most widely-quoted definitions of ritual abuse comes from the McFadyen paper:

> The involvement of children in physical, psychological and sexual abuse associated with repeated activities (rituals) which purport to relate the abuse to contexts of a religious, magical or supernatural kind (p.37).

Features of SRA, documented in a substantial and growing professional literature, include:

1. Highly organized, hierarchical cult structures, operating within and often between countries. The core membership is intergenerational but cults also recruit from outwith their ranks. Members are given specified roles in the hierarchy throughout their lives – not simply as children – and this poses particular challenges to feminists, because mothers and grandmothers play a key socialization role in intergenerational cults and because women and children are routinely involved as perpetrators of sexual, physical and emotional torture.

2. Belief systems which invert Christian moral values of good and evil and draw power from perversion and pain. Ceremonies in settings like graveyards, church crypts, forests and cellars feature frightening masks and costumes, dancing and chanting and include sexual orgies, animal sacrifice and also, it is widely claimed by survivors, human sacrifice. The bizarre, fantastic and, to many people medi-aeval features of such beliefs and rituals, have encouraged popular and media scepticism and a mistaken assumption that accepting these rituals take place also means believing that Satan and other evil spirits exist. Yet people do not assume they have to take on the belief systems of numerous other cults throughout the world whose existence they accept. Many writers on SRA choose the term 'satanist' rather than 'satanic', emphasizing the human followers of a cult rather than the involvement of any supernatural agency.

3. Forms of sexual, physical and emotional abuse of extreme severity and perversity, which evoke horror and nauseated revulsion. For instance: forced consumption of blood, faeces and body fluids, deprivation of sleep and food, consumption of animal and human flesh, bondage and electric shocks, imprisonment in confined spaces, killing of pets, coercion of children to torture other children.

4. Both the deliberate malevolence towards children (Mollon, 1994) and the revolting, sadistic nature of abusive practices cause many workers to question their basic, lifelong beliefs about the nature of human beings, and the limits of human behaviour. Those with reli-gious beliefs can also find them profoundly undermined.

5. Organized involvement in highly lucrative, large-scale child pornography, child prostitution and other organized crime like drug-dealing: 'benefits' which accrue very unequally within the hierarchy. These do not fully account for the baffling question of motivation, but they are pervasive features.

6. Highly-developed techniques of brainwashing and mind control, begun in infancy in intergenerational cults, designed to secure and

maintain absolute loyalty and secrecy for life. Systematic techniques include use of drugs and hypnosis, psychological confusion, torture and near-death experiences. The effects on many survivors of these mind control techniques are often bizarre and frightening to those who work with them – extreme terror, dissociative states, the emergence of many 'alters' in therapy (so-called multiple personality), gross self-harm, visual and auditory hallucinations.

7. Involvement in cult activity by highly respectable families, by wealthy and powerful people, and by some members of respected and trusted professions, including those within the child protection system: for instance, judges, lawyers, social workers, police, politicians, doctors and pathologists. This knowledge often proves the most disorienting, frightening and destructive of all: firstly, because personal judgments of others are turned upside-down – people may be leading entirely different lives, and may have entirely different motivations from the ones they present. Secondly, the very people entrusted with enforcing the child protection system may be undermining it from within. Who can be trusted? It is easy for workers to be overwhelmed with a paralysing, paranoiac conviction that nobody can be – even though the majority of professionals will not in fact be involved.

These and other features of SRA beliefs and practices are discussed in more detail in Coleman, (1994); Hudson, (1991); Katchen and Sakheim, (1992) and Tate, (1991).

Feminists have not simply had to judge all this overwhelming information about SRA. They have had simultaneously also to assess authors and vocal movements who deny the very existence of SRA and ascribe allegations to a 'witch-hunt', fomented by fundamentalist Christians, crusading social workers, assorted feminists, and self-aggrandising therapists (Jenkins and Maier-Katkin, 1991; Offshe and Waters, 1994; La Fontaine, 1998). Many workers with children and adults have been vilified and professionally discredited by courts and media for standing by their conviction that SRA exists (Tate, 1991) and this itself has proved highly intimidating, even traumatic, for them.

Priorities for feminists

Respect for survivor testimony

How should feminists respond to SRA, and what responsibilities do we have to adult and child survivors? First, I believe we must take seriously their trauma and their testimonies, and seek to understand the nature of their experience. We cannot make a principle of listening to, believing and respecting abused women in some contexts, then refuse to do so in others. This does *not* mean we must accept all the allegations and claims as literally true. Some remain unproven in our present state of knowledge: some beliefs in fantastic events are achieved by conjuring tricks and other forms of deception. Some practices will lie beyond the capacity of individual non-survivors to take on board. If so, I think there is no shame in admitting that honestly to survivors. But respecting the testimonies of children and adults does mean accepting their integrity and intelligence, and the reality of their serious life-trauma. It means listening closely to the evidence they give, and making the effort to interpret it in an informed way. If survivors find the courage to tell in the face of unimaginable intimidation, then surely we can find the courage to listen.

When SRA survivors and those prepared to stand beside them have already faced so much vilification from powerful lobbies who work to the benefit of abusive adults, they are doubly demoralized when feminists join the chorus of ridicule, as Louise Armstrong does in her analysis of SRA in *Rocking the Cradle of Sexual Politics* (Armstrong, 1996). This is only likely to contribute to the silencing of survivors, a silencing against which Armstrong has so fiercely protested in the rest of her courageous and outspoken writing on sexual abuse.

The Canadian Panel on Violence against Women (1993), which undertook a large-scale consultation exercise with women and their support organizations, took on board the 'compelling testimonies' of RA survivors. They point out (p.47):

> Survivors of ritual abuse continue to pay a high price for the disbelief they encounter. Without recognition and support it will be impossible for many to come to terms with their experiences. Adding further pain to those who have already been so injured seems at odds with any notion of a just or a more equitable society.

Maintaining our critical analysis and exposing falsehood

Second, we must maintain the basic principles of our feminist analysis in the face of shocking and disorienting information. In seeking to understand SRA and in particular the involvement of women, it is crucial to analyse its power dynamics as a hierarchical political and social system, and the nature of coercion within it. Who benefits most? Who pays the heaviest price? Who consumes the pornography? Who is mutilated in its making? (See Kelly in this volume). Asking such questions makes it easier to understand problematic issues about women's involvement. For instance, Kate Cook (1995), writing about the complexities of working with ritual abuse, points out the difficulty for adult women in leaving a satanic abuse group. They have usually been involved since birth, and their view of the world has been warped by lies told by their abusers who often claim all politicians, police and social workers rape children. So the women don't know whom to trust outside the group, and in any case it is extremely hard to find support. They may already be branded as liars, as hopelessly unreliable, as self-harmers and psychiatric cases.

It also becomes easier to comprehend how women might be involved in serious abuse of children when the extent to which even young children are forced to abuse each other, with dire punishments for refusal, is understood. Mothers are also told that if they do not hurt their own children, then someone else will hurt those children more. Many years of punishment, mind control and enforcement of strict obedience make people compliant and it can appear impossible to resist the following of orders. This is familiar to us from human behaviour under totalitarian regimes. This chapter describes several ways of understanding SRA which are helpful in explaining motivation and response, and making links with more familiar forms of gross repression. The behaviour of cult hierarchies can be seen to play out, in extreme form, the brutal group values of many societies. Ritual abuse practices have many links with forms of political torture and mind control techniques used by oppressive regimes throughout the world. Large-scale use of deception, lies and tricks in SRA provide mundane explanations of incredible accounts, and explain why survivors (and their supporters) lose trust in their own perceptions of what is real. All these 'ways of seeing' help us direct attention to familiar motivations for power and control, hedonistic gratification and large-scale financial gain.

Similarly, it is important for feminists to identify clearly the interests of the powerful lobbies who deny the existence of SRA, and vilify those convinced by the evidence that this gross form of organized exploitation is real. Whom does this propaganda benefit? Who pays the cost? We must critically scrutinize it continually for the very characteristics it ascribes to 'believers' – falsehood, gullibility and crusading zeal. For example: critics allege that a 'witch-hunt' (as they often term it) of international proportions has taken place against innocent parents (or innocent pagans) by crusading social workers and therapists. How strange, that it is the alleged perpetrators of the so called 'witch-hunt' who have been its objects of pursuit in the media, the courts and child-care agencies: it is social workers and therapists who have found their careers undermined or destroyed.

Again, anyone who has followed highly-publicized cases of alleged SRA has noticed that similar stories and conspiracy theories keep recurring mysteriously in the media to explain away the testimonies of children and women. These need to be carefully scrutinized instead of being accepted with gullibility. For instance, during the 'Orkney child abuse affair' (1991–92), which became the subject of an official Inquiry (Clyde 1992), claims or innuendo were repeatedly reported that one Christian basic grade social worker had influenced Orkney social work department and the Northern Constabulary into carrying out 'dawn raids' against four respectable families. The obvious fact was ignored that even had the worker sought this outcome, they lacked the professional status or power to achieve it. It was also widely reported that a conference on ritual abuse in Aberdeen had infused the social work department with beliefs about ritual abuse, yet the then social work director, Paul Lee, stated that none of his staff had attended it. Variants on these 'conspiracy theories' infused the BBC 'faction' drama *Flowers of the Forest* (broadcast 26 October 1996).

In Orkney at this time another story recurred: that the distinguished American child abuse specialist Roland Summit had inspired an international 'witch-hunt' by writing that if children denied abuse, this meant it had probably happened. Strangely, this exact claim surfaced in a *New Yorker* editorial of 3 October 1994:

> A psychiatrist named Roland Summit explained to the jury in the Kelly Michaels case that when children deny sexual abuse happened, the denial can be evidence that the abuses actually did occur.

Summit replied to the newspaper that he had been wholly uninvolved in this case and had said nothing to the jury: 'It would be fatuous to argue that denial is really confirmation in disguise. I have never said such a thing anywhere.' (*Accuracy About Abuse*, 14 February 1997) Sexual abuse is about lies, distortion and deception: SRA is founded on these things. We must not be naive but expect to find them in the public debate on SRA. Marjorie Orr is an outstanding and influential example of someone who has exposed many lies through painstaking research, especially about the 'false memory syndrome' lobby. Her regular *Accuracy About Abuse* newsletters have become key information sources for anyone seeking the facts in publicised cases or debates.

Yet she has been a lonely voice and in contrast, professional child-care agencies in the past decade have been effectively silenced by the intimidation and ridicule of the vocal sceptics. (Nelson, 1998) This has led lawyers, social workers and police to hold back from presenting evidence of ritual abuse in child protection court cases, for fear that all their evidence will be discredited. This is understandable but it also creates a form of collusion. Only by naming the phenomenon and presenting the evidence clearly and consistently, will credibility be established. Thus the simple act of standing up publicly to be counted in whatever work we do is tremendously important and makes a strong collective impact. As a journalist and a researcher, if anyone asks me sceptically if I believe SRA exists, I always say 'yes I do'. Usually this leads to an interested willingness to listen rather than simple rejection: often we will fail to convince people, but their thinking has been informed by the discussion. We only risk ridicule; survivors and protective parents have needed, and found, much greater courage.

Taking time to come to terms with our own trauma

Third, it is essential to ensure we ourselves are strong enough to stand beside survivors – by taking the time we need, with active support from others, to work through our own reactions of horror, disgust, fear and disbelief. These feelings are natural, are almost universal and need to be anticipated. In her survey of members of RAINS (Ritual Abuse Information, Network and Support), the psychologist Sheila Youngson found widespread reactions of fear, intimidation and disorientation among professionals. What they were hearing was 'overwhelming': inducing 'nausea, disgust and fear, professional helplessness and inadequacy' (Youngson, 1994). The sense of profound isolation, of possessing a terrible secret which nobody else wants to hear, has also been powerful for us all.

But we are not alone, and members of RAINS or other support networks have also found great strength from each other, from non-survivors and survivors alike, to recover from that initial, unforgettable trauma and accommodate terrible knowledge without being destroyed by it. The world never looks quite the same again, but you do come out the other side, and with a proper sense of proportion: SRA is a pernicious phenomenon, but it is still a minority form of sexual violence. It is also important and salutary for non-survivors to remember that their own trauma is slight in comparison with that of people who have lived the experience of SRA, or who have discovered as protective parents that their own children are doing so. While it is foolish to underrate our own need for continuing support, it is also self-deluding and disrespectful to argue that through isolation, trauma, professional vilification and silencing, professionals' experience becomes similar to that of survivors.

Empowering survivors and respecting their knowledge

Fourth, we should always work and campaign from the principle that survivors and their support groups must actively be consulted with respect for their own priorities, knowledge and experience. Our work should be closely informed by survivor knowledge and be geared towards empowerment rather than the creation of further dependency. This is a major issue in therapy and counselling, especially given the problems raised by indoctrination, mind control and dissociation in SRA.

Kate Cook's paper (1995), written with a survivor, is very helpful in suggesting strategies for supporting survivors which are based on a realistic feminist understanding of their experience. She argues against assuming women are safe now just because they are adults: they may still be victims of regular abuse. On the other hand, workers should not try and protect them 24-hours a day. Not only is this impossible, but it creates or perpetuates dependency. Just as women experiencing domestic violence need to take their own decisions to leave, so do women experiencing SRA. The challenges lie in enabling women to know they can do this for themselves and in finding appropriate ways to offer support. Again, the survivor activist Caryn Stardancer emphasizes the importance and empowering effect of encouraging survivors to take control of their own healing:

> The key to recovery from mind control is restoration of self-awareness and critical thinking. Understanding the methods and dynamics of mind control and conditioning is the first step in reasserting fundamental human rights (1996).

Survivors, she says, can themselves make use of methods to combat the tendency to dissociative states and trance logic. They can develop specific strategies giving them skills to desensitize triggers which maintain conditioned responses, replacing them with associations chosen by survivors. The SAFE newsletter, written by survivors for survivors, gives many examples of these techniques.

The empowerment of women survivors within conventional mental health systems is a particularly urgent issue for feminists (Russell, 1995) and one which receives strong impetus from developing knowledge about SRA. This knowledge enables us to identify many mental health symptoms as possible consequences of this form of abuse. There is not space here for discussion of this major issue, but it is gradually being more fully explored, especially in relation to 'multiple personality disorder' (Young *et al.* 1991; Mollon, 1996) Elsewhere I have discussed clues to an SRA history in certain phobias, eating disorders, obsessive compulsive disorders and hallucinatory symptoms (Nelson, 1996) Such post-traumatic effects, however, are widely misdiagnosed (for instance as borderline personality disorder) and oppressively treated in psychiatric hospitals, special hospitals and penal institutions. Campaigning for radical changes in the mental health system needs to become a priority.

Grounding our understanding of SRA in an analysis of other forms of oppression

I have suggested several important strategies for feminists in confronting the phenomenon of SRA. I believe they will be considerably assisted by a comparative analysis of other forms of oppression: therefore this chapter concludes with a more detailed look at comparative research. So long as SRA is seen as uniquely perverse, bizarre, fantastic and incomprehensible, perpetrators and their influential allies, for instance in the 'false memory syndrome' lobby, will continue successfully to persuade public and media alike that its very existence is patently absurd. Secondly, those who wish to stand by child and adult survivors will struggle to make sense of their knowledge, to analyse the dynamics of this abuse, to find reference-points to other known forms of human behaviour, or to plan campaigning strategies. It is thus extremely helpful to our understanding to make connections between SRA and other, more familiar, patterns of human exploitation. Three valuable examples follow.

Caryn Stardancer is founder and executive director of Survivorship, an American not-for-profit organization dedicated to campaigning, public education and support for survivors of RA. She describes RA as (1996): 'a rigid and ruthless hierarchy of power maintained by torture and terror, sustained by an elaborate series of lies.' In her provocative view, the cult reality is a microcosm of the denied reality of the dominant culture. It acts out society's blaming and subjugation of the weak, its objectification of gender, its demonizing of minorities, its abuse of children. In some societies these abuses are open and continuing (for example, female circumcision and purdah) and are justified by religious systems. In many countries, brutal rape in war has been and continues to be justified by claims of religious or racial superiority. In others extreme subjugation and degradation may appear under particular regimes (for example, under Nazism in Germany) or at certain times (the extreme, widespread sexual violence in the former Yugoslavia).

Stardancer has defined ritual abuse as any repeated, systematic mistreatment perpetrated in the name of an ideology, dogma or belief system. From her own experience, cult leaders were often members of the international élite class, who were wealthy because of their corruption. Child pornography and prostitution were essential and highly lucrative industries of these groups. This reinforces the point that there is no necessary contradiction between a genuine, quasi-religious belief system and mercenary motivations. It is not a matter of opportunist child abusers latching onto the activities of satanists who are 'pure believers'. A profoundly selfish and hedonistic belief-system, typical of satanist cults, itself rationalizes exploitation for motives of personal power and financial gain. At the same time, unconnected groups involved in large-scale organized crime, smuggling or drug-dealing, will find a vested interest in co-operating at intervals with SRA cults, and vice-versa. This serves to strengthen and expand international patterns of sexual exploitation.

In contrast to the status, wealth and influence of high-ranking cult members, Stardancer painted a picture of the social status of most women RA survivors which is a familiar and recognizable one to us. She ridiculed the myth that women reporting RA had been hypnotised by unscrupulous therapists. Few survivors in the USA even had health insurance, and a large proportion could not afford any therapy. Most barely made a living, and many were making what money they could in the sex industry. A vast number were poverty-stricken, and suffering physical injury-linked problems. Caryn says in her public speeches: 'I never forget the torture chamber as the background to this podium.' Her abuse has given her a thirst for justice and recharged her for the fight. She has come to know, after many years, the final triumph of sanity, happiness and love, and chosen to 'live in the land of recovery' (Stardancer, 1996).

Another very valuable means of understanding and contextualizing ritual abuse has come from Joan Golston, a clinical social worker who works in Seattle. She suggests reports of RA can be most fruitfully evaluated as allegations of systematic torture akin to brainwashing in wartime, or abuse of political dissidents by dictatorial regimes. Yet the international torture recovery community seems unaware of RA clients, and has had little dialogue with therapists treating RA or multiple personality disorders. In contrast to people in many other parts of the world, most people in the USA or Britain are unfamiliar with political torture. They are thus slow to recognize that the RA client may be a survivor of a process of formal domestic torture. Golston quotes Dr Inge Kemp Lunde, director of a torture recovery centre in Copenhagen, who sees the purpose of torture as: 'not primarily to extract information ... it is to destroy the victim's personality, to break him down, to create guilt and shame, to ensure he will never again be a leader.' (1992)

If we do not seriously consider the concept of torture, says Golston, we run the risk of accepting the severity of clients' psychological symptoms, minimizing the abusive acts which may have set these symptoms in motion. She contends RA abuse should be understood as a specific form of purposeful torture akin to thought reform, as in the destruction of Jewish people by the Nazis, or the use of electric shock, sexual assault and death threats during the imprisonment of political opponents by South American military dictatorships. When viewed in this light, RA may lose some of its controversial bizarreness, allowing us to proceed with research and treatment in concert with those involved in other forms of torture recovery. When we overlook existing knowledge about torture, she says, we deprive ourselves of a well documented data base.

She lists various forms of sexual torture including the known humiliation of forced nakedness, rape, use of degrading language, pregnancy, threats of death, and the 'good guy' routine which gives experience of dashed hope and general mistrust even towards agents of goodwill. (Many SRA survivors describe being rescued from the 'bad parent' by 'the good parent', who later abuses them with equal violence.) Golston describes the processes of torture: first initiation or breaking in to traumatize and break resistance, to damage family ties, to spread terror and compliance and to isolate. Victims must helplessly watch loved ones being brutalized. Then follows isolation, deprivation and confinement. Analysing comparative studies throughout the world, she says, reduces the sense of isolation and alienation among RA therapists – they are in touch with those who know torture as a terrible, but not uncommon, phenomenon (Golston, 1992).

A third way of understanding ritual abuse comes through exploring its pervasive use of deception, tricks and lies. Brenda Roberts (1996) makes the unbelievable comprehensible and attributes responsibility where it belongs – on human rather than demonic agency. She gives mundane explanations both for incredible beliefs and for incredible statements sincerely believed by child and adult survivors. Such beliefs – for instance, about flying in spaceships – discredit them with police, social workers, judges and the media, yet they may result from conjuring tricks, from sensory deprivation or from reality-changing drugs. Her work links to that of Golston, in that it enables us to relate to the ways victims' perceptions of reality are commonly changed by powerful and oppressive agents. Most people know something of the totalitarian thought control methods used by the Nazis and know too, that charismatic cult leaders have persuaded hundreds of followers to commit mass suicide. The force created by identification with the group, and with all-powerful leaders, is clear both from these examples, and from the history of the behaviour of many of the Japanese military in the Second World War.

The great strength of Roberts' presentations lies in making her audience painfully aware of the way we ourselves, or ordinary people we know of from similar cultures, can behave under lesser or shorter-term stress than experienced by RA survivors. Hostages captured by terrorists have identified with, or protected, their captors after a short time in an intense relationship with them. The American hostage Patty Hearst was even persuaded to rob a bank for the cause her captors espoused. In Northern Ireland, methods used by the British on internees during the 1970s – including sensory deprivation, wallstanding, hooding and 'white noise' – disoriented unusually tough paramilitary fighters within a week. Even accidental events can cause extreme disorientation and bizarre behaviour, such as hypothermia and exposure in mountaineers. Roberts also makes a powerful point about the profound effects sleep deprivation has on the mind: 'We are all', she says, 'only three nights away from psychosis.' The state induced by such sleep deprivation can mimic the symptoms of paranoid schizophrenia – a common diagnosis, not just among SRA survivors, but among survivors of 'ordinary' sexual abuse who are referred to the mental health system.

In SRA, Roberts says, an elaborate system of tricks destroys trust in one's own perceptions, and seems to demonstrate the total power of the group – including magical powers. The layers of trickery are extraordinary. Perpetrators may throw scalding water over victims and say it is cold water. When the victim is burned, she is told this is because she is so evil. In another example, a child was tricked into believing her cat was killed over and over again, yet it kept coming back to life (Roberts, 1996). Thus Sue Hutchinson, founder of the RA survivors' SAFE helpline, describes (personal communication) how often survivors will relate seeing figures at rituals with terrifying heads, such as demons or goats: 'I always ask, was he wearing trousers and shoes under the costume? And they say, oh.....yes..... now I remember.' (Hutchinson, 1996)

Non-survivors must be equally alert to the layers of lies and conjuring tricks – especially through the written word. In our case, we need to suspect not the ordinary shoes below the demon's costume, but the wolf in innocent sheep's clothing, the torturer in the respectable suit. Why is that so difficult, when in vicious political regimes throughout the world he is, after all, a commonplace? We cannot in isolation find the courage and influence to stand beside women and children to help expose those who have exploited them in the grossest of ways, but only through a collective act. Public declaration and public campaigning are powerful weapons against any system which relies on secrecy enforced by psychological terror: in SRA, Sue Hutchinson reminds us: 'the greatest fear is our own fear, and we must refuse to be bound by it'.

References

Action Against Abuse newsletters, Orr, M. (ed.) are available on subscription from AAA, PO Box 3125, London NW3 5 QB.

Armstrong, L. (1996) *Rocking the Cradle of Sexual Politics: What Happened When Women Said Incest*, London, The Women's Press.

Canadian Panel on Violence Against Women, (1993) *Changing the Landscape: Ending Violence – Achieving Equality*, Canadian Ministry of Supply and Services, Ottowa, Canada.

Clyde, Lord, (1992) *Report of the Inquiry into the Removal of Children from Orkney in February 1991*, London, HMSO.

Coleman, J. (1994) 'Satanic cult practices' in V. Sinason (ed.) *Treating Survivors of Satanist Abuse*, London, Routledge.

Cook, K. with 'The A Team' (1995–96) 'Survivors and supporters: working on ritual abuse' *Trouble and Strife*, 32, pp.46–52.

Finkelhor, D., L. Williams and N. Burns (1988) *Nursery Crimes: Sexual Abuse in Day Care*, California, Sage.

Golston, J. C. (1992) 'Comparative abuse: shedding light on ritual abuse through the study of torture methods in political repression, sexual sadism and genocide' *Treating Abuse Today*, 2(6).

Goodwin, J. (1994) 'Sadistic abuse: definition, recognition and treatment' in V. Sinason (ed.) (1994) *Treating Survivors of Satanist Abuse*, London, Routledge.

Hudson, P. (1991) *Ritual Child Abuse: Discovery Diagnosis and Treatment*, California, R&E Publishers.

Hutchinson, S. (1996) Personal communication.

Jenkins, P. and D. Maier-Katkin (1991) '"Occult survivors" the making of a myth' in J. T. Richardson, J. Best and D. G. Bramley (eds) *The Satanism Scare*. New York, Aldine de Gruyter.

Katchen, M. and D. Sakheim (1992) 'Satanic beliefs and practices' in D. Sakheim and S. Devine (eds) *Out of Darkness*, Concord, Lexington Books.

La Fontaine, J. (1998) *Speak of the Devil: Tales of Satanic Abuse in Contemporary England*, Cambridge, Cambridge University Press.

McFadyen, A., H. Hanks and C. James (1993) 'Ritual abuse: a definition' *Child Abuse Review*, 2(1), pp.35–41.

Mollon, P. (1994) 'The impact of evil' in V. Sinason (ed.) *Treating Survivors of Satanist Abuse*, London, Routledge.

Mollon, P. (1996) *Multiple Selves, Multiple Voices: Working with Trauma, Violence and Dissociation*, West Sussex, John Wiley.

Nelson, S. (1996) *Satanist Ritual Abuse: Challenges to the Mental Health System*, paper presented at the RAINS conference, 'Better the Devil You Know?' University of Warwick, 13–14 September 1996 (copies available from the author).

Nelson, S. (1998) 'Time to Break Professional Silences', *Child Abuse Review*, 7(3), pp.144–53.

Offshe, R. and E. Waters (1994) *Making Monsters*, New York, Scribner.

Roberts, B. (1996) *Deception, Tricks and Lies* paper presented to RAINS conference 'Better the Devil You Know?' University of Warwick, 13–14 September 1996. The author may be contacted at Hove Polyclinic, Nevill Avenue, Hove, Sussex BN 3 7HY.

Russell, D. (1995) *Women, Madness and Medicine*, Cambridge, Polity Press.

SAFE 'Safe Contact: Newsletter supporting survivors of ritual abuse', available quarterly from SAFE, PO Box 1557, Salisbury, Wilts SP1 2TP.

Stardancer, C. (1996) *Ritual Abuse: The Exploitation of Myth*, paper presented at the RAINS conference, 'Better the Devil You Know?' University of Warwick, 13–14 September 1996. Survivorship may be contacted at 3181 Mission 139, San Francisco, CA 94110, USA.

Tate, T. (1991) *Children for the Devil*, London, Methuen.

Young, W., R. Sachs, B. Braun and R. Watkins (1991) 'Patients reporting ritual abuse in childhood: a clinical syndrome: Report of 37 Cases', *Child Abuse and Neglect*, 15(3), pp.181–9.

Youngson, S. (1994) 'Ritual abuse: the personal and professional cost for workers' in V. Sinason (ed.) *Treating Survivors of Satanist Abuse*, London, Routledge.

4
Gender, Abuse and the Prostitution of Young People
Sheila Kershaw

Introduction

The last decade has witnessed many changes and none more distress-
ing than the increased reporting of sexual assault of children in and
out of the home (Barrett, 1995; Levy, 1995); the increase in the number
of women, children and young people working as prostitutes; and the
growth of a lucrative international sex industry in which vulnerable
groups worldwide are being used, abused and exploited, mostly for the
pleasure of adult men (Council of Europe, 1993; O'Connell Davidson,
1995). Other notable changes in the sex industry have surfaced
through developments in information technology such as the internet.
This has been of particular importance to pornographers and sex
abusers who have been among the most creative pioneers (see Kelly,
and also Nelson in this volume). Interestingly, according to the English
Collective of Prostitutes (1992), there has been a decline in the number
of men wanting sex with older women (much of this trend, but not all,
has been attributed to fear of HIV and AIDS). Yet at the same time an
increase has been noted in the number of young people being coerced
into prostitution. For example, a Council of Europe report (1993) highlights the trafficking and sexual exploitation of children, noting that
around the world, each day, thousands of young women and men are
being prostituted by individual or groups of men. Nearer home, tabloid
newspapers repeatedly report the discovery of sexual assault of young
people by male workers in community homes (Pritchard, 1998); of
sexual assault of children by priests (Davies, 1998) and cases of children and young people being sexually assaulted in their own homes by
people they know and trust. It is in the context of these developments
that the prostitution of young people should be seen.

Links between risk, prostitution and child sexual assault

Many studies describe the links between prostitution, risk taking behaviour and child sexual assault. Stein, Frost and Rees (1994) highlight the plight of young people abused at home or in care, who then run away, become homeless, penniless and workless, and who are forced into prostitution in order to survive. Vine (1996) raises concerns about sex abusers and their connection with the trafficking of children for sex, prostitution and pornography. Similarly research into risk taking behaviour (McKegany and Barnard, 1996) identified young people who had experienced child sexual assault, who used drugs and paid for them through prostitution. This process is not unlike that of young people who, because of abuse, reach adolescence with a low self esteem, feelings of worthlessness and as such may often engage in unsafe sexual behaviour that carries a high risk of HIV infection (Plant, 1990). In his work, Barrett (1995) links crime with sexual assault and prostitution. Lastly, but by no means least, research into the impact of changes in state benefits for younger people indicates that, because of abusive home circumstances, poverty and lack of formal education, some young people have little or no marketable skills and, without state benefit, leave home and fall prey to men ready to exploit them for their own pleasure and that of others. Perspectives on prostitution and the sex industry have widened therefore, moving from focusing solely on adult women to consider children and young people (Holmes and King, 1998/9; Sereny,1986).

Defining prostitution

Accurate definitions of prostitution, like definitions of sexual assault, are necessary for a variety of reasons. For example: to collate accurate information to enable us to begin to understand the behaviour of those who sexually exploit young people. Definitions are also necessary to highlight any need for legal changes to protect young people more effectively, to inform professional thinking and attitudes, and finally to target services proactively to meet the specific needs of sexually exploited young people.

Most people assume the word 'prostitution' refers to women and the selling of sexual services to men. However, research (Bloor et al., 1990; Harris, 1973; McKegany and Bloor, 1990) shows how young girls as well as boys also become involved in providing sexual services, although the latter is not as readily acknowledged or understood. Laws relating to prostitution were created around the notion that 'prostitute' meant adult women and set out to criminalize them rather than the male 'punters'. Thus girls and under-age young women working the streets, if cautioned twice, were labelled alongside their adult counterparts as 'common prostitutes', rather than seen as victims of child sexual assault. This means there needs to be a better understanding of young people's involvement in prostitution and a necessary starting point for this is an accurate definition of the nature of their entanglement and behaviour.

Looking through the research into prostitution, there does not seem to be a universal definition, only definitions proposed by researchers in terms of their own work. This multiplicity leads to diversity in our understanding. For example a dictionary definition of a prostitute is a: 'woman who offers her body to indiscriminate sexual intercourse especially for hire' (Concise Oxford Dictionary, 1975). This definition fails to highlight men's power and control over women and implies that her involvement in prostitution is an informed choice. It also implies prostitution, as a means of earning money, is only a secondary consideration.

Shaw and Butler (1998) offer a broader definition of prostitution: 'the exchange of sexual services, sometimes but by no means exclusively, sexual intercourse, for some kind of reward: money, drink, drugs, a meal or a bed for the night.' (p.181) Although this definition goes some way to identifying the nature and behaviour of young people involved in prostitution, the use of the word 'exchange' implies there is a level of consent. However, in law, young people under 16 years of age are not able to consent to sexual activity with adults, therefore their experience can only be defined in terms of abuse and exploitation. In my own work (Kershaw, 1999) many of the young men involved in prostitution appeared naive, needy and vulnerable, and were often recruited into a world of sex they did not fully understand.

Professionals involved in child protection work argue that the words 'children' and 'prostitution' should not be linked (The Children's Society, 1997), since adult prostitutes generally are not engaged in sexual behaviour in the same way as a child or young person. Consequently a child and young person should not be labelled in this way and instead be defined as exploited and sexually assaulted. Conversely, the adult demanding or enforcing sex should be recognized as a sexual abuser, guilty of contravening the 1959 Sexual Offences Act. As the law now stands, it seems young victims are more likely to be arrested than the men who abuse them. Changes in the interpretation of a young person's behaviour (that is, acknowledging their experience as one of sexual assault rather than anything else) would decriminalize them and would allow their experience to be transferred into the remit of child protection. On one level this strategy might seem a positive move to protect the young person from further abuse, yet Kelly (1999) feels this solution is too simplistic for such a complex issue. She questions any move to decriminalize a young person's involvement in prostitution, recognizing that the law provides the only basis for response. If there were no criminal framework, the police would have no responsibility or powers to respond. Kelly concludes that far more helpful would be a change in criminal legislation which would apply to punters and pimps, while civil legislation would be there to protect children and young people.

Similarities between prostituted young women and young men

Research and anecdotal evidence suggest similarities, but also significant differences, in the experiences of prostituted young women and young men. Common to both is that adult men usually make up the category of person paying for sex. Many appear to seek sex without any emotional ties or responsibility. As Gibson (1995) says in relation to 'rent boys':

> Some 'punters' seek boys for sex. They are usually the last men one might expect to be sexually involved with boys. Most do not identify as 'gay men'. Many say for example, that they are heterosexual and married: having a 'bit' before going home from work. It is a taboo area of sexuality, yet very common. (p.163)

Many underage prostitutes of both sexes are known to have come through the care system, and many are known to have been abused at home and/or in care. Comparing the research on the sexual assault of children, there is a strong suggestion that many young people who have been abused have often found themselves trapped into working in the sex industry. For example, Bagley and Young (1987), examining the possible links between childhood history of sexual assault and prostitution, found 73 per cent of former prostitutes had been sexually assaulted. Similarly, Silbert and Pines' (1981) study into the antecedents to prostitution found approximately 60 per cent of sex workers had been sexually assaulted as children. McMullan (1987), well known for his pioneering research with rent boys, recalls his childhood experiences of sexual assault, and how he later entered prostitution. Shaw and Butler (1998), believe that the way in which young people involve themselves in prostitution is more an issue of economic survival than sexual behaviour and that both life events and situational factors make young people vulnerable, and more open to a life working on the streets. Although there is no consensus as to the precise extent to which experiences of sexual assault as a child influence entry in to prostitution, no-one denies the strong links between the two (Shaw and Butler, 1998).

Many authors have attempted to 'profile' young people engaged in prostitution, and have assumed a variety of reasons for their involvement. Harris (1973) and Craft (1996) suggest that many young women and young men run away from overcrowded homes; many abscond from local authority care (see also Green, this volume). Many of these young people find themselves penniless, desperate, isolated and lonely. As already indicated, young people who were abused in their home, often later become involved in prostitution. Many of them find it hard to trust people easily, particularly adult men. Many of them sleep rough for long periods of time and (because of their vulnerability) are coerced and or trapped into providing sex for men (Bennello, 1994; Swann, 1997).

Risks

Not always in control of their own lives, some young people find themselves having sex with adults and are exposed to serious emotional and physical risks: for example, risks of physical assault, rape even murder (Lees and Gregory, 1993; Lees, 1996). In order to survive, many young people deny the risks, or else genuinely do not realise the dangers they face. Paul's experience was: 'I got beaten up a lot of times. I was forced to have sex and I was ripped off' (Paul, a rent boy cited in Gibson, 1995, p.76). Other research has detailed how both young and older women working as prostitutes have tales of violence and rape and (in many cases) of escapes from serious injury or death (Holmes and King, 1998/9).

Over and above assaults from violent men, prostituted young women also risk being arrested, fined, and/or sent to prison. Those with children have the added risk of being stigmatized and labelled as 'unfit mothers'. As a result, their children may be accommodated under the provisions of the Children Act (Department of Health, 1989) by local authority social service departments. From a wealth of research (Plant *et al.*, 1989), it is clear that the major health risks for young women and men involved in prostitution are drug and alcohol abuse. Research undertaken by Plant and colleagues, in 1990, into illicit drug use and sexual activity among male and female prostitutes in Edinburgh reports: 'Many were heavy drinkers and that illicit drug use was widespread .... the rent boys who drank most were least likely to use condoms.' (p.108)

Drugs are known to be used by clients in payment for sex and McKegany and Barnard's (1996) research found drugs were often offered to the boys as payment for unsafe sexual activity. Some boys would have sex to get money to buy drugs and give them to their regular partner; some were encouraged by clients to take drugs prior to engaging in sex. Only a minority of the rent boys in McKegany and Barnard's study were identified as high level injecting drug users, but many admitted to taking softer drugs such as ecstasy or 'dope'. A link between female prostitutes and drugs was also identified in this study: it appears that older women were more likely to use hard drugs (heroin, cocaine) than boys (Goldstein *et al.*, 1992). Swann's research (1997), indicates that many young women prostituted by pimps were often introduced to drugs and once entrapped into circumstances not previously imagined, drugs were used to control their behaviour.

The threat of sexually transmitted diseases including HIV is also a concern. Research by Plant *et al.*, (1990) focusing particularly on the links between HIV and AIDS and those working in the sex industry concluded that, although female prostitutes do have sexually trans-mitted diseases, evidence contradicts the myth about them being responsible for the spread of HIV. Female prostitutes aware of HIV infection use condoms as part of their job more than ever before, (although many admitted having unsafe sex with their regular partner). Tomlinson, Hillman and Harris (1989), based at a London hospital did similar research with 'rent boys' on safer sex practices and found that 50 per cent of the boys did not wear a condom. Research in Edinburgh (McKegany and Barnard, 1996) found that 5 per cent of the rent boys had HIV and Hall (1994), also indicated one in three 'rent boys' were HIV positive.

Differences and entry into sex work between prostituted young women and men

It is only when we examine the general differences between the experi-ences of young women and young men involved in prostitution, in terms of their entry, continuation, exit and the degree of control they have over the ways in which they carry out their work, that the gender hierarchies become clearer. Having already indicated how prostitution still exists for the almost exclusive use of adult men, those who 'service' are generally older women, young women, young men and children. In terms of entry, the literature suggests there are several routes into sex work for young women and men. Many young women from middle- and working-class backgrounds (Hopkins, 1996) are coerced into prostitution through boyfriends, or more subtly, through girlfriends already working. It is important to note however, that these girlfriends are usually themselves being coerced by their pimps to recruit new girls (Swann, 1997). Other girls enter through finding themselves in circumstances which have made them emotionally confused, in need of support and, at the same time, intensely vulnerable to being preyed upon. Swann (1997) highlights how many young girls are lured into the work this way, moving through a well-known process of being emotionally ensnared by apparent 'boyfriends' (who are in fact pimps), becoming dependent, losing control of their lives and finally becoming almost totally dominated. Milner and Milner (1972) examine a similar process – the way in which pimps change a women's identity to ensure her loyalty and obedience – referring to it as 'seasoning'. Through a process of disempowering the young woman, the 'boyfriend' (alias pimp) plays on the young woman's needs to such an extent that they fail to recognize themselves as victims, exploited and trapped, until it is too late. These processes are reminiscent not only of those through which women find themselves trapped in physically violent relationships (Hanmer, Radford and Stanko, 1989) but also of processes of grooming and entrapment (Finkelhor, 1984), whereby children are manipulated by men who later sexually assault them. Silbert and Pines (1983) take this further, suggesting a cycle of victimization of women which begins in childhood with physical, emotional and sexual assault, which continues in adult life through involvement in prostitution.

While the reasons for many young women and men entering prostitution are similar, it appears the process of becoming involved is very different. Although research is very scanty in terms of young men (there are many more questions than answers) it seems that most boys, particularly those who live on the streets, enter into it on their own and learn by trial and error. Sometimes they meet up with other boys surviving by similar means. Compared to young women, their career in prostitution is usually fairly short, sometimes only weeks. Clearly young men enjoy greater freedom of movement than young women and have a greater capacity to move in and out of street work. Gibson (1995) suggests boys generally remain in prostitution until such a time as they become 'unattractive' to men:

There is a lot of pressure for the boys to look as young as possible. The younger they are, the more physically and emotionally developed they appear, the more they are in demand. They have a sell-by date of up to about the age of nineteen. After that, new younger boys arrive on the scene, and there is very little demand for them from the 'punters'. (p.163)

On the other hand, both older and younger women find leaving prostitution more difficult:

Even with well-designed exit strategies and continuing support, there is considerable difficulty in breaking away from a lifestyle that is potentially lucrative or where there is extreme pressure from others to continue. (Barrett, 1995, p.24)

Swann (1997) quotes from a Canadian Government document (1984) concerned with child sexual assault and juvenile prostitution. The document defines a pimp as one who:

Exploits and cultivates the prostitute's vulnerability, her low self esteem, her feelings of helplessness and her need for love. The cost to the prostitute of working for a pimp goes far beyond the earnings she gives him; it amounts to the girl's forfeiture of her future. (Committee on Sexual Offences Against Children and Youths, 1984).

Pimps play a pivotal role in the sex industry, recruiting women and girls, living off the proceeds of their work and, through various means from co-option to coercion, controlling their earnings, lives and activities. Thus pimps are entrepreneurs of a sort, and women and children the medium through which they profit:

Her ponce (pimp) didn't work himself. He lived on social security and the proceeds of prostitution. And she found herself caught in a life from which she was unable to escape. Even on their wedding night he sent her out on the streets, and thereafter sent her out six nights a week. He kept her working till three days before the birth of each of her children. (Sandford, 1977, p.153)

As discussed earlier, the routes through which young women and men are prostituted are varied. For example, Lucy Burchell, age 16, was 'in love' with a man who promised to buy her a flat. He turned out to be a pimp. Within ten weeks of being prostituted, Lucy's decomposed body was found behind a nightclub (Hopkins, 1996). Other young women find themselves drifting into prostitution in order to meet their basic needs, or drug dependency, and are not recruited by pimps. However remaining independent and retaining control over their work is rare for many young female prostitutes. Very few manage to retain their independence.

Young men exit more easily than young women from prostitution, partly because demand for them falls off as they get older, partly because they are not subject to the control of a pimp, partly because they are more likely to be able to turn to burglary than women if they are drug dependent, and partly because they have a route out of prostitution without entirely leaving a world they know. Some can and do, become pimps for women prostitutes (AMOC, 1997). As such, these boys go through a rite of passage from 'boy' to 'man'; from exploited to exploiter. Women do not have this option. Very often women are prevented from leaving prostitution by their pimps, who need them to continue for financial reasons. Women often also have children and therefore need to earn more money to support their families than do single young men.

Miller *et al.*, (1995) suggest that with escalation in the availability and use of drugs, the traditional pimp/prostitute relationship has changed, in that drugs rather than pimps control prostitutes. However Scambler and Scambler (1997) contest this, saying that while women and young people are still highly exploited through the drug trade, the drug scene is very male dominated and that many drug dealers act in just the same way as pimps have previously. Kelly (1999) points out that drugs are also used by pimps to entrap young women into prostitution, and later used as a means of control. While many women and young people now trade sex for drugs, large numbers of women are forced to hand over a huge percentage of their earnings to dealers and still have to have sex with them.

From available evidence (Gibson, 1995; McMullan, 1988) it seems there are some similarities in the way in which young male street prostitutes carry out their 'business', but as already indicated there are significant differences. If young men have pimps, they appear less obvious than the men who control women. Thinking about where the activity takes place, more often than not, the boys can be seen hanging around public places which provide easy access to large groups of people and which also provide the boys and clients with a legitimate reason for being there (Coombes, 1974). In these places neither the young men or clients stand out, and are not easily identifiable to those not seeking sex. Such places include: railway stations, clubs, discos, parks, amusement arcades, public toilets, beaches, public swimming baths, Turkish baths and well-known coffee bars and large department stores. Many young men have been seen waiting outside telephone boxes or with mobile phones waiting for calls or instructions. These young men provide other men with sex and often receive payment (not always exclusively theirs) in money or other goods.

Women on the other hand often have much less anonymity and less freedom of movement. They can often be seen in 'red light' areas of cities, where men cruise in cars looking for sex. Pimps and or drug dealers linger near by. Swann's (1997) work with young women prostitutes records how some young women are totally hidden. They comprise what Gerrard (1996) refers to as an 'invisible' population of young, exploited female prostitutes. These are young women and girls who are lured in to prostitution by boyfriends after a long process of entrapment, and find themselves being: '... locked in rooms, humiliated and degraded – (having no toilet facilities) and experiencing extreme fear'. (Swann, 1997, p.9)

Entrapment is a far more common process than initially thought, as documented in Barnardo's Street and Lanes Project report (Swann, 1997) and on the whole appears to happen only to young women. Her boyfriend (or more accurately her pimp) totally dominates her life and controls her with absolute isolation and threats of violence. This process resonates with domestic violence and the way in which violent men control their partners (Mullender, 1996)

Conclusion

The issue of why pimps seem to be more invisible in the lives of young male sex workers is an interesting one. A great deal of research needs to be undertaken, which considers questions of power, gender, age and sexual orientation. Below are some hypotheses.

Once boys reach adolescence, in the minds of pimps they may start posing too great a threat (of some kind) to the pimp himself. Given that many of the boys are small and very young looking, this can hardly be a physical threat. Perhaps what the pimp does not have, if he is heterosexual, is an interest in sexually dominating the young man. Perhaps the young man is always a potential threat, because he is growing up to be an older man. Perhaps it suggests that not only are many 'rent boys' and their 'punters' heterosexual, but also most pimps are fiercely so: the problem is not with male sexuality, so much as male heterosexuality. It certainly suggests that whatever the actuality of women's vulnerability *vis à vis* that of young men, women, and especially young women, are far easier than young men for pimps to control through emotional manipulation, violence and rape. On the other hand there are questions about emotional and sexual relationships. Young men who recruit young girls in to prostitution are often good-looking, 'trendy', have money to spend, a car, and spoil the young women with gifts and expensive meals (Swann, 1997). Clearly, emotional vulnerability to apparently attractive young men is a large element in the successful recruitment of young women by these men. If most young male prostitutes are not homosexual, they will be less vulnerable to emotional manipulation by men.

Another crucial factor is demand. Young men it appears, tend to be less in demand from about the age of 18 or 19. (Is this because, for their heterosexual punters, they are beginning to look too much like themselves?) As such, they are perhaps not regarded as such a good business proposition as young women prostitutes. Generally, women can remain as prostitutes for much longer, because the demand, although in decline for older women, still remains. This, together with the 'pimp factor', affects the exit from prostitution for men and women.

It is clear that there are several factors common to young people lured, by whatever means, into prostitution. They include emotional and sexual assault, the use or threat of physical violence, exploitation and danger from adult men. The dangers range from recruitment into 'the game', through unsafe sex to murder. It is also clear that, while there are many similarities in the plight of prostituted young women and men, there are differences too. These differences tend to account for the hierarchy that generally exists among those involved in prostitution. At the top are those with the power and control, they are the pimps, drug dealers, and male punters. At the bottom, those who are the most vulnerable and the most dis-empowered, women, young women and girls. This points to an inequality in power between women and men. In this context, it is men demanding sex and women, regulated by other men, provide the service. This is not dissimilar to the role of women and young children in some households: thus, for some, it is seen as normal behaviour rather than exploitation and abuse. The power differential is inherited by boys as they reach full adulthood, a power which is seldom achieved by women prostitutes of any age. In this way, in the raw frontline of sexuality, the 'oldest profession' is still very old fashioned and women's history of exploitation still very clearly enshrined in custom, practice and belief.

References

Allen, D. M. (1980) 'Young male prostitutes: a psychosocial study', *Archives of Sexual Behaviour*, 9(5), pp.399–426.

AMOC (1997) *European Network Male Prostitution First Interim Report*, Amsterdam, AMOC.

Bagley, C. and L. Young (1987) 'Juvenile Prostitution and Child Sexual Abuse – A Controlled Study', *Canadian Journal of Community Mental Health*, 6, pp. 5–25.

Barnard, M. and N. McKegany (1990) Adolescent Sex and Injecting Drug Use: Risks for HIV Infection, *AIDS Care*, 2(2), pp.103–16.

Barrett, D. (1995) 'Child prostitution', *Highlight*, National Childrens Bureau.

Bennello, J. (1994) 'One in three rent boys has HIV', *The Independent on Sunday* 23 January 1994, 8.

Bloor, M., N. McKegany and M. Barnard (1990) 'An ethnographic study of HIV related risk practices among Glasgow rent boys and their clients: report of a pilot study', *AIDS Care*, 2(1), pp.131–7.

Burke, T. (1991) 'Streetwise on street life', *Journal of Young People Now*, November, pp.23–5.

The Childrens Society (1997) *Child Prostitution in Britain: Dilemmas and Practical Responses*, London, The Children's Society.

Committee on Sexual Offences Against Children and Youths (1984) *Sexual Offences Against Children*, Ottowa, Canadian Government Publishing Service.

Coombes, N. R. (1974) 'Male prostitution: a psychosocial view of behaviour' *American Journal of Orthopsychiatry*, 44(5), pp.782–9.

Council of Europe (1993) *Sex, Exploitation, Pornography and Prostitution of, and Trafficking of Children and Young Adults*, Strasbourg, Council of Europe.

Council of Europe (1994) *Street Children*, Strasbourg, Council of Europe.

Craft, M. (1996) 'Boy prostitutes and their fate' *British Journal of Psychiatry*, 112, pp.1111–14.

Davies, N. (1994) 'Children of the night' *The Guardian*, 15 March 1994, 6.

Davies, N. (1998) 'Is the Church forgiving sin or just turning a blind eye?' *The Guardian*, 4 June 1998, 6–7.

Davis, N. J. (1971) 'The prostitute: developing a deviant identity' in J. M. Henslin (ed.). *Studies in the Sociology of Sex*, New York, Appleton-Century-Crofts.

Department of Health (1989) *An Introduction to the Children Act 1989*, London, HMSO.

Donovan, K. (1991) *Hidden From View: An Exploration of the Little Known World of Young Male Prostitutes in Great Britain and Europe*, London, Home Office and West Midlands Police Publication.

English Collective of Prostitutes (1992) *Prostitute Women and Aids: Resisting the Virus of Repression*, London, Crossroads Books.

EUROPAP (1997) *Hustling For Health: Health and Social Services for Sex Workers (Draft Report)*, Ghent, Belgium, Department of Public Health, University of Ghent.

Finkelhor, D. (1984) *Child Sexual Abuse: New Theory and Research*, New York, Free Press.

Gerrard, N. (1996) 'Prostitution isn't just another job', *The Observer*, 4 August 1996, 26.

Gibson, B. (1995) *Male Order: Life Stories from Boys Who Sell Sex*, London, Cassell.

Goldstein, P. J., L. J. Ouellet and M. Fendrick (1992) 'From bag brides to skeezers: a historical perspective on sex for drugs behaviour', *Journal of Psychoactive Drugs*, 24(4), pp.349–61.

Hall, S. (1994) 'Prostitution', *The Independent*, 24 May 1994, 16.

Hanmer, J., J. Radford and E. A. Stanko (eds) (1989) *Women, Policing and Male Violence: International Perspectives*, London, Routledge.

Harris, M. (1973) *The Dilly Boys: Male Prostitution in Piccadilly*, London, Croom Helm.

Health Education Authority (1997) *Life on the Scene*, London, Health Education Authority.

Holmes, P. and V. King (1998/9) 'Giving a Damn', *Trouble and Strife*, 38, pp.28–31.

Hopkins, N. (1996) 'In six months this bright middle class girl sank into the seedy twilight world of teenage prostitution. So where did it all go wrong?' *Daily Mail*, 29 August 1996, 18.

Kelly, L. (1999) Personal communication.

Kershaw, S. (1999) 'Sex for sale', *Youth and Policy*, 63, pp.27–37.

Lees, S. (1996) 'Unreasonable doubt: the outcomes of rape trials' in M. Hester, L. Kelly and J. Radford (eds) *Women, Violence and Male Power*, Buckingham, Open University Press.

Lees, S. and J Gregory. (1993) *Rape and Sexual Assault: A Study of Attrition*, London, Islington Council.

Levy, A. (1995) 'Police investigate 80 social workers in a child sex enquiry' *Sunday Times*, 12 March 1995, 6.

London Rape Crisis Centre (1984) *Sexual Violence: The Reality for Women*, London, The Women's Press.

McKegany, N., M. Barnard and M. Bloor (1990) 'A comparison between HIV related risk behaviour and risk reduction between female working prostitutes and male rent boys in Glasgow', *Sociology of Health and Illness*, 12(3), pp.274–92.

McKegany, N. and M Barnard (1996) *Sex Work on the Streets: Prostitutes and their Clients*, Buckingham, Open University Press.

McKegany, N. and M. Bloor. (1990) 'A risky business', *Community Care*, 5 July 1990, pp.26–7.

McMullan, R. J. (1987) 'Youth prostitution: a balance of power', *Journal of Adolescence*, 10(1), pp.35–43.

McMullan, R. J. (1988) 'Boys involved in prostitution', *Youth and Policy*, 23, pp.39–41.

MESMAC (1990) *Men Who Have Sex With Men: Action in the Community: First Report.* London, MESMAC.

Miller, P., M. L. Plant, M. A. Plant and J. Duffy (1995) 'Alcohol, tobacco illicit drugs and sex: an analysis of risky behaviours among young adults'

International Journal of Addiction, 30, pp.239–58.

Milner, C. and R. Milner (1972) *Black Players*, Boston, Little Brown.

Morgan-Thomas, R., M. Plant and M. R. Plant (1990) 'Alcohol, AIDS and sex industry clients: results from a Scottish study', *Drug and Alcohol Dependence*, 26, pp.265–9.

Mullender, A. (1996) *Rethinking Domestic Violence: The Social Work and Probation Response*, London, Routledge.

National Youth In Care Project (1987) *Who Cares What I have to Say, Nobody Cares, Nobody Knew*, York, In Care Network.

Newman, C. (1989) *Young Runaways: Findings From Britain's First Safe House*, London, The Children's Society.

O'Connell Davidson, J. (1995) 'British sex tourists in Thailand' in M. Maynard and J. Purvis (eds) *(Hetero)Sexual Politics*, London, Taylor and Francis.

Plant, M. L. (ed.) (1990) *AIDS, Drugs and Prostitution*, London, Routledge.

Plant, M. L., M. A. Plant, D. Peck and J. Sellers (1989) 'The sex industry, alcohol and illicit drugs: implications for the spread of HIV infection', *British Journal of Adiction*, 84, pp.53–9.

Plant, M. L., M. A. Plant and R. M. Thomas (1990) 'Alcohol, AIDS risks and commercial sex: some preliminary results from a Scottish study', *Drug, Alcohol and Dependency*, 1, 25 February 1990, pp.51–5.

Plant, M. L. and M. A. Plant (1992) *Risk Takers: Alcohol, Drugs, Sex and Youth*, London, Routledge.

Pritchard, C. (1998) 'Matter of life and death', *Community Care* 14–20 May 1998, pp.20–1.

Redding, D. (1989) 'Reaching out to the rent scene', *Community Care*, 20 April 1989, pp.24–6.

Rees, G. (1993) *Hidden Truth: Young People's Experience of Running Away*, London, The Children's Society.

Sandford, J. (1977) *Prostitutes*, London, Abacus.

Scambler, G. and A. Scambler (eds) (1997) *Rethinking Prostitution: Purchasing Sex in the 1990s*, London, Routledge.

Sereny, G. (1986) *The Invisible Children: Child Prostitution in America, West Germany and Britain*, London, Pan Books.

Shaw, I. and I. Butler (1998) 'Understanding young people and prostitution: a foundation for practice', *British Journal of Social Work*, 28, pp.177–96.

Silbert, M. H. and A. M. Pines (1981) 'Sexual abuse as an antecedent to prostitution', *Child Abuse and Neglect*, 5, pp.407–11.

Silbert, M. H. and A. M. Pines (1983) 'Early sexual exploitation as an influence in prostitution', *Social Work*, July/August, pp.285–9.

Stein, M., N. Frost and G. Rees (1994) *Running the Risk: Young people on the Streets of Britain Today*, London, The Children's Society.

Streetwise Youth Project (1991) *Streetwise Youth Annual Report*, London, Streetwise Youth Project.

Swann, S. (1997) *Barnardo's Street and Lanes Project Report*, Ilford, Barnardo's.

Tomlinson, D. R., R. J. Hillman and J. R. Harris (1989) 'Setting up a support service for male prostitutes in London', *International Journal of Sexually Transmitted Diseases and AIDS*, 1 September 1989, 5, pp.360–1.

Vine, S. (1996) 'Abusers jailed in paedophile crackdown', *The Independent*, 31 July 1996, 15.

Part II
Examining Practice

5

Speaking Out, Coming Out and Being Outed

Joy Trotter

This chapter presents one of the major factors which inhibits social workers from collaborating effectively both with children who have been sexually assaulted, and with their non-abusing parents/carers: the silence about sexuality. Sexuality has been disregarded, dismissed and denied in the child sexual abuse literature and in the child protection practices of the last two decades. In an attempt to redress this inattention, some of the issues that arise for two key groups of people, parents and workers, are explored (the other key group – children – is addressed more fully elsewhere in this book). Of major importance for both groups is the privacy and protection of what is often profoundly personal information: the process by which some of this information becomes public is often arbitrary, the information is frequently inaccurate and the resulting responses can be damaging and dangerous.

The chapter begins with a brief examination of the terms and an attempt to define 'sexuality', a word which is used to mean a number of different things. It goes on to explore understandings and misunderstandings around some specific sexualities of particular relevance to the sexual assault of children, young women and young men. The relevance of feminisms for the author and how feminisms continue to influence theory and practice is then discussed, demonstrating the importance of personal accounts and gender analyses. After outlining some of the issues for parents and workers, the final part of the chapter offers some direction for realigning theory and some motivation for reshaping practice.

Linking results from a piece of research undertaken in 1992 with non-abusing mothers and fathers (Trotter, 1998a) and a study of antidiscriminatory practice among qualifying social work students and their practice teachers (Trotter, 1998b), with a preliminary search of the literature, has resulted in a fresh examination of sexuality issues and relationships. What emerges is an overwhelming inaccuracy and inconsistency around what is public (assumed or announced) and what is private, what is avoided and what is investigated, and what is deemed to be professional and what is personal.

It is essential to begin with an attempt to define 'sexuality'. Not unlike attempts to understand other similarly complex and, for some, unfamiliar areas of study (for example 'race' or 'disability'), it can be helpful to have some appreciation of history: our understanding and use of language for example, is influenced by its historical origins and past associations. It would be presumptuous to try and do justice to the history of sexuality within the confines of this chapter, but there is useful material available (Billington *et al.*, 1998; Coward, 1983; Gagnon and Parker, 1995; Griffin, 1993; Weeks,1986).

Perhaps because of the taboo nature of sex, or at least of talking about sex, it may not be a surprise to find that there are language problems of overlapping terminology – different authors use the same term to mean different things and different terms to mean the same. 'Sex' can refer to an act (usually heterosexual sexual intercourse), to a category of person (that by which species are either male or female), to a practice (a range of behaviours), or to gender (either of the 'divisions' of male or female). 'Sexuality' can mean sexiness or sexualness and is most often thought of in the context of biological capacity and/or reproductive potential. It is sometimes confused with 'gender' and/or 'sex' and all three terms have overlapping components: roles, identity, status, relational styles, attribution, biology and assignment for example. This last component – assignment – is, according to Nataf (1996) determined with almost haphazard indifference:

> [assignment is] the pronouncement of an individual's morphological sex based on a glance by a doctor at the time of birth, forming the subsequent registration of gender status. (p.17)

It is important to distinguish between the two dimensions of sexuality – sexual *behaviour* and sexual *identity*. The former is concerned with what you do (or don't do) in the bedroom (or wherever) and *may or may not* be anything to do with the latter. Sexual identity is: 'a consistent, enduring self-recognition of the meanings that sexual orientation and sexual behaviour have for oneself.' (Savin-Williams, 1990, p.3, quoted in Davies, 1996). The reason the two must be distinguished and may not be related, is because sexuality has two components: how someone regards themselves (as lesbian or bisexual or celibate or whatever) *and* how they are regarded by other(s) (as lesbian or bisexual or celibate or whatever). As one dictionary defines it 'sexual characteristics or activity' (Swannell, 1986), it is both 'what you do' *and* 'how you seem'. To add to the confusion, 'sexual orientation' is a term that is also used interchangeably with 'sexuality' but some believe it can be distinguished:

> a preponderance of sexual or erotic feelings, thoughts, fantasies, and/or behaviours.... It is present from an early age – perhaps at conception (Savin-Williams, 1990 p.3, quoted in Davies, 1996).

This term is sometimes used by organizations and agencies in their 'Equal Opportunity' or 'Managing Diversity' policies in lists of not-to-be-discriminated-against groups. Although the term is fairly succinct and easy to add to a list, its vagueness and breadth may be of particular difficulty to social work agencies however; if sexual orientation is not more specifically defined it could be interpreted as any sexual preferences or behaviours – including illegal ones.

Some specific sexualities

It is suggested that 'new' sexualities have emerged as a broader range of sexual identities have been affirmed and are emerging (Nataf, 1996; Plummer, 1996; Weeks, 1986): transsexuals, transvestites and sado-masochists are among the newer erotic minorities. Among other things, such developments have challenged society to rethink the criteria of appropriate and inappropriate behaviour and although it might have seemed logical for those concerned about child sexual assault to have contributed to this 'rethink', it has not happened. Apart from a few exceptions (see Kelly, this volume), academics and practitioners have added little to the discourse: other than to re-affirm that those who sexually assault children are different from the rest of us, and that child sexual assault is morally wrong. A government-funded inquiry report (Utting, 1997) failed to clarify, let alone specifically define, 'preferential paedophiles' (p.98).

Weeks (1986) argues that sexual behaviours should not be valued (or judged) on the grounds of morality or scientific analysis, but from a 'relational perspective' (p.82). He suggests that social factors and meaning should be considered and power relations should be analysed. It is in these areas that social work practitioners and academics could provide evidence and analysis for a greater understanding about adult sexuality, children's experiences and the meanings of relationships.

It is at this point that the relevance of feminist practice and feminist thought becomes clear. Feminists from a variety of backgrounds and disciplines have influenced theory and practice around child sexual assault, challenging dogmatic and often patriarchal 'truths' (for example Campbell, 1988; Herman, 1981; Russell, 1996). In social work too there have been many voices which have added to and inspired changes (for example Cavanagh and Cree, 1996; Driver and Droisen, 1989; Hooper, 1992; Hudson, 1989; Kelly, 1988). Leading experts in the world of child sexual assault theory are now acknowledging the crucial place feminism, and women generally, have had in the protection of children:

> ... I think what has made a big difference is that there are huge numbers of women working at all levels of the criminal justice system [in the US]. In a male system, people don't listen to children. (Finkelhor, quoted in Rafferty, 1997, p.30)

As a result of feminist influence, child sexual assault may be understood to be a gender-specific crime committed mostly by men and rooted in sexual inequality (Browne, 1994; Finkelhor 1986; Hedley and Dorkenoo, 1992; Kelly *et al.*, 1991). For some, this perspective continues to be overlooked or regarded as controversial (Atmore, 1996; Peterson *et al.*, 1993). For others, a sexist or more patriarchal analysis is maintained – by implying that sexual abuse by women is 'even worse' than by men (Elliott, 1993): or by arguing that 'families' are responsible for the abuse perpetrated by men (Patton, 1991). Some of the efforts to find virtually anyone other than men in families to write about, could almost be regarded as some form of diversionary tactic to keep the eye off the ball (NCH, 1992; Saradjian, 1996; Westcott, 1991). What is needed now is a re-establishment of the earlier feminists' assertions that the vast majority of child sexual assault is perpetrated by fathers (or father-figures) and other men in (or related to) families. What also needs to be analysed more clearly, is the sexuality of these men.

First, there is a need to consider heterosexual men. From the mid-1980s onwards there has been a systematic 'campaign', characterized by the active participation of increasingly pervasive and persuasive mass media (analysed by Kitzinger, 1996; Nava, 1988; Nelson, 1998), which has almost unanimously defended heterosexual men, and particularly fathers – whether it be specific individuals or some presumed homogeneous, beleaguered and innocent group. There is little doubt that the defense of the fathers is a defense of all heterosexual men – fathers are the champions of male heterosexuality – and that the rise of the men's rights movement has further fuelled the pro-father policies and ideologies (Bertoia and Drakich, 1995). It has been argued that the defense of fathers is also a defense of patriarchy (Collier, 1995; Field, 1995) and of the family (Robson, 1994a). Yet this position is clung to, in the face of overwhelming evidence about the relation of men to families and to children, (see Cox, this volume) by those who want to preserve the status quo; indeed it is necessary for them to do so in order to undermine research findings and feminist argument.

While most of the research indicates that sexual assault of children is mainly perpetrated by heterosexual men (Campbell, 1988; Finkelhor, 1983, 1986; McMullen, 1990), it is important to acknowledge that others are involved in this: for example celibate men (Cashman, 1993), and gay men (Sandfort, 1987). Discussion also needs to focus on 'paedophile' men. This term has become common parlance (as feminist research has brought child sexual assault to public attention), and the dominant image of the paedophile is a man who is external to the family and threatens both child and family life (McCollum, 1998). As already discussed, this image ill-fits the scale of the evidence, and is entirely contrary to the feminists' political analysis of child sexual assault as an issue of male power. However, presenting abusers as abnormal and/or sick individuals supports patriarchal, heterosexual sovereignty, and providing a neat label for them as 'paedophiles', legitimates this position (Kelly, 1996a; Potter, this volume): '... the more child sexual abuse was depicted as a horrible pathology, the less could 'ordinary' fathers be seen as enacting such deeds'. (Smart, 1989, p.52)

Children and sexuality

The feminist tradition, which emphasizes the importance of personal accounts, could be applied to work with perpetrators and alleged perpetrators (for example, presenting them with survivors' accounts). It could also be used to enable children's stories to be told in their own language (Barringer, 1992). This approach would also expose (among many other things) two deceptions: the comprehensive endorsement of heterosexual men, and the sexual 'innocence' of children.

Listening to children has been advocated for some time, at least among child care professionals (Bannister, 1992; Bannister *et al.*, 1990), yet little seems to have been documented about children's views on sex, other than from a victim standpoint. Adults' reluctance to even *think* about children and sex (let alone talk about it) without it being in the context of 'abuse', is widely accepted among social workers (Trotter, 1998c). This blinkered view contributes to the further pathologizing of sexually assaulted children – not only are they regarded as 'victims', they are denied any other form of sexual existence.

According to Jackson (1982), adults' avoidance of sexual issues in relation to children and young people contributes to their continued coercion and exploitation (see Kershaw, this volume), to their sexual guilt and to the oppression of women and children. She argues that children's need for sexual information should be acknowledged: 'there seems to be no justification for partitioning sex off from the rest of experience and concealing it from children'. (Jackson, 1982, pp.66–7).

Gradually, sex education has moved towards a more positive approach – sexual health instead of disease and damnation (National Curriculum Council 1990), yet despite this, it is still distant from the realities of young people's lives, and children are encouraged to be objective and academic rather than personal or experiential (Jackson, 1982). Kitzinger (1997), in a quintessential discussion of childhood and power, suggests that programmes designed to help children prevent themselves from being sexually assaulted manage to avoid mentioning the two key issues – 'sex' and 'power':

> The agility with which these programs are able to discuss sexual abuse *without* directly addressing either sex or power is testimony to the years of expertise built up around avoiding these two taboo subjects! (p.175)

More general sex education for children seems to be similarly inadequate (Martinson, 1994; Trudell, 1993), and despite the National Curriculum here in Britain, is still woefully deficient (Epstein, 1994; Winn *et al.*, 1995).

However, there are particular issues around sexuality for those children and young people who have been sexually assaulted. Mills and Karban (1996) point out:

> male victims of sexual abuse have entirely been portrayed as victims

and that the homosexual nature of the acts has contributed to their anxiety and distress (p.7).

They argue that there is no parallel concern for girls (see Karban and Horrocks, this volume); it is likely that many issues underpin this anomaly. First, the general heterosexist assumption that all boys are heterosexual and, building upon that inaccuracy, the further postulation that conjectures that their abusers are homosexual and that homosexual advances and involvements (towards heterosexuals) *cause* homosexuality. Second, a similar assumption that girls are all heterosexual, but with the additional quality of being 'seductive' or sexually dangerous to men (Mills and Karban, 1996). The contradiction between these two positions is profound: on the one hand sexually assaulted boys are seen to have been doubly victimized by being sexually assaulted and sexually tainted by *homosexual men*: on the other hand, girls have only marginally been victimized as they partially invited the assault and were not sexually tainted (as it is presumed that their attackers were *heterosexual men*).

This over-simple analysis omits to acknowledge that many abusers assault girls *and* boys, and may be *bisexual men* who, according to research:

> represent a group that is strikingly absent both from national studies of variations in sexual behaviour and from those who concentrate on men who have sex with men. (Sigma Research, 1996, p.21)

It is interesting to note that this research also found that one in eight of the men included in the study stated they were heterosexual, even though they had previously spoken of having sex with men; almost half of them might have been perceived as heterosexual (by neighbours or friends – or even family), as they lived with a female sexual partner.

Children and young people who experience the child protection system 'from the inside' by being accommodated may face even greater difficulties, especially girls, as female sexuality is often viewed as problematic (Mills and Karban, 1996). According to one researcher, many of the high proportion of girls who become parents within 18 months of leaving care are lesbians, and are responding to the feelings of denial and the pressures to conform with society's own heterosexual norms and behaviours (Biehal *et al.*, 1995). There may be a number of even greater incentives for lesbian and gay young people in care to engage in heterosexual sex: visibly maintaining a heterosexual façade may mean escaping the personal strains of coming out; avoiding the professionals' pathologising of them as the focus of the family's dysfunction; and elude the machismo and hyper-masculine offensive of many residential establishments (Davies, 1996; Green, 1995, and this volume; Savin-Williams, 1995). Most of these children will also face similar difficulties at school. Although many professionals and academics have not considered these issues, (see Berg and Nursten, 1996) research is beginning to expose considerable levels of homophobia and bullying experienced by lesbian and gay young people (Chaudhary, 1998; Epstein, 1994; Rivers, 1995; Trenchard and Warren, 1984).

Adults and sexuality

While there are many issues around the decision of lesbians and gay men to be open about their sexuality (whether they are service users/clients or social workers), some areas of social work practice carry more risks for the individual than others (Cosis Brown, 1998). Clearly anyone working in the child care field will be more exposed to the sharp edge of homophobia, and particularly so in relation to child sexual assault. Despite the fact that sexual assault of children is mainly perpetrated by heterosexual men, the view that gay men (in particular) have a tendency towards child sexual assault is still widely held (Sanderson, 1995).

This last point may be the most difficult of all, especially for gay workers (and fathers) who will be all too aware of the 'confusion' between paedophilia and homosexuality in the minds of many people. The additional dilemmas (that heterosexual workers and parents would not have to cope with) of personal uncertainty and vulnerability are unnecessary ordeals, and would not have to be endured if heterosexual social workers were better informed and less discriminatory in their practice. It is time that the positive contributions and particular skills that lesbian and gay workers and parents can bring to child protection work were acknowledged and welcomed. Heterosexual workers, in particular, need to update their attitudes and adjust their practice if partnerships are ever to be anything more than superficial.

Parents

In relation to children's sexual experiences, Martinson (1994), points out that fewer parents set limits on contact between same-sex friendships than they do on children with opposite-sex friends. He also reveals that most parents find the possibility of their children being homosexual disturbing, and fathers are more likely than mothers to caution their daughters and sons verbally about behaving like 'tomboys' or 'sissies':

> ... fear of homosexuality often prevented open and shared affection between fathers and sons and inhibited children's learning about their bodies. Most boys were discouraged from kissing, hugging, being gentle, or even asking for comfort or help. (p.63)

Non-abusing parents of sexually assaulted children are probably no better or worse than the rest of the population at dealing with or discussing sexual matters (Jackson, 1982), and many prefer to let school deal with such matters (Beavet and Thompson, 1996). However, their attitudes and influence can be powerful, whether they are informed and positive, or ill-informed and negative about sexual matters. Whatever the position held, professionals often expect a great deal from non-abusing parents, and from mothers in particular (Richardson and Bacon, 1991; Trotter, 1998a). Unfortunately, they often also continue to harbour suspicions and recriminations about culpability and/or collusion (Hooper, 1992; Kitzinger, 1991). Not only are parents of sexually assaulted children marginalized and stigmatized by social workers they come into contact with (Otway, 1996), they can be discriminated against in other ways (Trotter, 1996). As mostly white and heterosexual, child protection workers reflect the values held by society in general:

> All lesbian mothers live in constant fear of losing custody of their children, and of intimidation through threats of exposure.... As Black lesbian mothers,... there is always the threat that social services may interfere or decide to remove the child. Society already believes that Black women are neglectful, African-Caribbean mothers are child beaters, and that Asian mothers are too overbearing and restrictive. (Mason-John and Okorrowa, 1995, p.85)

The prejudice lesbian and gay non-abusing parents face in their interactions with social workers is seldom acknowledged and rarely challenged. It could be argued that social work organizations might be more informed about lesbian and gay lifestyles, yet in many social work agencies: 'heterosexist and homophobic policies, attitudes and behaviours are being condoned' (Trotter and Gilchrist, 1996, p.76). For example, research undertaken in 1992 with non-abusing mothers and fathers (Trotter, 1998a) involved nine parents, eight were heterosexual and one lesbian. At the end of the research period all except the lesbian mother were still caring for their children.

It is often suggested (Byerly, 1985) that lesbian mothers are even less capable than heterosexual mothers of protecting their children from sexual assault. Indeed it is not uncommon to hear that their sexuality may in itself be dangerous (Richardson, 1994) or even a form of sexual assault (Robson, 1994b). The lesbian mother in the 1992 research felt that she was 'suspected' of sexually abusing her children, but this was not the experience of the others.

> I'd got rid of my husband, and I found I couldn't handle being with the lads so I'd turned gay. Then I got that thrown in my face because I was a queer. So I had arguments with her. The social worker asked if I was sure I hadn't touched my son. I said of course I haven't what do you think I am? (*Susan*, in Trotter, 1998a, p.74)

According to Byerly (1985): 'Lesbian mothers say that their sexual preference often becomes an issue when incest is disclosed.' (Byerly, 1985, p.19) The issue may arise when statutory agencies attempt to assess suitability for parenting/protection, or may be used by the offender in attempts to discredit the mother (to the children he is abusing, to his family, to the statutory agencies and to others). It has been identified that lesbian mothers run a real risk of their children being removed from their care, regardless of the standard of that care (Rights of Women Lesbian Custody Group, 1986), and that gay men are stereotyped as: 'predators, child abusers and unfit to care for children.' (Logan and Kershaw, 1994, p.66).

Yet research suggests that children in lesbian or gay households seem to develop emotionally and physically just as well as children in heterosexual households (Bigner and Jacobsen, 1992; Patterson, 1992). There is no evidence that the social, emotional or sexual development of children raised by lesbians or gay men is in any way differently affected from the development of children raised by heterosexual women or men. Despite the pervasiveness of homophobia in society, most gay men and lesbians live similar lives to their heterosexual counterparts (Campion, 1995; Hanscombe and Forster, 1982; King, 1995; Patterson, 1995; Tasker and Golombok, 1991). Prejudice and discrimination against lesbian and gay parents continues to be endorsed by the media (Sanderson, 1995) and enshrined in the law. Collier outlines the heterosexism in the legal structures which govern child protection work:

> Those who fail to attain the ... sexual orientation to enter the comforting world of familial heterosexuality ... continue to speak in tongues alien to the notions of ... sexual propriety of the class of elite males (white upper/middle class) whose interest the law continues, in so many respects, to represent. (Collier, 1995, p.261)

It is not surprising therefore to find that government guidelines omit sexuality from their 'lists' of areas to 'respond positively' to. For example, the Guardians ad Litem: 'in their work with children and families ... positively responds to issues associated with gender, race, culture, religion, language and disability' (Social Services Inspectorate, 1995, p14), but is not required to do so with issues associated with sexuality. Presumably they are free to respond as negatively (or otherwise) as they see fit. All the parents in the 1992 research (Trotter, 1998a), experienced some rejection of their involvement in, or contribution to, their child's protection 'plan', but the lesbian mother's 'disclosures' to the abuser's family and the authorities were persistently dismissed.

Faced with the distress of the sexual assault of their child (Manon *et al.*, 1996), as well as with the heterosexist and homophobic attitudes of social workers, lesbian and gay parents may find it hard to focus on positive experiences in relation to sex and sexuality. They may even be 'outed' by the ensuing child protection procedures in areas of their lives that they would have preferred not to be. The thoroughness of child assault investigations (Department of Health *et al.*, 1999) mitigates against the majority of parents (even non-abusing ones) maintaining secrecy about their sexuality, especially if they are 'out' in other areas of their lives. This scrutiny does not apply to workers however, and given the scale of homophobia and the magnitude of ignorance in social work, many social workers will remain 'in the closet' at work (Cosis Brown, 1992). This invisibility, while perhaps suiting the employing agencies (Burrell, 1984; Hearn *et al.*, 1989), has many detrimental consequences for lesbians and gay men (Griffin and Zukas, 1993; Logan *et al.*, 1996), and may be particularly difficult when working with lesbian or gay parents. Heterosexual parents of lesbian and gay children who have been sexually assaulted might be confused and might have very little clear information or understanding about either sexual assault or their child's sexuality. It has been demonstrated that parents who turn to their family or community networks for support following the sexual assault of their child, can face disappointment (Richardson and Bacon, 1991). The evidence of response in relation to sexuality has many similarities (Chaffer and Garratt, 1997; Southall Black Sisters, 1990), but there are occasions when it may be more encouraging (Galford, 1994; Suriyaprakasam, 1995):

> There is a prevalent perception that it is much harder for Black communities to accept homosexuality; in fact, almost the opposite is true when the situation involves young people within the family. Black communities have had to face racism, adapting and modifying their cultural values to fit into a changing environment. This can give us more flexibility within our families to deal with all kinds of issues, including lesbianism. (Suriyaprakasam, p.101)

In some areas, perhaps in some way related to the confusion that many heterosexual adults experience, lesbian and gay adults have been specifically recruited as foster carers and adopters for sexually assaulted children. This move has not been widespread, at least not publicly, despite evidence which indicates that lesbian and gay carers make valuable contributions (Skeates and Jabri, 1988). However, even in the enlightened days of the early 1980s when at least the possibilities of adoption and fostering were endorsed, only lesbians were considered (not gay men), and then often only if they were 'single' (Hanscombe and Forster, 1982; Pringle, 1990). The Department of Health has shown some inconsistency in its policies: various documents reveal government discrimination against potential lesbian and gay foster carers and adopters (Department of Health, 1990, 1993). Most of the research and theoretical analysis continues to focus on 'family' placements and assumes the heterosexuality of carers in most cases (Byrne, 1997; McCracken and Reilly, 1998). There are however, occasionally, instances where logical and appropriate judgements are made (Cullen, 1997/98): these need to be increased if the best interests of children and young people (whatever their sexuality) are to be met.

Cosis Brown (1998) discusses a number of issues around lesbian and gay fostering and adoption, which are based on presumptions and, therefore, need to be carefully scrutinized. First, she argues that there appears to be a tendency for lesbian and gay foster carers to be given 'hard to place children', and wonders whether they are being regarded as second best. Second, she questions the presumption of many agencies, that all birth parents are homophobic (and therefore would resist placement with lesbian or gay carers). Finally, Cosis Brown suggests that there is one generalization that agencies could make (which might be justifiable) about lesbian and gay carers, and that is their experience and skill in dealing with stigma. She goes on to argue that many carers will have developed particular strengths in this area, and are, therefore, well-placed to help children in need of placement. These strengths may be of even greater relevance to those children and young people who have been sexually assaulted.

Workers

It is likely that social work and its institutions reflect the homophobia and heterosexism in society. Research in the United States has confirmed the incidence of homophobia among social workers (Mark, 1996; Sullivan, 1994); and closer to home, others are beginning to discuss the anti-lesbian and gay attitudes found in many social work settings (Cosis Brown, 1992; Logan *et al.*, 1996). Although many individuals and organizations claim to be otherwise, when pressures of politics or publicity loom close, hypocrisy and bigotry can be exposed (Field, 1995; O'Hare, Williams and Ezoviski, 1996). It is not surprising that social workers are uncertain about their work in relation to sexuality: it is a subject that even today remains virtually taboo in their training, their official guidelines, their textbooks and in their day-to-day work (Logan *et al.*, 1996). Many of the workers who have particularly close responsibilities to children who have been sexually assaulted, have little or no training at all (Parkin, 1989; Utting, 1991). When the notions of illegality, immorality and invisibility are also contemplated, it is perhaps astonishing that social workers *ever* consider it. The implications of this oversight, neglect or avoidance are numerous and various, and impact in different ways on service users, on the organizations and on the workers themselves.

In a study of 128 social work students' and practice teachers' final placement reports, (Trotter, 1998b) detailed analysis of the three reports which dealt with lesbian and gay issues revealed some of the implications of misunderstandings and partial (if not tokenistic) endeavours. Of these three reports, the one CQSW student chose to reveal that he was male and white and he described the gender and 'race' of all his clients. However his report did not reveal his own sexuality and described the sexuality of only one of the 16 clients, who was described as 'gay' (although a female client). The student's practice showed some appreciation of the issues, but with some naiveté (trying to help her find a 'local lesbian and gay network' and advising her that 'other women's groups' would reduce her isolation). His language in describing his involvement with this client revealed some difficulties which could be indicative of his own sexism (he referred to the client's previous partner as 'ex live-in lover') or homophobia (he felt it 'inevitable' that someone so 'openly gay' would stand out in a north-eastern community). The two DipSW reports gave evidence of work with 22 clients; the Probation student did not mention the sexualities of any of her ten clients, the HIV/AIDS Health Project student described the sexuality of six of the 12 clients she worked with (one lesbian, two gay men and three heterosexuals). Neither of the practice teachers nor either of the students said what their own sexualities were in the reports. Both students showed some awareness and ability in tackling issues around homophobia, although both of them seemed reluctant on occasions to be explicit about this (the Probation student tended to focus on the client's distress caused [supposedly] by *deceit* about his father being gay, rather than on his being gay).

These three students' reports illustrate what may be a general nervousness about lesbian and gay issues, and as none of them discussed their own sexualities, it may be assumed that they did not consider their personal impact on their clients to be relevant. Unfortunately, none of the students who were placed in child care or child protection settings, like the vast majority of the 128 students in the study, discussed lesbian and gay issues in their reports. On the whole, the subject of sexuality only arose if initiated by the clients and there was no routine consideration in supervision, planning, recording or face-to-face work. It was only when clients confirmed themselves as being lesbian or gay that these terms were used in the reports; otherwise sexuality was guessed at by the gender of the client's partner (if known). The reasons for this oversight or disregard may be numerous, and are likely to be complex, but denial, as one of the primary manifestations of homophobia, is likely to be a major factor.

It is important to note that none of the students who were placed in child care or child protection settings discussed lesbian and gay issues in their reports. It is likely that none of them considered them in their practice either, even though many of them were working with sexually assaulted children and young people. This omission may be linked to the problems qualified workers, and non-abusing parents also share, around talking to children about the 'sexualness' of their abuse and the sexual implications of the experience(s). Little seems to have been written about this. Manuals and training materials about child care and protection often overlook or skate over this part of the work (The Children's Society, 1989; HMSO, 1995; Open Learning Foundation 1994) and even those texts that focus on communication, or on sexuality, offer little more (Bremner and Hillin, 1993). It is likely that this gap in the literature reflects the gap in practice and although it is understandable, (to repress or reject trauma and taboo) it is unacceptable.

Discussion

In order to provide some direction for realigning theory, and some motivation for reshaping practice, I will conclude by outlining some of the implications of these issues for workers involved with the protection of children from sexual assault.

It is likely that most social work teams in most agencies and settings will be made up of staff who are mostly white, able-bodied and female (Langan and Day, 1992). It is also likely that they will spend most of their limited resources dealing with oppression and discrimination relating to 'race', disability and gender. If lesbian or gay workers are present, they are likely to be assumed to be heterosexual and are likely to feel insecure in their agencies. If they are 'out', they are likely to be in lower status roles (part-time, second-in-charge, assistant, and so on). 'Out' staff may also be regarded differently from heterosexual colleagues, thought of as being biased in favour of other minority groups, or informally classed as 'second class' professionals. 'Out' staff may also be treated differently, their workload may be restricted to lesbian and gay issues or they may be encouraged or assumed to concentrate on equal opportunities areas. As pointed out elsewhere (Trotter and Gilchrist, 1996) these trends may be especially so for disabled and/or black lesbians and gay men.

It is also likely that there is a similar percentage of lesbian and gay people in social work as in society as a whole (at least 10 per cent), yet their invisibility is striking. While the low numbers of black workers and disabled workers also need to be challenged and increased, the low numbers of 'out' lesbian and gay workers in child protection is particularly relevant. Absence of role models or affirmative images and literature is an issue in all areas of young people's lives – school, youth groups, sport centres, but lesbian and gay role models are particularly absent among the professionals (and their agencies) that become involved with sexually assaulted children and young people: police, social workers, doctors, solicitors (Suriyaprakasam, 1995). Misinformation about sexual abusers, misrepresentations of lesbians and gay men and misguided fears about 'causes' of homosexuality can seriously mislead children, (and their parents) who may already be confused and distressed following sexual assault.

Not surprisingly, many lesbian and gay workers are wary of coming out at work (Sone, 1993). As already discussed, many out lesbian and gay workers are faced with discrimination, higher expectations (particularly relating to 'political correctness') and silence. According to practitioners and researchers the silence can amount to a conspiracy of such magnitude for some workers that it becomes detrimental to their mental health. However, rather than finishing this chapter by focusing on lesbian and gay workers (and indeed on a 'negative' consequence of being lesbian or gay in social work), I will concentrate on heterosexual workers – and the contributions they do and can make.

Conclusion

I will assume that the workers who have failed to gain any understanding or information about the importance of lesbian and gay issues in social work, are heterosexual. It is crucial that this assumption is considered and acknowledged, in order that it can be dealt with. The impact of such unaware and untrained workers on service users is multi-faceted, whatever the sexuality of the service user. As discussed already, the issues for non-abusing parents are numerous and profound.

The implications for work with children may be even greater, particularly around misinformation For example, contrary to the beliefs of most heterosexual adults, not all young lesbian and gay people experience a 'difficult' adolescence (Trenchard and Warren, 1984). Indeed, many lesbian and gay young people have no doubt about their identity and are confident about their relationships. According to Dunne (1997), there is an interrelationship between educational opportunities and interpretations of sexuality. Those young women who questioned the givenness of heterosexuality during their schooling experienced being 'different', and this mobilized and liberated them:

'... the early problematising of a conventional heterosexual future is an important source of empowerment.' (p.72) Questioning the givenness of heterosexuality, or 'compulsory heterosexuality' as Rich termed it (1984) might be one of the keys to preventing child sexual assault and might be a starting point for further research.

In the meantime, there is no doubt of the impact that ill-informed, unaware and untrained heterosexual workers have on their clients and colleagues, particularly if agencies have bulldozed them into accepting an equal opportunities policy on lesbian and gay issues. If workers are not convinced about the decisions they are expected to make, and if they are also faced with controversy and hostility, they are unlikely to be effective in child protection (Cosis Brown, 1991). There are heterosexual workers who are informed and trained in lesbian and gay issues and their efforts need to be acknowledged and affirmed. These workers can play a key role in identifying and exposing sexual abusers, providing sensitive and appropriate services to clients, and supporting their lesbian and gay colleagues by opposing homophobia and heterosexism in their agencies and challenging the compulsory nature of heterosexuality. The majority of heterosexual workers, however, need to examine the issues and re-examine their practice. They might begin by speaking out about homophobia.

References

Archer, J. (ed.) (1994) *Male Violence*, London, Routledge.

Atmore, C. (1996) 'Cross-cultural media-tions: media coverage of two child sexual abuse controversies in New Zealand/Aotearoa' *Child Abuse Review*, 5(5), pp.334–45.

Bannister, A. (ed.) (1992) *From Hearing to Healing*, London, Longman/NSPCC.

Bannister, A., K. Barret and E. Shearer. (eds) (1990) *Listening to Children*, London, Longman.

Barringer, C. E. (1992) 'Speaking of incest: it's not enough to say the word' *Feminism and Psychology*, 2 (2), pp.183–8.

Beavet, T. and J. Thompson (1996) 'Parents talking: sex education in secondary schools' *Pastoral Care*, December, pp.11–18.

Berg, I. and J. Nursten (eds) (1996) *Unwillingly to School* (4th edn), London, Gaskell.

Bertoia, C. E. and J. Drakich (1995) 'The fathers' rights movement' in W. Marsiglio (ed.) *Fatherhood: Contemporary Theory, Research, and Social Policy*, London, Sage.

Biehal, N., J. Clayden, M. Stein and J. Wade (1995) *Moving On: Young People and Leaving Care Schemes*, London, HMSO.

Bigner, J. J. and R. B. Jacobsen (1992) 'Adult responses to child behavior and attitudes towards fathering: gay and nongay fathers' *Journal of Homosexuality*, 23, pp.99–112.

Billington, R., J. Hockey and S. Strawbridge (1998) *Exploring Self and Society*, London, Macmillan.

Bremner, J. and A. Hillin (1993) *Sexuality, Young People and Care*, Lyme Regis, Russell House Publishing.

Browne, K. (1994) 'Child sexual abuse' in J. Archer (ed.) *Male Violence*, London, Routledge.

Burrell, G. (1984) 'Sex and organizational analysis' *Organizational Studies*, 5(2), pp.97–118.

Byerly, C. B. (1985) *The Mother's Book. How to Survive the Incest of Your Child*, London, Kendal/Hunt.

Byrne, S. (1997) 'Single-person adoption' *Adoption and Fostering*, 21(1), 50.

Campbell, B. (1988) *Unofficial Secrets: Child Sexual Abuse – The Cleveland Case*, London, Virago.

Campion, M. J. (1995) *Who's Fit to be a Parent*, London, Routledge.

Cashman, H. (1993) *Christianity and Child Sexual Abuse*, London, SPCK.

Cavanagh, K. and V. E. Cree (1996) *Working with Men: Feminism and Social Work*, London, Routledge.

Chaffer, A. and D. Garratt (1997) 'A friend in need' in D. Garratt, J. Roche and S. Tucker (eds) *Changing Experiences of Youth*, Buckingham, Open University Press.

Chaudhary, V. (1998) *Bullying of gays 'rife in schools'*, The Guardian, 13 March 1998, 8.

The Children's Society (1989) *Working With Sexually Abused Children: a Resource Pack for Professionals*, London, The Children's Society.

Collier, R. (1995) *Masculinity, Law and the Family*, London, Routledge.

Cosis Brown, H. (1991) 'Competent child-focused practice: working with lesbian and gay carers' *Adoption and Fostering*, 15(2), pp.11–17.

Cosis Brown, H. (1992) 'Lesbians, the state and social work practice' in M. Langan and L. Day (eds) *Women, Oppression and Social Work*, London, Routledge.

Cosis Brown, H. (1998) *Social Work and Sexuality: Working with Lesbians and Gay Men*, London, Macmillan.

Coward, R. (1983) *Patriarchal Precedents: Sexuality and Social Relations*, London, Routledge and Kegan Paul.

Cullen, D. (1997/98) 'Adoption: prospective adopter living in lesbian relationship; whether contrary to public policy' *Adoption and Fostering* 21(4), p.62.

Davies, D. (1996) 'Working with young people' in D. Davies and C. Neal *Pink Therapy: A Guide for Counsellors and Therapists Working with Lesbian, Gay and Bisexual Clients*, Buckingham, Open University Press.

Department of Health (1990) *Consultation Paper No 16: Foster Placement (Guidance and Regulations)*, London, HMSO.

Department of Health, Home Office, Department for Education and Employment (1999) *Working Together to Safeguard Children: A Guide to Inter-Agency Working to Safeguard and Promote the Welfare of Children*, London, HMSO.

Department of Health (1993) *Adoption: The Future*, London, HMSO.

Department of Health, Social Services Inspectorate (1995) *The Challenge of Partnership in Child Protection: Practice Guide*, London, HMSO.

Driver, E. and A. Droisen (eds) (1989) *Child Sexual Abuse: Feminist Perspectives*, London, Macmillan.

Dunne, G. A. (1997) *Lesbian Lifestyles: Women's Work and the Politics of Sexuality*,

London, Macmillan.

Elliott, M. (ed.) (1993) *Female Sexual Abuse of Children: The Ultimate Taboo*, London, Longman.

Epstein, D. (ed.) (1994) *Challenging Lesbian and Gay Inequalities in Education*, Buckingham, Open University Press.

Field, N. (1995) *Over the Rainbow: Money, Class and Homophobia*, London, Pluto Press.

Finkelhor, D. (ed.) (1983) *The Dark Side of Families*, London, Sage.

Finkelhor, D. (1986) *A Sourcebook on Child Sexual Abuse*, London, Sage.

Gagnon, J. H. and R. G. Parker (1995) *Conceiving Sexuality*, London, Routledge.

Galford, E. (1994) 'Out and proud in the Athens of the North' in E. Healey and A. Mason (eds) *Stonewall 25: The Making of the Lesbian and Gay Community in Britain*, London, Virago.

Green, L. (1995) *Sexuality and Residential Childcare – Oppression Through Repression or Protection?* paper presented at 'Youth 2000' Conference, University of Teesside, July 1995.

Griffin, G. (1993) 'History with a difference: telling lesbian *her*stories' in G. Griffin (ed.) *Outwrite: Lesbianism and Popular Culture*, London, Pluto Press.

Griffin, C. and M. Zukas (eds) (1993) 'Coming out in psychology: lesbian psychologists talk' *Feminism and Psychology*, 3(1), pp.111–33.

Hanscombe, G. E. and J. Forster (1982) *Rocking the Cradle: Lesbian Mothers: A Challenge in Family Living*, London, Sheba.

Hearn, J., D. Sheppard, P. Tancred-Sheriff and G. Burrell (eds) (1989) *The Sexuality of Organization*, London, Sage.

Hedley, R. and E. Dorkenoo (1992) *Child Protection and Female Genital Mutilation*, London, Forward Press.

Herman, J. L. (1981) *Father–Daughter Incest*, Cambridge MA, Harvard University.

HMSO (1995) *Looking After Children: Good Parenting, Good Outcomes*, London, HMSO.

Hooper, C.-A. (1992) *Mothers Surviving Child Sexual Abuse*, London, Routledge.

Hudson, A. (1989) *Changing Perspectives: Feminism, Gender and Social Work*, London, Unwin Hyman.

Jackson, S. (1982) *Childhood and Sexuality*, London, Basil Blackwell.

Kelly, L. (1988) *Surviving Sexual Violence*, Cambridge, Polity Press.

Kelly, L. (1996a) 'Weasel words: paedophiles and the cycle of abuse', *Trouble and Strife*, 33, 44–9.

Kelly, L., L. Regan and S. Burton (1991) *An Exploratory Study of the Prevalence of Sexual Abuse in a Sample of 16–21 Year Olds*, London, Child Abuse and Woman Abuse Studies Unit, University of North London.

King, M. B. (1995) 'Parents who are gay or lesbian' in P. Reder and C. Lucey (eds) *Assessment of Parenting*, London, Routledge.

Kitzinger, J. (1991) 'Child sexual abuse and the trials of motherhood' in S. Wyke and J. Hewison (eds) *Child Health Matters*, Buckingham, Open University Press.

Kitzinger, J. (1996) 'Media representations of sexual abuse risks' *Child Abuse Review*, 5(5), pp.319–33.

Kitzinger, J. (1997) 'Who are you kidding? Children, power and the struggle against sexual abuse' in A. James and A. Prout (eds) *Constructing and Reconstructing Childhood: Contemporary Issues in the Sociological Study of Childhood*, London, Falmer Press.

Langan, M. and L. Day (eds) (1992) *Women, Oppression and Social Work: Issues in Anti-Discriminatory Practice*, London, Routledge.

Logan, J. and S. Kershaw (1994) 'Heterosexism and social work education: the invisible challenge' *Social Work Education*, 13(3), pp.61–80.

Logan, J., S. Kershaw, K. Karban, S. Mills, J. Trotter and M. Sinclair (1996) *Confronting Prejudice: Lesbian and Gay Issues in Social Work Education*, Aldershot, Arena.

Manon, I. G. and J. McIntyre, P. Firestone, M. Liaezinska, R. Ensom and G. Wells (1996) 'Secondary traumatization in parents following the disclosure of extrafamilial child sexual abuse: initial effects', *Child Abuse and Neglect*, 20(11), pp.1095–109.

Mark, R. (1996) *Research Made Simple: A Handbook for Social Workers*, Thousand Oaks California, Sage.

Martinson, F. M. (1994) *The Sexual Life of Children*, London, Bergin and Garvey.

Mason-John, V. and A. Okorrowa (1995) 'A minefield in the garden: Black lesbian sexuality' in V. Mason-John (ed.) *Talking Black: Lesbians of African and Asian Descent Speak Out*, London, Casson.

McCollum, H. (1998) 'What the papers say', *Trouble and Strife*, 37, pp.31–9.

McCracken, S. and I. Reilly (1998) 'The systemic family approach to foster care assessment: a review and update', *Adoption and Fostering*, 22(3), p 16.

McMullen, R. J. U. (1990) *Male Rape*, London, Gay Men's Press.

Mills, S. and K. Karban (1996) *Developing Feminist Practice in Residential Child Care: Swimming Against the Tide?* Paper given at 'Feminism and Social Work in the Year 2000: Conflicts and Controversies' Conference, Teesside University, October 1996.

Nataf, Z. I. (1996) *Lesbians Talk: Transgender*, London, Scarlet Press.

National Curriculum Council (1990) *Curriculum Guidance 5: Health Education*, Department for Education, London, HMSO.

Nava, M. (1988) 'Cleveland and the press: outrage and anxiety in the reporting of child sexual abuse' *Feminist Review Special Issue on Child Sexual Abuse*, 28, pp.103–21.

NCH (National Children's Homes) (1992) *The Report of the Committee of Enquiry into Children and Young People who Sexually Abuse Other Children*, London, NCH.

Nelson, S. (1998) 'Time to break professional silences', *Child Abuse Review*, 7(3), pp.144–53.

O'Hare, T., C. L. Williams and A. Ezoviski (1996) 'Fear of AIDS and homophobia: implications for direct practice and advocacy', *Social Work*, 41(1), pp.51–8.

Open Learning Foundation, (1994) *Social Work with Children and Families*, Birmingham, BASW.

Otway, O. (1996) 'Social work with children and families: from child welfare to child protection' in N. Parton (ed.) *Social Theory, Social Change and Social Work*, London, Routledge.

Parkin, W. (1989) 'Private experiences in the public domain: sexuality and residential care organizations' in J. Hearn, D. L. Sheppard, P. Tancred-Sheriff and G. Burrell (eds) *The Sexuality of Organization*, London, Sage.

Patterson, C. J. (1992) 'Children of lesbian and gay parents' *Child Development*, 63, pp.1025–42.

Patterson, C. J. (1995) 'Lesbian mothers, gay fathers, and their children' in A. R. D'Augelli and C. Patterson (eds) *Lesbian, Gay and Bisexual Identities over the Lifespan*, Oxford, Oxford University.

Patton, M. Q. (ed.) (1991) *Family Sexual Abuse*, London, Sage.

Peterson, R. F., S. M. Basta and T. A. Dykstra (1993) 'Mothers of molested children: some comparisons of personality characteristics' *Child Abuse and Neglect*, 17, pp.409–18.

Plummer, K. (1996) 'Foreword' to W. Simon *Postmodern Sexualities*, London, Routledge.

Pringle, K. (1990) *Managing to Survive: Developing a Resource for Sexually Abused Young People*, Newcastle upon Tyne, Barnardo's.

Rafferty, J. (1997) 'Ritual denial' *The Guardian*, 22 March 1997, pp.26–35.

Rich, A. (1984) 'Compulsory heterosexuality and lesbian existence' in A. Snitow, C. Stansell and S. Thompson (eds) *Introducing Women's Studies*, London, Macmillan.

Richardson, D. (1994) 'Lesbians, HIV and AIDS' in L. Doyal, J. Naidoo and T. Wilton (eds) *AIDS: Setting a Feminist Agenda*, London, Taylor and Francis.

Richardson, S. and H. Bacon (eds) (1991) *Child Sexual Abuse: Whose Problem?* Birmingham, Venture Press.

Rights of Women Lesbian Custody Group (1986) *Lesbian Mothers' Legal Handbook*, London, The Women's Press.

Rivers, I. (1995) 'The victimization of gay teenagers in schools: homophobia in education', *Pastoral Care*, March, pp.35–41.

Robson, R. (1994a) 'Resisting the family: repositioning lesbians in legal theory', *Signs*, Summer, pp.975–96.

Robson, R. (1994b) 'Mother: the legal domestication of lesbian existence' in C. Card (ed.) *Adventures in Lesbian Philosophy*, Indiana, Indiana University.

Russell, D. E. H. (1996) 'Between a rock and a hard place: the politics of white feminists conducting research on black women in South Africa' in S. Wilkinson and C. Kitzinger (eds) *Representing the Other*, London, Sage.

Sanderson, T. (1995) *Mediawatch*, London, Cassell.

Sandfort, T. (1987) 'Pedophilia and the gay movement', *Journal of Homosexuality*, 13, pp.89–110.

Saradjian, J. (1996) *Women Who Sexually Abuse Children*, West Sussex, John Wiley.

Savin-Williams, R. C. (1995) 'Lesbian, gay male, and bisexual adolescents' in A. R. D'Augelli and C. J. Patterson (eds) *Lesbian, Gay and Bisexual Identities Over the Lifespan*, Oxford, Oxford University Press.

Sigma Research, (1996) *Behaviourally Bisexual Men in the UK: Identifying Needs for HIV Prevention*, London, Health Education Authority.

Skeates, J. and D. Jabri (eds) (1988) *Fostering and Adoption by Lesbians and Gay Men*, London, Strategic Policy Unit.

Smart, C. (1989) *Feminism and the Power of Law*, London, Routledge.

Sone, K. (1993) 'Coming out at work', *Community Care*, 7 October 1993, pp.18–19.

Southall Black Sisters (1990) *Against the Grain: 1979–1989*, London, Southall Black Sisters.

Sullivan, T. R. (1994) 'Obstacles to effective child welfare service with gay and lesbian youths', *Child Welfare*, LXXlll (4), pp.291–304.

Suriyaprakasam, S. (1995) 'Some of us are younger' in V. Mason-John (ed.) *Talking Black: Lesbians of African and Asian Descent Speak Out*, London, Casson.

Swannell, J. (ed.) (1986) *The Little Oxford Dictionary*, Oxford, Oxford University.

Tasker, F. L. and S. Golombok (1991) 'Children raised by lesbian mothers: the empirical evidence', *Family Law*, May, pp.184–7.

Trenchard, L. and H. Warren (1984) *Something to Tell You: The Experiences and Needs of Young Lesbians and Gay Men in London*, London, London Gay Teenage Group.

Trotter, J. (1996) *Illusive Partnerships: Gender and Sexuality Issues Relating to Child Sexual Abuse and Child Protection Practices*, paper presented at ISPCAN Conference, Dublin, August 1996.

Trotter, J. (1997) 'The failure of social work researchers, teachers and practitioners to acknowledge or engage non-abusing fathers: a preliminary discussion' *Social Work Education*, 16(2), pp.63–76.

Trotter, J. (1998a) *No One's Listening: Mothers, Fathers and Child Sexual Abuse*, London, Whiting and Birch.

Trotter, J. (1998b) 'Learning and practising, or just saying the words?' *Journal of Practice Teaching in Health and Social Work*, 1(2), pp.31–47.

Trotter, J. (1998c) *Pass, Fail or Bypass: Avoiding and Assuming Children's Sexuality in Schools*, paper presented at 'Child Welfare and Social Action' Conference, University of Liverpool, July 1998.

Trotter, J. and Gilchrist, J. (1996) 'Assessing DipSW students: anti-discriminatory practice in relation to lesbian and gay issues' *Social Work Education*, 15(1), pp.75–82.

Trudell, B. N. (1993) *Doing Sex Education*, London, Routledge.

Utting, W. (1991) *Children in the Public Care, A Review of Residential Child Care*, London, HMSO.

Utting, W. (1997) *People Like Us: The Report of the Review of the Safeguards for Children Living Away from Home*, London, HMSO.

Weeks, J. (1986) *Sexuality*, London, Routledge.

Westcott, H. (1991) *Institutional Abuse of Children – From Research to Policy*, London, NSPCC.

Winn, S., D. Roker and J. Coleman (1995) 'Knowledge about puberty and sexual development in 11–16 year-olds: implications for health and sex education in schools', *Educational Studies*, 21(2), pp.187–201.

6

Communication – a Key Towards Better Understanding

Varsha Nighoskar

As recognition of child sexual assault has grown during the two last decades, (see Kelly, this volume) so has awareness of the complex dilemmas it raises for all those employed in child protection work; professionals have had to acquire greater humility in the face of their own failures and mistakes. Feminists, who have played an important part in achieving public recognition for this issue, have attempted to counter definitions that blame children and women for sexual assaults perpetrated by men: 'locating child sexual abuse within the broader problem of men's violence against women and children and in its context in a male-dominated society.' (Hooper, 1992, p.2) Feminists have had some success in attempting to redefine the power relations in child sexual assault by shifting the focus from a 'family problem' to one of masculinity. For example, it is well documented that sexual assaults on children are predominantly committed by men. Research (Kelly *et al.*, 1991) found that among younger abusers, 85 per cent were male, and among adults, 95 per cent were men. Patterns of violence tend to reflect and reinforce existing power relations in society and groups, and child sexual assault is no exception.

In the context of child sexual assault, it appears that mothers are the primary adult actors in child protection (Hooper, 1992; Trotter; 1998) and may be more likely than professionals to be told of abuse. Where professionals do get involved in cases of familial abuse, mothers are still a key factor; the decisions to remove children from home depend crucially on the ability and willingness of mothers to protect them from further contact with the abuser (see Potter, this volume). One study of such decisions found that the mother's belief and her co-operation with agencies were the two most significant factors, more important than the severity or frequency of abuse (Pellegrin and Wagner, 1990).

The history of child sexual assault reflects the development of a strong emphasis on policy responses and on interagency and multi-disciplinary co-operation in the management of cases. According to Frost (1990), lack of co-ordination greatly hinders inter-agency communication in child protection, and it is this factor on which I will concentrate in this chapter, exploring how gender effects the process and outcomes of assessment and intervention.

Communication is an important tool, and even when sophisticated multi-agency packages have been devised, the success and failure of casework can rest upon the quality of the communications. My concern is primarily about professionals' lack of knowledge and sensitivity when faced with learning disabled parents and how resulting breakdowns in communication can eventually lead to unsuccessful outcomes for all involved.

Some of my experiences (as a female, Asian social worker) with mothers who are learning disabled, found communication to be the primary factor for breakdown of working relationships, not only between professionals and parents but also among professionals themselves. As a result, children were not always successfully protected. In my experience, some professionals appear to believe that learning disability is the main factor responsible for poor parenting. They assume that if parents are learning disabled, whether mild or moderate, they are not capable of looking after their children and parents are not given a fair chance to prove their abilities. In the individual case that I will later discuss, although regular meetings, intensive work and packages of support were introduced, there was something vital missing – good communication skills within and between agencies and with parents. All this can result in abuse being overlooked. Two sets of guidelines will be introduced later in the chapter which aim to improve communication skills with women who are learning disabled and with women from different cultural backgrounds.

Communication between people is a process in which a sense of meaning, a rapport and the possibility of a developing relationship is quite high (Lishman, 1994). However, in some cases the communication breaks down and shared meaning never develops. Language is a powerful tool which can have both social and personal consequences for individuals, thus the responsibility is on professionals to learn as many communication skills as possible and be conscious about the terminology used. An inability to communicate might also result in a child remaining at risk of sexual assault (Knutson and Sullivan, 1993). Professionals convey their own attitudes and prejudices through verbal and non-verbal communication, the latter can be equally powerful (Sands and Nuccio, 1992); for example, I attended a child protection conference where all professionals were already seated when the mother entered the room. This in itself is a powerful state-ment. Following this, a few minutes later one of the professionals got up and opened the windows, saying: 'This room is so smelly.' The person close to the mother shifted her chair slightly away from her; someone looked directly at the mother, and said laughingly: 'Someone would think you [mother] had not had a wash.' This was an extremely humiliating experience for this particular woman.

In any communication system, there will be barriers to overcome, due to factors such as age, sex, race, disability. These can be very specific around learning disabilities and parenting (Booth and Booth, 1997), and especially for black women and mothers (Williams, 1992). Hence these barriers must be recognized as such and strategies designed to deal with them. Where a person with a disability has been abused, there are likely to be additional issues. Professionals must be able to distinguish which aspects arise from the abuse and which are due to being disabled (Kennedy and Kelly, 1992). From the profes-sional point of view, the need to avoid any prior assumptions during the assessment process is very important.

The most important condition for successful practice is the quality of the relationship between a child's family and the responsible profes-sionals. It appears that the recurrence of abuse tends to be less common in those homes where there is an agreement between the professionals and the family to be honest with each other (Hallett, 1995). A great deal of research has shown that clients will co-operate even if it is against their obvious personal interests, as long as they see the process as just, and there are no conflicting messages or mis-information given to them by different agencies (Westcott, 1995). Contradictory and conflicting information can only increase parents' sense of confusion and feelings of helplessness over the situation. Hence it is imperative that parents have opportunities to change their perceptions and see professionals in a more positive light, especially in a child protection situation.

Gender issues

There is among some social workers a tendency to blame women for men's behaviour. For example, Westcott and Merry (1996) suggest that it is common to hear that women who do not give their male partners sexual satisfaction are driving them to incest and other types of sexual assault. In my experience of working with women who were mildly learning-disabled and had children, many seemed genuinely unaware that the mistreatment they themselves had received or were receiving, was in fact abuse. Most of these women had been subject to sexual assault by either their father or a close male relative; there remained some confusion about what was abuse and what was love and affection. We as professionals need to provide information, advice, education and support to mothers who have suffered or are suffering abuse, on the long-term effects for themselves and their children. According to Westcott (1993), research is available which shows that disabled children suffer from the same long-term and short-term effects of sexual abuse as their non-disabled peers. This means that it is the responsibility of the professionals is to disentangle whether the behaviour arises from their abuse, or their disability, or from their experience of a disabling society (Kennedy and Kelly, 1992). This is a difficult area as the learning disability is never the only factor, indeed mothers often experience a pattern of separation, loss and abuse in childhood which continues into their adult lives. As already indicated, professionals involved feel that learning disability is the key to parenting problems which can lead to family blaming, rather than locating the responsibility for the assault directly with the male abuser. Some of these issues will be illustrated in a case study later in this chapter where a learning disabled woman experienced discrimination, not only at the hands of her husband, but also from professionals (see also Oko, this volume).

Cultural issues

Interdisciplinary work is crucial in a multicultural society as there are language differences, cultural differences, and varying norms. The Department of Health (1995) places great importance on sensitivity to issues of 'race' and ethnicity, and advises: 'All professionals need to be aware of the power diffferentials which exist between workers and families from different cultural, ethnic and racial grouping.' (p.24). Staff in health and welfare services work with a large number of people from racial minority communities. It is therefore paramount that services operate from a multiracial/cultural perspective. Professionals must be equipped with knowledge and skills in order to meet the necessary requirements of an individual, irrespective of racial or cultural origin. As Ahmed (1986) has commented:

… an important difficulty in cross cultural communication is learning to differentiate between aspects of behaviour which are associated with consistent cultural patterns and those associated with individual personality differences (p.24).

Begum (1991) believes that professionals find it easier to deal with issues concerning learning disabilities for black disabled children, rather than dealing with racial and cultural issues. Furthermore, it is my experience that when racial and cultural issues come to the fore, many white workers expect their black colleagues to rescue them and do the work. Rather than wanting it on a platter from their black co-workers, good practice would mean that white workers take responsibility to educate and inform themselves. Thus, white and black professionals could work together and be joint specialists in race issues.

In those agencies where staff have not informed and educated themselves about race issues, working in partnership becomes virtually impossible where there are also the dual elements of abuse and learning disability. In my experience, many families are difficult to understand because their family structures are tight and rigid, and this includes Asian families. Such closed families may be reluctant to contact outside agencies for help but instead may chose to 'sort out our own problems' or seek answers within religious and cultural traditions. Many religious and cultural traditions cause problems for women and girls as their voices are not heard. As women, we are all products of our socialization, where our identities are moulded according to patriarchal society. This can be especially so in Asian communities (Ahluwalia and Gupta, 1997; Southall Black Sisters, 1990). Radical organisations like Newham Asian Women's Project have campaigned for improvements and, despite continued exclusion from agency planning, have resisted and overcome many barriers (Binney *et al.*, 1988; Social Services Inspectorate, 1998; Southall Black Sisters, 1990). In order to work effectively with different races and cultures, professionals have to be aware of, and analyse their own preconceived ideas and beliefs, about the constitution of a family. Professionals might have the skills to work effectively in family settings, but may not have appropriate support themselves or appropriate services available for the families. Communication and especially language skills, are particularly important for learning disabled people who may be relying on a worker to speak on their behalf. Black staff who are of similar background to those of their clients are vital in any organization.

Experience has shown that employing staff who can communicate in the clients' own languages may increase the take up of services by those who are non-English speaking (Sheik, 1986).

Cultural issues for interagency communication

In my own work experience with learning disabled people of different racial/cultural backgrounds, who are also parents, I have developed the following useful check-list.

1. Antidiscriminatory practice is about accepting people and providing services based on their individual need.
2. Workers should challenge their own preconceived ideas about sexism, racism and disability.
3. Workers should seek out coalitions, alliances and interest groups for solidarity in the face of persistent racist argument, especially when representing Black people.
4. Workers should be committed to change, by challenging the dominant socio-cultural systems which encourage gender stereotyping.
5. Workers should work in partnership with other agencies, fully utilising their skills and knowledge.
6. Representatives from black communities, disability campaigning groups, religious organizations and women's groups must be included in service planning.
7. Information must be available in all appropriate languages.
8. Workers must recognize their attitudes, prejudices and stereotypes when communicating verbally and non-verbally.
9. Properly trained interpreters must be employed and available.

In the following case-study a number of details, including the client's name, have been altered. This was a woman I worked with some years ago and hopefully the communication issues, which in practice I had to address, have been maintained.

'Mary'

Mary came to my attention for help with 'poor parenting skills', and I worked as a consultant with her and with the workers involved the case for several months. The purpose of my involvement was to provide a detailed assessment of Mary's circumstances in order that interventions could be appropriately planned, implemented and monitored. She was married aged 17 and at the age of 20 had three children (all of whom were subjects of child protection investigations).

During the ensuing assessment, it became apparent that in addition to social services, other agencies (the home care team, nursery nurses and health visitor) were also involved. Before meeting Mary, I asked a simple question: 'Will Mary be able to read if we send an appointment letter?' But she had never been asked, and none of the workers involved with her knew. I heard comments such as: 'She comes to the nursery and we tell her the time of our next visit' or 'We just drop in, as she is a housewife and is usually at home'. These examples emphasize that consciously or unconsciously, Mary had been already judged on a number of levels:

a) since she is a housewife and at home, assumptions are made that she will not mind people dropping in without prior notice.
b) since Mary is learning disabled, no one bothered to ask if she could read.
c) since Mary is both a housewife and learning disabled, she may not refuse entry to anyone or have any privacy.

These judgements highlight the importance of proper communication, and general good practice.

Mary was also criticized for not following agency procedures and professional norms. For example, in meetings, Mary was never given positives or encouragement for even the slightest success, but was reprimanded for anything she had 'failed' to do. One cannot help but ask whether anyone bothered to find out if Mary actually understood what was being discussed in the meetings, especially in the reports that were normally presented in meetings? Did anyone bother to observe any non-verbal signs in Mary's behaviour about whether she was understanding what was being said? Did Mary really have any chance of being successful? The first stage of assessment provided detailed information about Mary's background, and workers came to understand her better. As a child Mary had moved house many times: because of this her education had suffered, resulting in her inability to read. Mary had also been sexually assaulted by her father and had married young, possibly to get away from it. Unfortunately for Mary, sexual assaults continued in her marriage, this time by her husband: together with physically and emotionally abusive experiences. Unsurprisingly, Mary had very low self-esteem and lacked confidence. Mary tried to comply with her husband's demands, and this resulted in her children and her home taking secondary positions. However, despite the sexual assaults and her Catholic upbringing, Mary was able to manage contraception and knew she only wanted three children. The assessment confirmed what had been suspected: Mary understood better if things were demonstrated to her.

The next stage was to involve all agencies in improving communications with Mary. It was agreed, after some discussion involving all parties, that the care team would be asked to label the household items and housework tasks, and also to have pictures alongside the work. For example, soiled clothes were pictured by drawing dirty clothes and this label was attached to her laundry bag. Similarly, another bag where the clothes needed ironing was illustrated by a picture of an iron. Also, Mary was given the choice of days that she would prefer the home team to visit her and a chart was drawn up so that all people involved were aware of who was visiting Mary on which days. All the procedures were printed on charts with photos to demonstrate each step and a tick chart for Mary to tick if she thought she had done it properly. All of this enabled Mary to feel more in control of her own actions.

Professionals were also discouraged from judging Mary by their own standards. In meetings, certain professionals felt it was their 'duty' to comment on the state of the house. For example: 'Mary had not dusted the house properly.' My questions to these professionals were: 'by whose standard?' and also (if the main purpose of our involvement was to protect the children and Mary from being abused): 'is the dust going to have a more detrimental effect than the abuse itself?' Another worker made the assumption: 'I suppose it's no good talking to her about contraception, her being a Catholic.' My question to her was: 'Why didn't you read the assessment properly, instead of making assumptions?' (See also Oko, this volume). The health visitor was asked to advise Mary about the children's needs by using visual aids. Mary also went on an assertiveness training course where she met other learning disabled mothers. Video tapes and role playing (for teaching basic parenting skills) were used.

From here on in at meetings, irrespective of Mary's presence, negative statements were challenged and everyone was encouraged to tell the facts rather than what they thought might have happened. Reasons were given for Mary not completing tasks and statements such as: 'she has never done it' or 'she can't do it' were prevented. Training was provided for professionals, to help them understand how to better communicate with Mary including, for example, not using jargon. According to research carried out by a number of authors (Booth and Booth, 1997; Gath, 1988; Tymchuck, 1992; Tymchuck and Andron, 1992), there is ample evidence to show that parents with learning disabilities can be competent parents. However, there is real difficulty for social workers and health visitors in knowing how much weight to give the learning disability of a parent when working with families. This is mainly due to the lack of training professionals receive in this field, and to the fact that most of the research about parents and learning disabilities has focused on the child's disability not the parents' (for example, Rose and Jones, 1994). Consequently there is a tendency to offer help which pays little regard to the learning disability: for example, by using written agreements which cannot be read, let alone be understood.

One other factor which was highlighted in Mary's case was the lack of information each agency seemed to have. This was apparent when no-one knew if Mary could read or not, about her history of sexual assault, or even about any on-going domestic violence. It is not uncommon for professionals to be ignorant about their clients' histories (Millard, 1994), or about domestic violence (Mullender, 1996; Pahl, 1985). In 1993 (when this work with Mary was undertaken) the critical links between domestic violence and child protection were largely unrecognized by professionals (Kelly, 1994). The gathering and exchanging of information are, therefore, important features of communication which can greatly enhance good professional and client relationships, especially in cases of child sexual assault. Yet research indicates that once an inquiry is complete, particularly if it is inconclusive, communication fades (Hallett, 1995). In my experience parents were rarely told when the investigation was over or what had been decided. A procedure for informing parents about the conclusion of the process would help reduce the trauma.

Inter-agency communications

There is a need for closer attention by all professionals to work together and improve communication. For most professionals, the training involves very little interdisciplinary work, and therefore the contact with other agencies is limited. I have outlined below guidelines for agencies to improve their communication with clients and each other, especially in meetings.

1. In meetings workers must be aware of the patterns of interaction i.e. who talks to whom, who initiates the interchange and the frequency of such interchanges in order to gain an assessment of power distribution. If the parents are being ignored or not given the opportunity to voice their opinion, workers need to take appropriate action.

2. Professionals must be aware of covert agendas in meetings i.e. prior assumptions made point scoring.
3. Workers should seek out coalitions, alliances and interest groups for solidarity in the face of persistent masculine argument, especially when representing women.
4. Professionals must avoid repetition and superficial responses which might patronize the client.
5. Professionals must be acutely aware not to use jargon as a source of power as it alienates the client.

Conclusion

First, when many agencies come together, there is usually the potential for conflict with other professionals whose values and attitudes may be different. Workers must try and overcome these as the clients' needs are of paramount importance, while acknowledging that agencies will have different agendas. Second, procedures guiding inter-agency work suffer from problems of interpretation, emphasis and discretionary decisionmaking. Third, in inter-agency meetings, presentational issues are always important. Sometimes crucial decisions are made based solely on how arguments are presented. Fourth, the interconnections between race, culture, gender and disability can be complex and intense, especially in work involving domestic violence and child sexual assault, not least because of attitudes which stem from ignorance. Education and training to increase knowledge and understanding must be insisted upon. Finally, to reiterate points made earlier, it is imperative to be aware of multiple oppressions, and to attain clear and unequivocal communication in all areas of practice.

References

Ahluwalia, K. and R. Gupta (1997) *Circle of Light: The Autobiography of Kiranjit Ahluwalia*, London, Harper Collins.

Ahmed, S. (1986) 'Cultural racism in work with Asian women and girls' in S. Ahmed, J. Cheetham and J. Small (eds), *Social Work with Black Children and their Families*, London, Batsford.

Begum, N. (1991) 'Setting the context: disability and the Children Act 1989' in S. Macdonald (ed.), *All Equal Under the Act? A Practical Guide to the Children Act 1989 for Social Workers*, London, Race Equality Unit.

Binney, V., G. Harkell and J. Nixon (1988) *Leaving Violent Men: A Study of Refuges and Housing for Abused Women*, Bristol, Women's Aid Federation.

Booth, T. and W. Booth (1997) *Exceptional Childhoods, Unexceptional Children:*

Growing Up with Parents who have Learning Difficulties, London, Family Policies Study Centre.

Department of Health, Social Services Inspectorate (1995) *The Challenge of Partnership in Child Protection: Practice Guide*, London, HMSO.

Frost, N. (1990) 'Official intervention and child protection : the relationship between state and family in contemporary Britain' in Violence Against Children Study Group (eds) *Taking Child Abuse Seriously*, London, Unwin Hyman.

Gath, A. (1988) 'Mentally handicapped people as parents: is mental retardation a bar to adequate parenting?' *Journal of Child Psychology and Psychiatry*, 29, pp.739–44.

Hallett, C. (1995) *Interagency Co-ordination and Child Protection*, London, HMSO.

Hooper, C-A. (1992) *Mothers Surviving Child Sexual Abuse*, London, Routledge.

Kelly, L. (1994) 'The interconnectedness of domestic violence and child abuse: challenges for research, policy and practice' in A. Mullender and R. Morley (eds) *Children Living with Domestic Violence: Putting Men's Abuse of Women on the Child Care Agenda*, London, Whiting and Birch.

Kelly, L., L. Regan and S. Burton (1991) *An Exploratory Study of the Prevalence of Sexual Abuse in a Sample of 16–21 Year Olds*, London, Child and Woman Abuse Studies Unit, University of North London.

Kennedy, M. and L. Kelly (eds) (1992) 'Special Issue on Abuse and Children with Disabilities', *Child Abuse Review*, 1(3).

Knutson, J. F. and P. M. Sullivan (1993) 'Communicative disorders as a risk factor in abuse' *Topics in Language Disorders*, 13(4), pp.1–14.

Lishman, J. (1994) *Communication in Social Work*, Basingstoke, Macmillan.

Millard, L. (1994) 'Between ourselves: experiences of a women's group on sexuality and sexual abuse' in A. Craft (ed.) *Sexuality and Learning Disabilities*, London, Routledge.

Mullender, A. (1996) *Rethinking Domestic Violence: The Social Work and Probation Response*, London, Routledge.

Pahl, J. (1985) 'Refuges for battered women: ideology and action', in *Feminist Review*, 19, pp.25–43.

Pellegrin, A. and W. G. Wagner (1990) 'Child sexual abuse: factors affecting victims' removal from home', *Child Abuse and Neglect*, 14, pp.53–60.

Rose, J. and C. Jones (1994) 'Working with parents' in A. Craft (ed.) *Sexuality and Learning Disabilities*, London, Routledge.

Sands, R. and K. Nuccio (1992) 'Postmodern feminist theory and social work' *Journal of National Association of Social Workers*, 37(6), pp.481–576.

Sheik, S. (1986) 'An Asian Mothers' Self Help Group' in S. Ahmed, J. Cheetham and J. Small (eds) *Social Work with Black Children and Their Families*, London, Batsford.

Social Services Inspectorate (1998) *Partners in Planning: Approaches to Planning Services for Children and their Families*, London, Department of Health.

Southall Black Sisters (1990) *Against the Grain: a Celebration of Survival and Struggle (1979–1989)*, Southall, Southall Black Sisters.

Trotter, J. (1998) *No-one's Listening: Mothers, Fathers and Child Sexual Abuse*, London, Whiting and Birch.

Tymchuck, A. (1992) 'Predicting adequacy of parenting by parents with mental retardation', *Child Abuse and Neglect*, 16, pp.165–78.

Tymchuck, A. and L. Andron (1992) 'Project parenting: child interactional training with mothers who are mentally handicapped' *Mental Handicap Research*, 5(1), pp.4–32.

Westcott, H. (1993) *Abuse of Children and Adults with Disability*, London, NSPCC.

Westcott, H. (1995) 'Perceptions of child protection casework: views from children, parents and practitioners' in C. Cloke and M. Davies (eds) *Participation and Empowerment in Child Protection*, London, Pitman.

Westcott, H. and C. Merry (1996) *This Far and No Further: Towards Ending the Abuse of Disabled Children*, Birmingham, Venture Press.

Williams, F. (1992) 'Women with learning difficulties are women too', in M. Langan and L. Day (eds) *Women, Oppression and Social Work: Issues in Anti-Discriminatory Practice*, London, Routledge.

7

Work with Abusers: How Do We Talk About 'Rehabilitation'?[1]

Gillian Hirst

Varying perspectives

Following a television programme in 1998 about the naming of 'paedophiles'[2] in a number of communities, I received a telephone call from a woman asking whether I could confirm that there was a paedophile living in her vicinity. I replied that this was almost inevitably the case and began to talk about prevalence of child sexual assault and child protection strategies. Her purpose in phoning, however, was not to increase general knowledge: she asked for his name and address – information I could not give – to share with the other local mothers. The tone of subsequent news coverage suggested that a violent response to the man in question was not ruled out. Rehabilitation was barely discussed and often, in the face of actual (or potential) victimization of community members through sexual assault, with the need to support and protect those individuals, any intervention to change the behaviour of the perpetrator is under-standably not seen as a priority. Working with known abusers to reduce the risk of reoffending, however, remains one strand in the protection of women, children and men, from harm. Such work can complement other strategies rooted in politics, policing, education, health and social services, and many who undertake interventions with abusers can accommodate them within a feminist understanding of sexual assault. Contributing to the rehabilitation of sexually abusive men by the Probation Service represents, therefore, one preventative role. Other roles result from different employment responsibilities, community membership or political office. In seeking to prevent harm, the priority can remain the same although activities may differ within the various settings.

This chapter seeks to establish the extent to which probation practice in the area of sexual assault reflects feminist understandings, by
analysing the often implicit beliefs which appear to underpin the work
undertaken. To make this assessment, consideration will be given to
the manner in which the men, women, girls and boys who either
perpetrate, or are victimized by, sexual assault are portrayed: as individual people or as objects of concern; distinguished by a diversity of
personal characteristics or aggregated on the basis of one feature; digni-
fied by a name or anonymous. Contemporary feminist thought would
seem to be evident where there is a greater degree of specific attention
to individual people and their circumstances; where both differences
and commonalities are taken into account. This has been a lesson hard
learnt from the alienation of black women, disabled women and
lesbian women, from some developments in the women's movement
which paid insufficient attention to diverse experiences (Langan and
Day, 1992; Oko, this volume). The extent to which gender is highlighted within work with perpetrators could also indicate the
prevailing level of feminist consciousness. Additionally, feminist
approaches to practice imply a holistic framework, setting individual
actions within a context of a person's total experience of the world,
where work on several fronts may be simultaneous ('multi-modal').
This is reflected, in my view, in the assessment and intervention skills
taught through social work qualifying training and by reference to
'professional' intervention by trained workers. The chapter will thus
also explore any apparent narrowing of focus or trend toward the
exclusive application of a single technique to one area of problematic
behaviour without a general sense of overarching purpose or understanding of the wider causes of sexual abuse. The intention is to link
interpretation of the language used with the theoretical underpinnings
of practice and draw out the implications for practice itself.

Feminist politics being rooted in the personal experience, a feminist
analysis of any work must include an appreciation of the author's
perspective in order that the sources upon which she has chosen to
draw, and the inferences she has made, are appropriately weighted.
The reader may thus wish to know that my own form of feminism is a
blend of interpretation, guided by an appreciation of power imbalance
maintained by structures and institutions, with actions guided by
pragmatism and compromise! I am a mother, in a heterosexual relationship, white, without significant disability, middle class, without
religious affiliation and married for the second time. I have been
employed within Probation Services for 18 years in total; as a probation

officer for seven and then senior probation officer for another ten. I do not believe any one person is either wholly bad or wholly good and advocate holistic approaches to work with offenders. I believe imprisonment is inevitably a damaging experience. It is also my view, however, that where we cannot affect people's thinking and behaviour sufficiently to ensure the protection of others from serious harm, we require the most humane form of containment available.

My understanding of feminist approaches, and my experience of work with people who commit sex offences, lead me to believe it is important that they should, while observing the appropriate confidentialities, be described as members of the human race: that is, with a name, gender and status (adult, adolescent, child), the type of sexual offending they perpetrate, their sexual orientation and whether they are black or white. In referring to victims and survivors, I believe it is important to convey a sense of respect for them, an awareness of the damaging nature of the sexual assault(s) they have suffered, and a recognition that they are more than simply the sum of abusive experiences; that they are individuals as well as members of groups or categories. Pithers (1994) talks of the need mentally to: '... keep the victim in the room' while working with perpetrators and I believe this holds true for writing about this work also. Again, with due regard to confidentiality, this means giving attention to individuality (for example: age, a name, gender, race, physical and learning abilities, sexual orientation) when describing victims and survivors. I am aged 40 – 20 years ago my thinking was more mainstream, ten years ago it was more radical. I see feminist analyses as reflecting the diversity of women's experiences rather than as a constraining dogma for interpretation. In my view, debate within feminist discourse(s) is healthy.

It has been my experience that there are three contributory factors in the acquisition of the label of 'offender' within the criminal justice system: these being structural (to do with opportunities and scope for choice); individual (the exercise of choice within constraints); and pure chance (whether opportunities arise and if one is reported, apprehended and prosecuted). In order for an offence to be committed, I believe there are three prerequisites: the person must have the opportunity; they must also have the inclination, that is: they must believe the ends they are seeking will be met by the illegal means chosen; and their perceptions of self must be such as to accommodate being the kind of person that acts in that particular illegal manner. In terms of sexually abusive offending these prerequisites are linked to (respectively): grooming of the environment and other people; arousal patterns; and rationalization. (Finkelhor, 1986) The Probation Service is the only organization with a statutory duty to supervise in the community people who have been convicted of sexual offences. Supervision can be under Probation Orders (or Combination Orders) or on Licence following a prison sentence. The clearest expression of the purpose of such supervision is found within the National Standards for the Supervision of Probation Orders (Home Office, 1995): to secure the rehabilitation of the offender; to protect the public from harm from the offender; and to prevent the offender from committing further offences.

Engaging directly with the people who commit sexually abusive offences can pose two particular challenges to women and men whose analysis of the incidence of, and response to, sexual assault is informed by feminist approaches. First, there is the question of giving rehabilitation priority over punishment in the sentencing of convicted offenders. In a sentencing culture – where the perceived seriousness of offences is reflected in the range of disposals, from fines and discharges for the least serious to imprisonment for the most – a feminist understanding of the serious nature of sexually abusive offences would call for this to be reflected in the use of the greatest penalties. I would argue however, that this immediate response is flawed by the lack of any feminist analysis of the Criminal Justice System itself, of which the sentencing of people convicted of sexually abusive offences is only a part. I would further advocate the adoption of Carlen's (1989) 'women-wise penology' which promotes a form of Criminal Justice having as one aim: '… that penal regulation of lawbreaking men is not such that it brutalizes them and makes them even more physically or ideologically oppressive toward women in the future.' (p.112)

In this context, support for the use of community sentences as an appropriate option for rehabilitating men who commit sexually abusive offences would not seem out of place, although it is recognized that, in the lack of a more humane form of containment, a prison sentence does afford temporary protection for individual women and children from a particular offender. As is customary within feminist analyses, therefore, an 'either/or' dichotomy oversimplifies the issues. Second, there is the need to engage with the reality that a very small proportion of people so convicted are women. At first glance this may not sit very comfortably with a feminist analysis of sexual assault as a misuse of the power held by the individual as a result of the status conferred by institutionalized structures. The experience of the incidence of sexual assault committed by women being used to distract attention from the need to engage with the reality of it being an offence primarily committed by men (in my experience predominantly heterosexual men) against women and children has been recorded elsewhere (Hirst and Cox, 1996). However, a feminist analysis does not imply that disadvantage of itself brings with it sainthood, understanding or even a simple concern for others; like privilege it is what you make of it – only harder! While the aetiology of sexual assault committed by women requires proper examination, and the definition of abuse to which I subscribe – lack of consent and equality with the presence of coercion (Ryan 1990) – means women are also capable of abuse in situations where they wield power, the more fruitful line of enquiry is to identify why so few women are in fact perpetrators of sexual assault (see Cox, this volume). Such research is likely to bring far more benefits to the development of work with the majority of perpetrators – that is, men – as well as to work with women.

The field of enquiry

Given the way in which sexual assault was made public, by the less powerful parties (mainly women, girls and boys) speaking out about their experience of being harmed by men, there could be a justifiable expectation that the work done by the Probation Service with those who commit sex offences would take an approach based on feminist understandings. The purpose of this chapter, as stated above, is to identify the extent to which probation practice, and its underlying principles, do reflect feminisms. The method by which I have approached this task is to examine the longest standing professional publication which is readily available to probation practitioners: *Probation Journal*. Wykes, (1995) identifies the advantages of close examination of language in order to elicit something of the values and beliefs of the authors and their expectations of audiences. Accordingly, I have adopted a method of formal counting of particular terms as well as an interpretive reading of texts in an attempt to uncover the context within which work with men who commit sexually abusive offences is set. I have also considered the practice described in order to assess the extent to which holistic understandings of causal factors are balanced with a belief in personal responsibility for behaviour – both of which I believe to be cornerstones of feminist practice.

Probation Journal is published quarterly and I began by examining the 56 issues circulated since October 1982 when I became a subscriber by virtue of membership of the National Association of Probation Officers. NAPO is both the recognized trade union and professional association for Probation Officer and Probation Service Officer grades. More than a third of these issues carried at least one article about aspects of sexual assault. Authors mirrored to a great extent a developing knowledge of sexual assault, methods of work and underpinning theory which reflected my own: hearing first from Ray Wyre in the mid 1980s about the risk represented by discharged, and untreated, prisoners (before he went on to become the Director of the only residential treatment facility in this country specifically for men convicted of sex offences); joining the Regional Offender Treatment Association in 1989 and seeing it develop in 1991 into an influential national body (NOTA); being involved during that time in a group-work project with sexually abusive adolescent young men; and attending a training event led by Stephen Wolf in 1991 which highlighted the role of cognition in sexual offending.

The huge volume of material within *Probation Journal* meant subsequently that I had to confine a detailed analysis to those articles published between March 1991 and December 1996. This amounted to 15 articles, reflecting a degree of attention given to sexually abusive offending in excess of that given to other types of offending in this period (for example burglary, theft, assault or arson) and also disproportionate to the prevalence of such perpetrators within Probation Service caseloads where 'sex offenders' made up only 5 per cent of the national Probation Service caseload in 1995 (Proctor and Flaxington, 1996). Moreover, 1991 had certain features which commend it as a starting point. By then there was no doubt that sex offending was being taken seriously. Barker and Morgan (1991) point out that the '... proportion of convicted sexual offenders receiving immediate custodial sentences increased from 20% in 1979 to 33% in 1989.' (p.171) Morrison (1992) indicates that between 1983 and 1987, according to the NSPCC, children placed on 'at risk' registers for sexual abuse increased by 800 per cent (122). Lancaster (1995) points out that by 1991 there were 63 'probation-run sex offender treatment programmes' in operation (79). Furthermore, the 1991 Criminal Justice Act emerged as the result of a clear shift in sentencing policy toward a 'just deserts' model.

Within this framework, however, there was an approach of bifurcation, separating violent and sexual offences from those against property or otherwise of lesser identifiable risk to the public. This meant violent and sexual offences could attract a more punitive sentence (that is, more restricting of liberty) than might otherwise have been the case. Sections of the 1991 Act demanded more of the Probation Service: Schedule 1A4 allowed for people convicted of sex offences to be required to attend specific additional programmes for up to the entire length of time that the Probation Order is in force; Section 44 allowed sentencers to extend supervision of such people after a prison sentence to a point beyond the norm for other people released on licence. In 1991 Her Majesty's Inspectorate of Probation (Home Office, 1991) published the report of a thematic inspection demonstrating central interest in how such work was undertaken. This interest has continued, and my finishing point (December 1996), follows the publication of the consultation document by the Home Office in June 1996 concerning the 'sentencing and supervision of sex offenders', which subsequently led to the 1997 Sex Offender Act.

The 15 articles cover the following areas: work with defendants on bail; surveys of practice, research and evaluation activity (Barker and Morgan, 1991; Fisher, 1995; Proctor, 1994; Proctor and Flaxington, 1996); practice developments, specific methods and considerations (Kennington, 1994; Lancaster, 1995; Monk-Shepherd, 1995; Perry, 1993; White, 1992); the groupwork strategy in prisons (Sabor, 1992); staff training (Mark, 1992); managing practice (Morrison, 1992); and descriptions of aetiology (Dunkerley *et al.*, 1994). Some pieces which related to wider 'domestic' violence (including sexual assault) or to victim contact, but not specifically to sexually abusive offending, were excluded.

References to individuals

As stated earlier, my understanding of feminist approaches and my experience of work with people who commit sex offences means that I am particularly interested in the terms and descriptions used in writing about them, and about those whom they have assaulted. In total the 15 articles use 1034 words to refer to people who commit sex offences, sometimes in combination as for example 'child sex offenders'. Few of these words (31) could be said to reflect what these people have in common with other members of the human race rather than what sets them apart, that is references to them as 'people' (16) and 'individuals' (15). The use of the word 'individual' is also important in identifying that people who commit sex offences are unique, even among offenders of that type, as well as often sharing common characteristics with others who sexually assault others. In practice, to prevent the objectification of victims and survivors when talking to men about the women or children they have abused, real names are used. This is seen as an important step, both in assisting men to avoid distancing themselves from the fact that real women, girls or boys suffered from their actions and in recognizing the humanity of those victims and survivors. In view of this, I would have expected to find sexual abusers referred to by name within the case material (in articles with a national audience, 'John' or 'Dave', for example, would not compromise confidentiality). The lack of such references could, therefore, be seen as a distancing mechanism on the part of the authors and, therefore, indicative of a lack of feminist understandings.

Another example of distancing could be that the greatest number of words (474) were used to describe the status of the person within the general criminal justice system as opposed to within the community; most of these references being to 'offenders' (419) and other examples being 'alleged', 'convicted', 'defendant', 'prisoner'. While these latter distinctions are often important given the area covered by the article in question, in at least half of the cases where 'offender' is used it is done so without other qualification (for example 'sexual offender') and as such would seem to take as the prime consideration in describing the person that they have broken the law, rather than that they have harmed a vulnerable person. Another large number of words (86) describe the perpetrator's relationship to the Probation Service, most of these being 'client', 'client group' or 'clientele' (69), while there are also isolated incidences of the use of 'participant', 'consumer' and 'case'. Again these terms serve to aggregate and anonymise rather than individualize the people being discussed, and do not contextualize their behaviour in the way that uses of 'abuser' (29) or 'perpetrator' (74) would. These latter terms imply an explicit understanding of the power dynamics involved in sexual assault, but they are clearly used comparatively less frequently than the more general terms like 'offender'.

Feminist interpretation would require attention to the relatively powerful status of men committing sexually abusive offences, but within the articles there are only three references to 'adults' and two to 'adolescents' in describing abusers. The inference, where it is not explicitly stated that adolescents committing sexual assault are at issue, is that adult perpetrators are under discussion. This lack of detail, however, combines with the scant use of terms such as 'parent' (2), 'father' (2) or 'stranger' (1), to make little differentiation between one 'offender' and another and to mask the power they wield by virtue of their position. Looking at the age status specified when offences themselves are described, references make clear that they were against children generally (52), more often than against members of a particular age group or gender within the child population: 'schoolgirls' (2); 'girls' (2) or 'boys' (10); 'infant' (1); 'teenager' (1). An explicitly feminist approach to writing, requiring greater attention to be drawn to the advantage the perpetrator has over his victim, by specifying his status, their gender and their age more clearly, is thus not evident.

A feminist analysis of sexual assault puts victims and survivors centre-stage. However, although there are articles which talk about the primacy of the 'victim' (Monk-Shepherd 1995), some of the depersonalizing terms used to describe people who commit sexually abusive offences are echoed in the references to the children and adults who suffer as a result of their actions. There are again no references to their actual names or unique identities, the words used reflecting, in most instances, their objectification through abuse. Of 295 references to the women, men, girls and boys who had been abused, there are many uses of the word 'victim' (140) and scant use of 'survivor' (2), other generic terms comprise 'party' (6), 'partner'(1) and 'the abused' (1). Although some references to victims and survivors within the case material do state their age, gender and relationship to the perpetrator (for example '15 year-old daughter') mostly there is little real sense of an actual child conveyed. While this may seem less, or more, relevant according to the nature of the piece, I would argue that any writing in this area should consistently convey a sense of concern about real people's lives, rather than a sense of detachment.

It is, however, the lack of specificity in relation to gender in the articles that I found most surprising. In all there appear to be a fair number of references to gender (198): most (192) of these being attributive, making clear that a person under discussion was male (115) or female (77), the remainder being references to the concept of gender. In the main, there is an implicit inference that the people described as committing sex offences are men but this is only made clear by 8.6 per cent of the words used to describe them: 'men'(27), 'he/him/himself' (51), 'male' (8), 'fathers/stepfathers' (2), 'Mr X' (1). All other references to perpetrators of sexual assault are gender neutral apart from those which make clear that women are under discussion: 'woman' (1) and 'female' (4) – the ratio being 1:25, (female specific to male specific references) whereas one estimate of the ratio of female to male sexual abusers is 1:100 (Proctor and Flaxington 1996).

With regard to the gender of victims and survivors, around one-sixth (59) of the total number of references (295) make clear that the sexual assault under discussion was against girls or, much less commonly, women: 'she/her/herself' (21), 'girls' (12), 'daughter' (13) and 'women' (3). About half as many references (22) make the male gender explicit in discussing those who had been sexually assaulted: 'he/him/himself' (10), 'boys' (10), 'stepson' (1) and 'men' (1). There is thus a greater degree of specificity of gender when discussing victims and survivors than when discussing perpetrators, despite the apparently more even spread across genders of victim experience than perpetration. Could it be the influence of patriarchal relations that make it apparently more noteworthy when a member of the male gender is abused than when he abuses? (see Karban and Horrocks, this volume). The numbers of references to victims and survivors as boys is certainly out of proportion to their apparent prevalence (Finkelhor, 1986; Russell, 1983).

A simple count of gendered terms reveals that their use obscures the importance of the prevalence of males among adults and adolescents convicted of sexually abusive offending and the prevalence of women and girls among victims and survivors. This is a factor that is otherwise not ignored by the authors. For example, Morrison (1992) states: '… male socialization is a central issue in the treatment of offenders' (p.124). Nevertheless, articles which link childhood experience of sexual assault with subsequent perpetration do not pay attention to the apparent lack of such a link among girls and women. Fisher (1995) found that 70 per cent of men included in their study had suffered sexually assaultive experiences as children, but she is astonishingly gender neutral in writing:

> … although the cause of sexual offending is complex, this finding underlines the concern that sex offenders are adequately treated in order that they do not create further victims who may themselves go on to be perpetrators of sexual abuse. (Fisher, 1995 p.4)

Equally, Monk Shepherd (1995) refers to: '… the cycle of abuse where one generation's victim can become the next generation's abuser …' (p.29) without highlighting that this is evidently not the case with girls – she having made clear that, in all her work experience, victims and survivors had been female and perpetrators male.

That is not to say that the role of gender in sexual assault is overwhelmingly ignored in the articles examined. Perry (1993), for example, states that:

... distorted views ... sexualising children and objectifying women ... (are connected with) ... internalised attitudes about being the more powerful gender ... (and that) ... the sex offender does not hold those beliefs because he is a sex offender; he holds them because he is a man. (p.140)

Diversity

Taking a broader look at references that imply diversity among the perpetrators of sexually abusive offences, the victims and survivors and those undertaking rehabilitative work with them, there is again much more that is left unspecified than made explicit. This means that the use of terms which reflect the diversity of the communities within which probation practice takes place, highlights black women and men, gay men and lesbian women, disabled women and men, and to some extent any woman, as 'other', against an implied norm of white, heterosexual men without disabilities. The term 'diversity' itself is used only once. 'Race' is given attention on few occasions (12), among which people are referred to as 'black' (6) and 'white'(3), but mention is rarely made of other factors connected with race or ethnicity: 'ethnic minority group' (1), 'racism' (1) and 'race awareness'(1). 'Sexuality' is mentioned a similar number of times (15). Sexual orientation is referred to less, through the description of people as 'homosexual' (4), 'gay' (1), 'bisexual' (1) and 'heterosexual' (1). Being disabled is referred to rarely, comprising the description of people as having physical difficulties (1) and learning difficulties (3). To summarise, although all articles contain at least some reference to gender, only three refer to race or skin colour, one to disability and three to sexual orientation, while four refer more generally to sexuality. This lack of attention to the diversity among the people described is at odds with a feminist understanding which would take more account of such factors.

In terms of engaging with sexual orientation, however, there is a clear shift from the probation world of 1982 to that of the 1990s. Crolley and Paley (1982), in 'Sexual Problems and the Probation Service', focus on how probation officers deal with 'homosexuality', 'incest', 'indecent assault' and 'sexual advances', almost as if all were equally deviant. They made an apparent assumption that gay men and lesbian women were exclusively service users, not service providers. In contrast, Kennington (1994) talks of the needs of lesbian and gay offenders in a manner that implies lesbian and gay probation workers not only exist, but represent a valuable resource. He also raises the issues that:

negative views of black sexuality exist and racism inhibits black offenders in predominantly white groups ... [and] ... homophobia may inhibit the effective involvement of homosexuals in group work (p.82).

This suggests that, a decade later on from the work of Crolley and Paley, probation officers were taking responsibility to respond to disadvantage proactively and to appreciate diversity, thereby reflecting feminist understandings in this area.

References to sexually abusive offending

In describing the sexually abusive illegal behaviour that is the focus of probation intervention, as with the description of perpetrators, victims and survivors, it is again the relationship to the criminal justice system that is highlighted most often in the words chosen (sometimes in conjunction, for example 'sex offence', 'child sexual abuse'). 'Offence' or 'offending' is used in almost one third of the instances (139), although 'crime' is rarely used (4). The particular nature of the offence is also seldom specified, for example: 'rape' (5), 'incest' (6), 'indecent assault' (17) and 'buggery' (2). That the behaviour is abusive as well as illegal is reflected somewhat less often in references: 'abuse' or 'abusive' (67), 'perpetration' (3) and 'victimisation' (3). The sexual nature of the abusive behaviour is only sometimes made explicit by the prefix 'sex' or 'sexual' (78) while the prefix 'child' or suffix 'against children' to terms describing this behaviour (29) does not make clear those defining characteristics of the offence. Very rarely are inherently condemning terms used to describe offences: 'deviant' (3), 'improper' (1), 'anti- social' (1), 'damage' (1), 'harm' (1). What we could see as the distancing technique of using the word 'behaviour' (often, but not always, as 'offending behaviour') is more in evidence (38).

From a feminist perspective, looking for detail that differentiates between people on the basis of the offence they have committed reveals 'offender', 'abuser' and the like being prefixed by 'incest' (1), 'familial' or 'nonfamilial' (3), 'child' (18), 'rapist' (9) and 'exhibitionist' (1). Mostly however, where these terms are qualified, it is again by the use of the more general 'sexual' (176) – the imprecise term of 'sexual offender', for example, presumably implying sexual assault and not including those illegal (at the time the pieces were written) but consenting acts such as homosexual activity among young men between 16 and 18. This general lack of differentiation is important in two aspects: first, a proper appreciation of the nature of sexually abusive offending can be lost if descriptions are predominantly lacking in detail; second, different types of offending may respond to different interventions as discussed below.

References to practice

The selection of terminology to describe what the probation service offers to courts, communities and people under supervision to assist in their rehabilitation (that is its activity), together with the description of targets of intervention and methods, ranges enormously in level of detail and tangibility. Of the total number of words used to describe probation activity (664), while a good number (143) are accounted for by the generic term 'work', there are substantially more (202) uses of 'programme' to imply a more structured activity. The often used word 'group' (104) to describe what is offered makes clear the prevalence of a groupwork approach, while the confidence of the authors and/or probation officers in the capacity for rehabilitation is suggested by the use of the words 'treatment', 'therapy' or 'therapeutic' (131 in total) as opposed to the more limited description: 'supervision' (18). Clearly probation officers are doing more than simply monitoring the movements of men who commit sexually abusive offences.

The care/control debate is not rehearsed in stark terms in the description of this area of probation activity: 'care' is the term used in only one instance, as is 'surveillance', while 'correction' and 'intervention' are both used twice. However, the apparent confidence in the process of rehabilitation, rather than punishment or monitoring, is not reflected by a significant number of references to the underpinning theoretical bases of the work. Five articles name no theory at all. One describes the application of transactional analysis theory; one refers to both attachment and loss theory and crisis intervention; and one speaks of a psychodynamic approach. However, eight of the articles make reference to cognitive behavioural theory, of which two separately refer to 'cognitive' approaches and two to 'behavioural' or 'behaviourist' approaches although Fisher (1995) describes probation officers being more comfortable with a cognitive, rather than behaviour modification, focus. Only one article explicitly describes the theory underpinning the activity as 'feminist' although, as already described, feminist interpretations of power dynamics do underpin a significant amount of the writing.

Among the methods described, the greatest reference is to 'groupwork' (42). More limited references to other methods suggest that groupwork is viewed as the primary method for dealing with sexually abusive offenders: 'co-work' – that is, more than one probation officer or others involved in group or individual programmes – (24), 'individual' or 'one-to-one' work (7), 'family work' (4). The methods used within these settings are described in terms which encompass a range of practices along a continuum from what could be seen as tougher approaches of: 'confrontation' (11), 'challenging' (13), 'tackling' (5); through the more neutral forms of: 'training' (2), 'educating or teaching' (9), 'questioning' or 'obtaining explanations' (6) 'interviewing' (2): to the apparently softer techniques of: 'non-confrontation' (1), 'counselling' (2), 'persuading' or 'encouraging' (2), or 'helping' (1). Methods relating to cognitive approaches (for example 'altering perceptions'), behavioural ones (for example 'reconditioning') or a combination of the two (for example 'covert sensitization') are mentioned in seven of the articles and represent the most common references to types of practice.

Although readers of the articles may find internal tensions caused by terms employed, the above reflects the balance of the overall tone in the pieces examined. That the references to methods do err toward what could traditionally be seen as a more masculine end of the continuum (confrontation) rather than feminine (educating) is explored by some writers who question not only the worker's motivation in adopting a confrontational stance, but also the effectiveness of an approach which can only be perceived as adversarial. This is not to imply that men are more active in confrontation than women. Indeed, in my experience, women adopting a feminist analysis often use confrontational techniques. This does not, however, obviate the need to explore the efficacy of such interventions. Sheath (1990), exploring the attractions of confrontation ('especially for male workers') concludes '... if we are to protect women and children from sexual assault then nonce-bashing (sic) will have to take a back seat.' (p.162)

Mark (1992) advises:

> ... it may be wise to resist the temptation to storm the barricades too quickly by demanding that the client instantly gives up defences that are necessary for psychological survival ... an adversarial approach is the very stuff that the client's resistance feeds on. (p.10).

Fisher (1995) provides a description of the elements characteristic of effective treatment which include:

... an atmosphere where members felt encouraged and respected as individuals and did not feel that they were viewed solely as sex offenders ... [and] ... care should be taken as to the timing of work on developing victim empathy. If this is undertaken too soon the effect may be counter-therapeutic. In the early stages of treatment, offenders may not have come to terms with the consequences of what they have done and may become more defensive and likely to blame the victim as a coping strategy. (p.6)

This accords in my view with a feminist approach; such thoughtful balancing of intervention is important. The probation officer is employed to help the perpetrator help themselves stop offending in the manner that, within the value base of the Service, is most likely to be effective. It is precisely that value base, expressed by the Home Office (1997) as: '... to challenge attitudes and behaviour which result in crime and cause distress to victims' that can lead probation officers, in the face of unacceptable expressions or views, to forbid these to be verbalized from the outset, rather than use discussions to inform a baseline assessment against which change can be measured and interventions planned to alter often structurally reinforced thinking errors. I believe probation officers are abusing their power if they use interactions with perpetrators simply to make their own stance clear. It is also important in assessment to hear and note the perpetrators' perceptions without correction in the first instance, particularly when dangerousness is to be accurately assessed. It would be ironic indeed if meeting the probation officer's need to mount a clear and immediate challenge to the perpetrator's attitudes led to an increase in risk of reoffending (through hardening attitudes to victims in a defensive response) rather than a decrease (through eliciting commitment to treatment). Probation officers need to ensure their actions facilitate, rather than preclude, change in the perpetrator, and that they are strategic rather than immediate in response. 'Being oneself' is not enough when employed to give a service, particularly one as important as the protection of girls, boys and women.

The concentration on cognition and changing behaviour described above is confirmed, for the most part, in the aspects of the lives or personalities of sexually abusive men that are referred to as being targeted. Eleven of the articles refer to a focus on the belief system, attitudes and values or thought processes, of the individual. Five of those refer specifically to victim empathy and three to fantasy. Other targets are only referred to in isolated instances, for example: 'social skills' (2), 'assertiveness' (1), 'employment' (1), 'access' to family (2), 'communication skills' (1), 'anger management' (1), 'stress management' (1), 'substance abuse' (1), 'relationship skills' (1). This suggests a narrowing of the focus onto individual cognition, in keeping with the notions of where the Probation Service can have an influence. However, there is also a suggestion that programmes with this cognitive focus do not distinguish between different types of motivation and rationalization, for example by differentiating between sexually abusive offending against women, or against girls or boys. For example, Barker and Morgan (1991) note that differences in programmes:

> ... revolve around whether programmes are exclusive to offenders against children or open to all types of sex offenders ... [and] that ... approximately one third of programmes restrict their intake to offenders against children, many of them as part of a conscious effort to focus on child protection (p.174).

However, Proctor (1994), describing four years of the Cherwell Group, makes clear that, while most participants had been convicted of offences against children, men who offended against adult women were also included. Kennington (1994) confirms this trend, suggesting that there are advantages in a uniform approach to different types of perpetrator '... child abusers and rapists of adults attended the same programme as similarities are believed to outweigh differences and differences enhance discussion.' (p.83) Fisher (1995) also notes this trend but indicates that 88 per cent of the men in programmes studied had committed sexual offences against children. Perpetrators of offences against children do seem thus to be the majority of programme participants, and Fisher (1995) questions the logic of not paying greater attention to the type of sexual assault men have committed when assigning to treatment '... rapists tended to be treated with offenders who abused children. Evidence suggests that programmes designed for child molesters have little impact on rapists.' (p.6) Nevertheless, Proctor (1996) indicates that almost three-quarters of probation programmes were shown by the ACOP (Association of Chief Officers of Probation) survey to accept rapists. Although Proctor also implies that some programmes accept 'female sexual offenders', I find it inconceivable that women who sexually assault children could have as appropriate a service as their male counterparts, if expected to share the same treatment facility. This belief is based on my knowledge of women's responses to probation programmes in mixed gender groups generally (Hirst, 1996) and a specific study of treatment for women who have committed sexual assault (Mathews *et al.*, 1989). Again, then, a characteristically feminist attention to detail is justified by its impact on effectiveness while narrowing the focus onto commonality, rather than exploring difference, can apparently lead to less effective services.

References to frameworks

My reading is that this narrowing of focus is reflected in less attention to the external environment. I scrutinized the articles for attention to political, ideological or philosophical factors in setting a context for work with men who commit sexually abusive offences and increasingly discovered a political vacuum. While seven articles referred to beliefs, often in terms of those of perpetrators, only a third referred to 'philosophy' or 'ideology', four to 'principles', four to 'values' or a 'value base' and two to 'ethics'. Just four articles discussed social structural factors and four (not all the same as before), social roles. A minority (five) articles referred to 'culture' and six to one or more of 'concepts', 'models', 'analysis' or 'theory'. Although I would argue that the role of a probation officer is such that, in the course of employment, it is most legitimate to engage with sexual assault at an individual level in working to rehabilitate known perpetrators, it is nevertheless one of the main areas where the backdrop of patriarchal relations, institutionalized oppression and internalized cultural norms are particularly relevant. However, while eight articles referred to the 'power' dimension, eight to 'control' and two to 'conflict', only one spoke of 'deconstruction', 'critique', 'elitism', 'exploitation', 'marginalisation' or 'alienation', respectively. Perhaps even more surprisingly, only three articles referred to 'anti-discriminatory', 'anti-oppressive' or 'non-discriminatory' practice, two to 'heterosexism', one to 'racism', two to 'prejudice' and astonishingly *none* to 'sexism' (although three refer to 'gender awareness').

The often apparently apolitical stance is underlined further in that, while two thirds of the articles make neutral reference to 'perspectives', 'assumptions', 'opinions', 'feelings', 'attitudes' or 'views', less set these in a structural context by the use of 'blaming' or 'scapegoating' (three), 'collusion' (three), 'orthodoxy' (one), 'convention' (one) and 'tradition' (one). Ten articles talk of risk to children, women and the public, their protection and/or the need to prevent harm but only five refer to vulnerability. Three articles refer to politics or politicians, three to public concern. Although ten articles talk about responsibility in one form or another, only one mentions 'morality'. The response to sexual assault can only, in my opinion, be a moral issue and, while discussion of morality can be simplistically equated with conservatism, feminist understandings would suggest a need to engage with it. Cox, (in this volume), refers to the wave-like phenomenon of political awareness of child sexual assault, describing how Gordon (1989) links this with the strength of the feminist movement at particular times. There is no doubt that the political climate through the 1990s had a profound effect upon the Probation Service. Lancaster (1995) writes of '... a clear impression that the Probation Service will be forced to eschew its rehabilitative functions in favour of control, surveillance and case-management.' (p.79)

Summary and conclusion

As I write under the first Labour administration for many years, it seems timely to consider whether we are 'condemning more and understanding less' in the field of child sexual assault. Although there is an absence of explicit reference to the contextual features of power relations in the pieces examined, influenced no doubt by the accusations of political correctness earlier this decade (Phillips, 1993), the concern to balance personal responsibility and the contributory societal features referred to above, does give some indication that sexually abusive offending is not being divorced from its wider context in Britain in the 1990s. Four articles do refer to 'understanding', while the attention paid to 'collusion' suggests that this is not in any sense permissive.

In December 1995, the then Home Secretary abolished the requirement for Probation Officers to hold a recognized social work qualification (Dews and Watt,1995). A qualifying structure was not put back into place until 1998 when the Diploma in Probation Studies was finalised. There was thus a gap in recruitment and training after the rejection, by the centre, of generic training which has led to a temporary shortfall in qualified probation officers. Against this background, it is interesting to consider how members of the Probation Service working in the area of rehabilitating people who commit sex offences are referred to, either by themselves or outside commentators. The use of the word 'officer' (61) can be seen to confirm both the level of qualification (historically CQSW or Diploma in Social Work equivalent and Diploma in Probation Studies for the future) and the unique role of

Officer of the Court in both supervision and rehabilitation. It is, however, used comparatively less than the total of more generic terms: 'worker' (89), 'teams' (25), 'practitioner' (11) and 'staff' (58), or terms describing the activity undertaken: 'therapist' (9), 'programme deliverer' (2), 'groupworker or 'group leader' (4), 'co-worker' (2), 'keyworker' (2). 'Probation' prefixes 'officer' and other terms relatively often (52) but there are many where the grade of worker, level of qualification or nature of employment are, at best, implicit in the context. Compared with the article by Crolley and Paley (1982), where (probation) officers are referred to constantly (53) and described as working in a 'profession', there is scant use of the term 'professional' in the articles of the 1990s. Mark (1992) makes one reference to the probation worker as a 'professional' and describes some responses as 'unprofessional': Kennington (1994) talks of the Officer's 'professional' opinion while Morrison (1992) and Lancaster (1995) ascribe 'professional' only to bodies or individuals outside the Probation Service. In 1991 Barker and Morgan had stressed the need for particular skills in addition to generic training: '... working with sex offenders demands special skills above those acquired by probation officers through basic training or through their work with other offenders.' (p.174)

By 1995, however, Lancaster highlights the prevalence of not applying the full assessment skills borne of social work training, stating:

> ... in my experience, groupwork projects largely concentrate on someone's behaviour in the here-and-now ... [as opposed to taking account of] ... developmental, familial, individual and societal factors (p.80).

Sabor (1992), wrote of the prison programmes ignoring the social context of sexual assault and also highlighted the value of a broad qualifying base: 'Probation Officers are fortunate in having a substantial basic training in groupwork, counselling and recording skills as a foundation for this work.' (p.16) Morrison (1992) raises similar concerns:

> Work with sex offenders appears unfortunately to have become abstracted from the main body of correctional treatment work, resulting in de-skilling for both practitioners and managers. The nature of sex offending and our approach to it has been conceptualised as being very different to other types offending, thereby negating previous knowledge and experience in dealing with entrenched and anti-social behaviour. (p.124)

Fisher (1995), on the other hand, states of behavioural techniques:

> The reason why these techniques were not in evidence in many of the programmes may have been due to the fact that fantasy modification techniques require specialised psychological knowledge and training. (p.3)

Accordingly, the trend that I determine within the *Probation Journal*, as a result of the language used and the concepts presented, is one where there is increasingly a tension between the probation officer as case manager, (who commissions services on the basis of a professional and holistic assessment undertaking some – but not necessarily all – of the interventions themself), and that of the probation worker as skilled technician in a discrete area of practice operating solely on an individual basis without reference to wider societal factors. This interpretation is strengthened by the fact that, while seven articles make reference to 'effectiveness' only four refer to 'strategy' and three to 'policy', three to 'resources' and two to 'commitment'. The context of the work does seem to be taking a backseat to the efforts of probation officers themselves, despite the increase in internal policy statements. (In 1992 Morrison indicated that six of the 56 probation areas had policy statements relating to the management of sex offenders and by 1996, Proctor and Flaxington were indicating an increase to 46). This again supports the notion that feminist understandings may be in a period of ebb rather than flow.

Within a coherent strategy there would be scope for both skilled case managers and technicians with more focused skills in work with people who commit sexually abusive offences. Probation officers, as case managers, can make holistic assessments and manage a multi-modal approach to reduce the risk of reoffending in all areas of a person's life. Technicians can be used to fill any gaps in practice as identified, for example, by Fisher (1995) who points out that: '... most of the programmes ... had little or no behavioural component' (p.3). Probation officers could commission psychological services to undertake parts of: assessments (for example measuring arousal); interventions (such as masturbatory reconditioning); and evaluation (by measuring behavioural change). Officers could simultaneously capitalize on their strengths in work with cognition, skills development and relapse prevention. This combination could do much, not only to increase, but also demonstrate, effectiveness through the synthesis of different disciplines and approaches that sits so comfortably with a feminist analysis.

The advantages of the trend toward measuring effectiveness in individual cases centre around holding probation officers and perpetrators of sexually abusive offenders to account by investigating measurable changes in behaviour, thus focusing on a reduction of risk to women, girls and boys. This becomes a disadvantage only if it means that the factors outside the individual which contribute to sexual abuse are ignored or if, in fact, abuse is replicated in the individual's dealings with the probation service. Although, only two articles refer explicitly to 'feminism', feminist approaches have much to offer in the reconciling of these tensions. McColl and Hargreaves (1993) discuss NAPO's guidelines on 'Work with Men who Abuse Women and Children', stating that '... the document presented a feminist perspective ... which places the abuse of male adult or parental power at the core of sexual offending.' (p.15) As stated above, the advantage of premising work on feminist understandings is that it becomes inclusive rather than exclusive. This approach allows the probation officer and probation managers to retain a sense of the wider politics and the immediate practice with individual men, the place for the professional and the scope for skilled technicians undertaking specific tasks within an overall assessment. Feminist understandings allow for denunciation of offending; actions to protect vulnerable women, girls, boys and men; and rehabilitation of the men who commit sexual abuse. Proctor and Flaxington (1996) clarify '... for most services, work with sex offenders is strategically rooted in child protection and the prevention of further harm to victims.' (p.216)

There is more than one means of achieving this and it is important to keep the widest view of all the factors involved, particularly when the role of the individual worker runs the risk of narrowing the focus, blurring difference and holding only the minority to account. Thus the Probation Service does need generically trained people, both working directly and co-ordinating other interventions, with men and the small number of women who are charged and/or convicted in connection with sexually abusive offending to take account, in keeping with feminist understandings, of individual circumstances and societal factors which inhibit or foster abuse and the overarching need to protect vulnerable groups from the more powerful.

Notes

1. The National Standards for the Supervision of Offenders in the Community (Home Office, 1995) charges the Probation Service with three essential tasks:

preventing re-offending by the offender; by protecting the public from harm from the offender; and securing the rehabilitation of offenders.

2. Unfortunately, despite proper academic and professional concern about the use of the term 'paedophile', (Gallagher 1998; Kelly, 1996a) its frequent use in the media has apparently resonated with the majority of the public, who continue to use this unhelpful term.

References

Barker, M. and R. Morgan (1991) 'Probation practice with sex offenders surveyed' in *Probation Journal*, 38(4), pp.171–7.

Carlen, P. (1989) 'Feminist jurisprudence or women-wise penology?' *Probation Journal*, 36(3), pp.110–14.

Crolley, T. and J. Paley (1982) 'Sexual problems and the probation service', *Probation Journal*, 29(4), pp.133–7.

Dews, V. and J. Watt (1995) *Review of Probation Officer Recruitment and Qualifying Training*, London, Home Office.

Dunkerley, A., F. Graham, P. Doyle, T. Gooch and R. Kennington (1994) 'Learning from perpetrators of child sexual abuse', *Probation Journal*, 41(3), pp.147–51.

Finkelhor, D. (1986) *A Sourcebook on Child Sexual Abuse*, California, Sage.

Fisher, D. (1995) 'The Therapeutic Impact of Sex Offender Treatment', *Probation Journal*, 42(1), pp.2–6.

Gallagher, B. (1998) 'Paedophiles: what's the problem?' *NOTANEWS*, 28, pp.3–7.

Gordon, L. (1989) *Heroes of Their Own Lives: The Politics and History of Family Violence*, London, Virago.

Hirst, G. (1996) 'Moving Forward: How Did We Do That?' *Probation Journal*, 43(2), pp.58–63.

Hirst, G. and P. Cox (1996) 'Hearing all sides of the story: the challenge of integrating teaching on sexual aggression into social work qualifying training', *Journal of Sexual Aggression*, 2(1), pp.33–48.

Home Office (1995) *National Standards for the Supervision of Offenders in the Community*, London, Home Office.

Home Office (1996) *Sentencing and Supervision of Sex Offenders: A Consultation Document*, CM 3304, London, HMSO.

Home Office (1997) *The Three Year Plan for the Probation Service 1997–2000*, London, Home Office.

Kelly, L. (1996a) 'Weasel words: paedophiles and the cycle of abuse', *Trouble and Strife*, 33, pp.44–9.

Kennington, R. (1994) 'Northumbria sex offender team', *Probation Journal*, 41(2), pp.81–5.

Lancaster, E. (1995) 'Working with sex offenders: where do we go from here', *Probation Journal*, 42(2), pp.79–82.

Langan, M. and L. Day (eds) (1992) *Women, Oppression and Social Work: Issues in Anti-Discriminatory Practice*, London, Routledge.

Mark, P. (1992) 'Training staff to work with sex offenders', *Probation Journal*, 39(1), pp.7–13.

Mathews, R., J. Kinder Mathews, and K. Speltz (1989) *Female Sexual Offenders: An Exploratory Study*, Vermont, The Safer Society Press.

McColl, A. and R. Hargreaves (1993) 'Explaining sex offending in court reports', *Probation Journal*, 40(1), pp.15–21.

Monk-Shepherd, R. (1995) 'Mediation in prison following incest', *Probation Journal*, 42(1), pp.26–30.

Morrison, T. (1992) 'Managing sex offenders: the challenge for managers', *Probation Journal*, 39(3), pp.122–8.

Perry, T. (1993) 'Congruent behaviour: male worker and sex offender', *Probation Journal*, 40(3), pp.140–2.

Phillips, M. (1993) 'Oppressive urge to stop oppression', *The Observer*, 1 August 1993, 3.

Pithers, W. D. (1994) 'Treatment of Sex Offenders' Conference Speech, Birmingham, September 1994.

Proctor, E. (1994) 'Sex offender programmes: do they work?' *Probation Journal*, 41(1), pp.31–2.

Proctor, E. and F. Flaxington (1996) 'Progressing work with sex offenders', *Probation Journal*, 43 (4), pp.216–17.

Russell, D. (1983) 'The incidence and prevalence of intrafamilial and extra-familial abuse of female children', *Child Abuse and Neglect*, 7, pp.133–46.

Ryan, G. (1990) 'Developing integrated treatment programmes', *Audiotapes of ROTA Conference*, NOTA.

Sabor, M. (1992) 'The sex offender treatment programme in prisons'. *Probation Journal*, 39(1), pp.14–18.

Sheath, M. (1990) '"Confrontative" work with sex offenders: legitimised nonce bashing?' *Probation Journal*, 37(3), pp.159–62.

White, C. (1992) 'A T.A. approach to child sex abusers', *Probation Journal*, 39(1), pp.36–40.

Wykes, M. (1995) 'Passion, marriage and murder: analysing the press discourse', in R. E. Dobash, R. Dobash and L. Noakes (1995) *Gender and Crime*, Cardiff University of Wales Press, Cardiff.

8

Silenced Voice/Zero Choice – Young Women in Residential Care

Lorraine Green

Introduction

Historically, little research has been conducted into sexuality and sexual assault in residential child care (Bloom, 1992; Bullock *et al.*, 1993; Parkin, 1989; White, 1987). This deficit has begun to be redressed by contemporary research: there have been numerous scandals relating to the sexual assault of children by staff in these settings, for example Frank Beck in Leicestershire, and residential staff in Clwyd (Boseley, 1996; Corby *et al.*, 1998; Karban and Horrocks in this volume). Subsequent inquiries (Utting, 1991, 1997; Warner, 1992) appear to have changed very little and to have been conducted in a 'judico-legal' framework. Insightful studies of the sexuality of young women have been conducted by a number of feminist researchers based in schools (Halson, 1991; Lees, 1986, 1993). Such studies have been noticeably absent with regard to residential care settings. The only studies relating exclusively to young women and residential child care have been specifically around prostitution. These studies have shown that the treatment young women received in residential care increased the possibility of these young women either becoming involved initially in prostitution or becoming more deeply entrenched in it (Jesson, 1993; O'Neill, 1994: O'Neill *et al.*,1995).

The research this chapter is based upon aims to embrace a wider and more interconnected view of sexuality and sexual assault within children's homes, rather than concentrating on just one aspect of sexuality, or manifestation of sexual behaviour, such as prostitution or sexual orientation (for example, Jesson on prostitution, 1993, and McMillen on homosexuality, 1991). The factors which will be examined are the young women's past sexual experiences prior to reception into care, how the care system, including residential care, responds to the young women both generally and with regard to sexuality and sexual assault, and the combined effects both family and 'in care' experiences have on their sexual behaviour, vulnerability to sexual exploitation and attitudes.

Even though a limited range of factors have been concentrated on for the purposes of this chapter, it is seen as important not to view sexuality in a unitary or essentialist way, as a type of behaviour, a 'performative' act or a biological imperative. 'Sexuality' will therefore be treated as a socially constructed phenomenon (Vance, 1995; Weeks, 1986), shaped by the particular social, historical and spatial locations in which it is embedded and within which it is produced (Foucault, 1977).

Methodology

The findings in this chapter emanate from qualitative research conducted between 1994 and 1996. This involved ethnographic field-work in two children's homes situated in two different local authorities, as well as a large number of non-ethnographic interviews. The ethnographic studies encompassed participant observation of staff and children, formal interviews, and documentary analysis of agency documents such as log books and care plans. Most of the interviews conducted within the ethnographies were with staff and social workers. Formal interviewing of children was dropped because they often seemed to give inaccurate accounts, if their accounts were cross triangulated (Robson, 1993). This may have been because the children associated the notion of interviews with 'oppressive' police and child protection interviews. These seemingly inaccurate accounts may also link with the hypothesis that young people are more 'moral' about themselves and less so regarding their peers when being interviewed about sexual behaviour (Moore and Rosenthal, 1993). In addition, a wide range of non-ethnographic interviews with external/internal managers, residential and other agency workers, and ex-residents, were also conducted. These were one-off interviews with previously unknown residents who had no connection with the ethnographic settings. Of the non-ethnographic residential respondents, the major-ity of residential workers were accessed via contact with social work students from three different universities. The ex-residents were contacted via voluntary organizations and social services contacts.

Overall, 103 interviews including both ethnographic and non-ethnographic interviews took place. Because a minority of the respondents were interviewed in small groups or couples the number of respondents interviewed totalled 110. Of these 65 were residential or ex-residential workers and managers, 7 were social workers, 9 were children in care, 15 were ex-residents and 9 constituted 'other' personnel. These 'other' respondents did not fit into any of the above categories but had extensive relevant experience of, or knowledge about residents or ex-residents. They included HW workers who had conducted sexuality work with children in homes and workers with prostitutes and 'rent boys', many of whom had care backgrounds (see also Kershaw, this volume). The majority of these 'other' respondents were accessed via snowball sampling. Data was accessed from over one hundred settings and over 15 local authorities and voluntary organizations regarding contemporary and past experiences. The majority of settings were provided by local authorities.

This chapter will initially chronologically contextualize the young women's past family and 'in care' biographies in terms of assault. The research relates to young women accommodated in residential care (children's homes), most of whom were aged between 11 and 17. How the care settings respond or fail to respond to sexuality issues and the reasons why will then be evaluated. The sexual behaviour and beliefs of the young women will be outlined and described in conjunction with factors that influence them. The conclusion will bring together the preceding sections and summarise how and why young women in care are sexually vulnerable, as well as discussing theoretical, policy and practice implications.

Abused objects

> I think it's fair to say most of these girls have probably been sold or abused before they come into the institution. Perhaps not on the streets, but within their families, their peer group or their family's social group. Very few come into care who haven't experienced sex. Even if they haven't been used within those groups they may have been unprotected from sex in the past by their families. So these young women may have been raped once *or* twice by strangers because the parents have let them as kids play out until eleven or twelve at night.

This remark made by a social worker with substantial experience of working with children in care, was corroborated by many female residents and ex-residents. Within this chapter it is mainly sexual assault and exploitation that will be alluded to, although it is important to point out that different types of abuse are often interconnected, and that even non-sexual assault can increase emotional and sexual vulnerability (Parkin and Green, 1994). The influence sexually abusive home lives had on the young women's subsequent sexual behaviour was recognized and commented on by some, but not all of them:

> I didn't really go out with lads before but with being abused and stuff I started to sleep around.... I thought it was right. And because my parents and no one else had ever loved me that was my only way of showing love. But finally I realised it wasn't and stopped doing that. (female resident, aged 14)

> I had this boyfriend in the first children's home I was in but he just treated me like shit. He'd see me, he'd want to sleep with me and then he'd flick off and not want to see me. At that stage because it were the first sexual relationship I'd had after me dad had abused me, I didn't, well, I couldn't stop him. I guess I just went along with it. (female resident, aged 16)

When the young women entered the care system they talked about continuing experiences of assault:

> They're all arseholes. I've been in care for two and a half years and not once has anyone suggested I have any say in where I go to live. They've moved me about all over the place. And kids in care just get treated like objects and kicked from pillar to post and back again. And then they just move us somewhere else where they can forget about us for six to eight months. (female resident, aged 15)

The above quotation exemplifies the objectification many young women in care felt. Being treated as an object was linked not only to frequent moves but also to lack of involvement they had in important decisions that were made about their lives. Many young women also talked about feeling negatively labelled and stigmatized with regard to their care status and the residential homes they lived in, of internalizing the stigmatizing label and of wanting to make themselves invisible:

> I thought I should hide as I got to the front door. You were seen to be naughty if you ended up in a children's home and even the kids

used to say: 'What have you done then?' (female ex-resident, aged 25)

Many of them had also spent time in foster care prior to residential care and some had felt negatively and differentially treated, for example, given different food from the rest of the family or told they were 'bad' or 'wicked'. Sexually abusive and exploitative scenarios by members of the foster families were also sometimes outlined.

Residential and social work staff located the above experiences of the children in a failure by the system to plan adequately or provide suitable accommodation for children 'in care':

> There is planning in that we plan the admissions but we only plan a lot of the admissions because there is nowhere else for that child to go. So you might have a 14/15 year old with emergency carers and they can't stay there. But there isn't any other foster placements available to them so you do a planned admission to here. But only in about 5 per cent of the cases is the home an ideal wanted placement. (Social worker working with children in care.)

Thus abusive family experiences were compounded further when the children entered the care system, where they felt disempowered, uncared for and insecure. When placed in residential homes this was rarely a first, wanted or planned, placement. Residential care was therefore frequently perceived by residential staff, social workers and the young women themselves as a last resort, a fact corroborated by previous researchers (Aymer, 1992). The young women perceived the children's homes as a 'dumping-ground' and as evidence that no one wanted them. Therefore common experiences of the operation of the care system included not only objectification, but stigmatization, alienation, disempowerment, and both psychological and geographical instability.

Goldfish bowls or militaristic microcosms?

One important and continually replicated feature was the high institutionalization of the settings (Goffman, 1961, 1969; Parkin and Green, 1994, 1997). Both current and young women ex-residents talked of great isolation, of 'living in a world within a world' or a 'goldfish bowl' and of having few contacts outside the children's homes. Few had regular contact with parents or people from their original community, the frequency and quality of social work contacts varied considerably and educational attendance was sporadic or non-existent (Jackson, 1987). Additionally, staff talked about their perceived isolation and of having minimal contact with other parts of the organization. Workers and ex-residents also described the experience as akin to living or working in a prison and many homes were characterized by surveillance/containment features such as locked doors, alarm systems and patrolling by staff at night. Workers sometimes said they felt like army or prison guards as they walked around with bunches of keys jingling at their waists; they perceived their remit to be solely one of control and not of care or development:

> The fact that the only compulsory training course is 'control and restraint' tells you so much. That we aren't here to work with people sensitively. It's more a case of policing the building, keeping the lid on things – not really doing anything constructively. (residential worker)

In the following example a residential worker describes how many homes catered for the children's basic physical needs and responded to bureaucratic pressures, but did little else:

> I think the staff do the day to day things and the administration very well but in terms of giving a little bit of input, support and encouragement, not a lot of it goes on. That mentality is basically the norm and people can't see any different. That's the way they have always worked, so why change it? (residential worker).

The emphasis in these settings was thus around both organizational and community isolation, control and containment, surveillance, and enforced conformity to institutional norms through rigidity and regimentation. One effect of these institutionalized practices was to set up divisive staff and children's cultures, with each culture distrusting and dehumanising the other. The children's behaviour thus was often being treated punitively and as evidence of intrinsic individual pathology and/or past abusive backgrounds, but was rarely perceived as a response to the institutionalized treatment they received. Staff cultures were often described by staff as hard and 'macho' with any exposure of vulnerability or sensitivity to self, peers or children being seen as weakness and an inability to do the job. Such a finding accords closely with how staff cultures in prison regimes operate (Carter, 1997), and thus further contributes to staff finding it very difficult to work sensitively with the children in their care.

Children's cultures were comprised of a combination of conformity to an institutionalized regime and simultaneous resistance to it. One aspect of their culture was the 'buzz' phenomenon. Here the children 'managed' boredom and emotional distress through a continual search for momentary excitement, or by artificial suppression or elevation of emotion. They fuelled this largely through the winding-up of staff, abusing each other, sexual encounters, criminal behaviour and excessive consumption of drugs and alcohol. Children's cultures were also characterized by excessive bullying, 'top dogs' and a policed cultural conformity within. There did not appear to be a specific gendered component to this hierarchical bullying as young women as well as young men occupied 'top dog' positions in the individual homes. However to some extent young men were more liable to occupy 'top dog' positions because of their ability to utilize strength and size and well as intimidating and manipulating tactics. However, in one home, a small young woman managed to intimidate and command considerable obedience from young men, who were sometimes considerably bigger than she was.

Worker management of sexuality: panic and invisibility

Responses by staff to sexual activity varied considerably but the prime emphasis was on control and prohibition. This was influenced not only by institutionalized practices, but also by the location of the homes within public realm organizations, where the rules of the public sphere superseded and overarched those of the private realm (Parkin, 1989; Parkin and Green, 1994). Within homes located within the private realm, for example the nuclear family, some forms of hierarchic male-dominated adult sexuality and sexual activity are seen as acceptable.

With children's homes being publicly located, the myth of the asexual organization predominates and sexuality is publicly proscribed and denied. Alternatively certain manifestations of it are covertly condoned or punitively policed (Hearn and Parkin, 1995). Most of the staff had received little, if any, training on how to talk to the children about sexuality and sexual assault, and organizational guidelines or policies on sexuality were rarely to be found or were of little practical use. Such deficits appeared to be linked to the public/private dichotomy debate and anomaly, as well as the poor researching of residential homes (Berridge and Brodie, 1996) and their institutional-izing remit. Many staff felt ill equipped to work with the children on sexuality and sexual assault issues and were embarrassed about broach-ing the subject. When staff did intervene in sexual issues their intervention seemed to be clearly informed by individual morals, by fear of scandal and by an overall atmosphere of institutionalization.

Some staff would look the other way, others would intervene puni-tively, particularly if they were witness to sexual activity in the building. Others would not talk to the young women in terms of what their sexual activity meant to them, but would sometimes offer tech-nical contraceptive advice, 'march' the young women to family planning clinics, or warn of the possible dangers or consequences of sexual activity. Sex education or contraceptive advice prior to 'known about' sexual activity was rare. The situation was further complicated by the fact that the staff and children used different languages to talk about sex, staff often talking about sex in euphemisms or annotated phrases such as 'be careful'. One young woman who had a stomach upset and could not take her contraceptive pill was advised to use a sheath but had no idea what a sheath was. There was additionally a clear gender bias in the way sexuality was dealt with. Women workers disproportionately tended to deal with sexuality issues but only with selective issues with regard to young women residents. They would generally only intervene if young women were known to be sexually active, and their intervention would tend to centre around punitive comments or technical contraceptive advice to prevent pregnancy. The only time male resident sexuality was ever responded to by either male or female staff was if it involved same sex sexual activity or the discovery of a young man and woman resident 'in flagrante' in the home. Staff responses to this would involve immediate separation and sometimes also punitive sanctions.

The effect of neither female nor male staff responding to adolescent male sexuality, and of female staff selectively and reactively respond-ing to female sexuality, was to create a situation whereby male sexuality was hidden, made invisible and rendered unproblematic. In contrast female sexuality was highlighted and condemned. This emerged in the interviews when male staff were asked to talk generally about sexuality: 'Certainly female sexuality wasn't something I was ever involved in or would have expected to be involved in. It was handled by the women staff and seen as women's business.' (male resi-dential worker) Male workers not only tended to ignore the sexuality of residents in terms of working sensitively with them, they also were more likely to make punitive value judgements about female sexuality. Simultaneously they implicitly seemed to accept exploitative, male sexuality by leaving it unchallenged or justifying it in essentialist 'boys will be boys' tonalities. They thus appeared to have embraced constructivist, societal stereotypes about the differential and immutable sexual natures of men and women and the sexual double standard (Choi and Nicholson, 1994). Their responses to young women residents involved in prostitution constitutes one example of this as these young women tended to be seen in a very lowly manner by male staff and their behaviour subsequently interpreted as immoral and deviant rather than as evidence of their exploitation:

> ... if you were talking to lad in the home the staff, more likely the male staff, would say: 'don't you know she charges £15, so you better start saving your money up.' They never did anything in the way of talking to you to try and understand why you were doing it. Just sly comments and dirty looks. (ex-resident, age 17).

Male workers also continually voiced fears that they would be subject to allegations of sexual impropriety from young women residents, despite the fact that this fear was totally out of proportion with the actual fictitious allegations made. This led to many individual male workers refusing to be alone with young women at any time or offering them physical affection and comfort when upset. Sometimes the organization reinforced this through policies which stipulated two men should not be on duty together or be in a room alone with young women residents. Such a position was organizationally seen to safeguard against sexual assault, but much contradictory evidence manifested itself to show this was not the case. Such contact avoiding behaviour also led to the young women being at risk in terms of men being unprepared to intervene in situations where the young women were in possible, physical danger:

> She was semi-conscious in the toilet and had been sick everywhere and I knew I had to get her into bed.... She only had a pair of flimsy shorts and a little top on.... I couldn't leave her there but I thought if I touched her to move her, I might be in bother. So what I had to do was to knock two other girls up to get them to carry her to bed. I know it wasn't fair on them but I'd rather do that than compromise myself. (male residential worker)

Such behaviour made the potentially sexually exploitative nature of men's sexuality even less visible, by reconstructing it as men's vulnerability to false allegations. Through these discursive strategies, male workers were then depicted as potential victims needing protection rather than being seen as potential offenders or professionals with responsibilities. However, male residents were not perceived in the same way. Many young men were abusive sexually to both female staff and young women residents as well as other resident young men who they feminized and labelled 'poufs' if they did not conform to their stereotypical visions of masculinity. However despite their potential for abusive behaviour, concealing the young men's sexuality also detracted from attention being paid to their vulnerability to potential sexual assault from other resident young men and from adult sexual offenders operating both within and outside the homes.

How workers manage sexuality issues is, therefore, determined by a number of factors. These include the institutionalized nature of settings and their ambiguous and blurred location between public and private locations, with the rules of the public predominating. Organizational support is also an important factor because without adequate information, training and guidelines, workers tend to fall back on their own morals or to err on the side of caution by reacting prohibitively to anything of a sexual nature, particularly the sexual activity or exploitation of young women. Internalized and unchallenged conceptions of 'naturalistic' gendered sexualities also affect workers' responses and result in male sexuality remaining unscrutinized and submerged, while certain aspects of female sexuality are exaggerated and condemned.

The young people's sexual explorations, encounters and exploitations

Such institutionalized practices, combined with past care and family experiences of abuse, had a significant effect on sexuality and sexual exploitation. This related to the children inhabiting and relating to specific parochial, institutional cultures which had sexual norms and values that, in some ways differed from those in wider society, and in other ways magnified and exacerbated what occurred in wider society. Sexual exploitation by both adults and peers was often tolerated, or not seen as abuse, because it was the only way the children felt they could gain affection from anyone. Peer male/female rape and sexual assault was also often seen as the norm and rarely challenged, and the young women frequently used sex as a commodity to trade for either money or material assets such as alcohol and cigarettes.

Adult/child abuse

Young women were thus often unable to define and recognize both past and contemporary adult/child sexually abusive behaviour:

> At first I didn't see what the worker did as abuse. I don't think I saw it as abuse for a very long time. At first I saw it as attention and affection and thought it was quite nice but then it got violent and I didn't like it, but I didn't know what to do. (female ex-resident, aged 32)

The young women also felt that even if they did recognize and disclose sexual assault, because of antagonistic and divisive staff/child cultures, there was little chance that they would be understood or protected (see also Trotter, this volume). Some of the young women tried to disclose and were not understood. Others were responded to in a negative manner because staff were unaware what they should do, and others felt they could not tell anyone:

> I tried to tell them this is why I did this and this is why I wanted out. I said my uncle comes over and he likes to play with me and they said: 'that's nice'. I just didn't have the vocabulary to say this man's abusing me. So I'd say: 'this man takes me for walks and he buys me ice creams.... He takes me a lot for walks and he takes me down the cemetery.' That was my way of trying to tell them. But nobody picked up on that and I'm bloody angry that they didn't. (female ex-resident, aged 33)

Heterosexual peer sexual activity

Relationships between male and female residents were also exploitative, with the young women often feeling unable to refuse young men's sexual advances, misinterpreting them as love, or using them to procure affection. Conversely, many of the young men seemed to perceive sex as a conquest and physical experience, entirely divorced from love:

> I know I flirt with the lads but when they come on heavy, I just can't say no. I've had countless one night stands in the last couple

of years. I don't want to have sex with them but I'm scared if I don't they'll get violent and force me, like what happened before. So I just go along with it and sometimes it's just for having someone there being with me. (female resident, aged 15)

A lot of young women talked about being coerced into sexual activity:

I've woken up a lot times in care and I know it sounds disgusting but there's been a lad trying to put his penis in my mouth. You just had to stick up for yourself at the end of the day and I got my brother to sort them out. They mainly used to do it to the new girls that came in. (female ex-resident, aged 21)

In other homes young women colluded with and sometimes even joined in with young men raping their young women peers. Due to the institutionalized nature of the homes and the differential cultural standards such behaviour was often seen as the norm and was rarely consciously conceptualized as abuse or assault:

I've known girls since leaving talk about being forced into sex.... And if you were outside a kids' home that would be seen as rape but in a kid's home it's just par for the course. Standards are a joke in kids' homes. Things that would shock people elsewhere are seen as the norm. (ex-residential worker)

In a way I guess it's abuse if you're pushing someone into sex who doesn't want it, which is what happened. But you just got to accept it and saw it as normal. Other kids would join in with it and if a lad was forcing a girl into having sex the other kids would hold the door shut. (female ex-resident, aged 17)

The young women would also police and attempt to control each other's sexual behaviour, but rarely blamed the young men if they were unfaithful. In one home a group of young women resorted to beating up another resident because she had slept with one of their boyfriends, but no blame or responsibility was attributed to the boyfriend:

Kate's just a fucking dirty slag. She slept with Rita's boyfriend, Tom, so we had to jump her and teach her a lesson.... You can't blame Tom though, men just can't help themselves. If it's offered to them on a plate they take it. (from fieldnotes)

Other young women and ex-residents talked about having no sense of control or ownership over their own bodies; of being unable to say no because they did not know they could say no. They assumed sex with the young men in the home was just the norm – something that happened to everyone:

> We would do it with anybody either outside or inside the home. It was just something you did.... It wasn't for sex. It was for attention and affection.... We saw it as something that happened that we had no control over, you had to go along with it. We didn't know how to say no and we didn't know we could. It was like we had been trained. (female ex-resident, aged 32)

Sex as commodity trade

Prostitution was only perceived by residents and ex-residents as such when financial exchange was involved. Yet many of both current and ex-residents, as well as staff, talked about the young women having sex in exchange for affection, alcohol, drugs, cigarettes or sometimes even for a bag of chips. Such exchanges, except debatably sex in exchange for affection, could be conceptualized as a form of informal prostitution:

> She used to say: 'I'll give you a blow job for a packet of fags'.... We used to negotiate stuff like: 'Are you going to do it until I come or are you going to stop?' and that ... there was no love or emotional feelings, it were like a trade off all the time. (male ex-resident, aged 27)

> [Sex] was an easy commodity, so it did go on. I think a lot of kids did it for that because they needed somebody. Even if it was for five minutes or the whole night you needed somebody. Everybody does and that was the only way we had with each other. (female ex-resident)

Heterosexual activity between the young women and young men in the home was thus often an implicit trade-in for conquest and physical pleasure on the young men's side, and affection or material commodities on the young women's side. However the young men tended not always to keep their side of the bargain:

> It was always important for the girls to know you were going out

with them before they let you have sex with them and then to let everyone know that I used to say: 'Yes, fine, no problem if that's what you want.' Eventually I'd get what I wanted out of it. A lot of the lads would finish with them as soon as they'd had a shag and the girls would get really mad. (male ex-resident)

The women, in particular, were also highly vulnerable to sexual exploitation from outsiders, the main categories being drug pushers, child sexual offenders and pimps. Their isolation from 'everyday' community living, vulnerability caused by past sexual and emotional assaults, a search for love and affection, a desire to rile and rebel against staff and a search for excitement, and artificial emotional highs from drugs, rendered them easy prey for these men. Some young women ex-residents talked about being lured into prostitution by a constant (initial) supply of drugs, being taken out for drinks and to night-clubs which they found exciting, as well as believing (again initially) that these men loved them and would care for them: 'A lot of it's by force, because the pimps, black or white, make you think they love you and then they force you into prostitution and then you've got no choice and you can't get out.' (female ex-resident). Others talked about peer pressure within the home: one example was a young women whose clothes were thrown out of the window and her possessions burned because she refused to be involved in prostitution. Although the sexual exploitation of young women residents by male outsiders did not take place within institutional confines, these young women were often targeted as captive prey by such men because of their marked locational visibility as well as their emotional vulnerability. Sometimes, as shown above, female prostitution was also a cultural sexual norm within the young people's cultures.

Same sex female sexual activity

Lesbian or same sex, female, sexual activity was very closeted and covert in the homes. In one of the homes, there was a rumour that one new resident was lesbian. Following this, all the other young women initially refused to share a room with her. Two ex-residents, who as adults identified as lesbian, also talked about how difficult it was to identify as lesbian while living in a children's home. One of them kept it secret for fear of getting beaten up:

I would have been a dead girl if any of the other kids had found out I was gay. One of me mates came out as gay in a children's home and every day she used to get her head kicked in. (16 year old ex-resident)

Another was beaten up by the children and treated extremely punitively by the staff:

The head of the home dragged me into her office and told me it was illegal to be a dyke until you were twenty one ... she went overboard when she heard I was getting involved with people who were HIV. She called a meeting with the staff and the kids which resulted in me getting beaten up by a bunch of hysterical kids.... The kids had taken the piss before but when they found out about the HIV stuff it got really nasty – one big, fucking fight and I had to fight my way out of the home. (ex-resident, aged 25)

Silenced voice: zero choice

Young women in residential care seem highly vulnerable to sexual assault and exploitation. A number of factors contribute to this vulnerability. These include poor assertiveness skills, a lack of knowledge and information around sexuality, little physical affection, psychological or social care, an institutionalized care culture and the acceptance of traditional gendered perceptions of femininity and women's sexual behaviour. Mixed sex institutions, and the placement of known young men offenders with already victimized women and younger men also exacerbates this vulnerability. The low self esteem and poor assertiveness skills of the young women are linked to past experiences of sexual and other forms of abuse; the disempowering and destabilizing experience of frequent moves and lack of consultation within the care system, followed by institutional living, which increases passivity as well as rebellion. The young women often search for love and affection from any source it can be found, while simultaneously attempting to block out painful emotions or artificially reproduce emotional highs through an unrelenting search for excitement and excessive drug and alcohol use.

These factors render the young women vulnerable to exploitation of a sexual nature from both within and outside the system. Pimps and pushers from the outside target and exploit the young women by promising love and affection, while simultaneously getting them addicted to drugs to ensure compliance and dependency. The young men within the homes see women as commodified forms of sexual conquest (Evans, 1993) and use them to feed their own emotional and sexual needs. Consequently they are rarely able to offer the young women the stability or love they crave or even any form of respect. Many staff, in particular the male staff, are unable to offer any form of physical affection, and the organizational and locational emphasis on containment and control also mitigates against staff building-up relationships of trust and affection with the children. This further increases their sexual vulnerability as they tend to trade in sex in exchange for affection. In addition when the young women do seek to meet unfulfilled needs through multiple sexual encounters and involvement with drug dealers and pimps, they tend either to be ignored, subject to punitive and moralistic treatment or given technical contraceptive advice. This is ineffective and does not help them look at how they are being exploited, or why they are behaving in particular ways. Female heterosexual activity detected within the home is also (initially) 'pushed out' and treated punitively, as is lesbian activity, which residents recognize is likely to engender even more negative reactions from both peers and staff.

The behaviour and responses of the young women can be conceptualized as the result of their passage through a continuum of abuse which occurs in different locations. They initially enter the care system with a biography of abuse and the way the care system 'processes' and objectifies children 'in care' further exacerbates their feelings of powerlessness and experiences of abuse. When they are admitted to residential care they enter into an insular, institutional culture, subdivided into antagonistic and divisive staff/children's subcultures. Both of these cultures are abusive, so these children not only receive abuse in terms of exploitation and bullying from their own culture but also are dehumanized and objectified by the staff culture. Because of the parochial nature of the institutional culture, which has few outside points of reference, the young women often come to accept abusive practices as inevitable and as the norm. This further disadvantages them in terms of survival, with few opportunities to develop self-preservation strategies against sexually exploitative peers or adult 'outsiders' and 'insiders'.

In view of these factors young women in residential care seem to be even more at risk of sexual exploitation than their non-institutionalized women counterparts. These women are also vulnerable because of inadequate and moralistic sex education and the internalization and acceptance of gender stereotyped prescriptions of femininity and female sexual behaviour (Halson, 1991; Lees, 1986, 1993). However, young women in residential care are substantially more disadvantaged because of the impact of past abusive intrafamilial and 'in care' experiences.

Theoretical implications

Important theoretical directions include acknowledgement and incorporation of Goffman's theory of institutionalization (1961, 1969) which relates to the treatment and responses of children and staff, both generally and with regard to sexuality. Important parallels with Goffman include: the rigidity and regimentation of the settings; isolation from the wider community; dehumanizing treatment and stigmatization of the young women, and divisive staff and resident cultures. Goffman's theories also relate to the way in which children's cultures operate. The young women attempt to procure affection and esteem from sexually exploitative 'outsiders' such as pimps, child sexual offenders and drug pushers, and from 'insiders', as well as rebelling against staff via proscribed sexual behaviour.

Foucault's writings on disciplinary discourses (Foucault, 1977) relate closely to these institutionalized regimes and to the punitive, controlling methods they employ. Foucault's discourses around sexuality are also important, as they inform and influence both staff and children's beliefs about sexuality and their corresponding sexual behaviour (Foucault, 1981). One particular discourse adopted by young women and their male peers, as well as staff, is the belief that male sexuality is primordial, overriding and not subject to individual control. This equates closely to Dyer's (1985) illustration of the male 'sexual incontinence' theory. Contradictory discourses about men and male sexuality also coexist with the above, and sometimes supersede them in terms of practice and policy. These include the unsubstantiated belief that men are highly likely to be subject to false allegations of sexual impropriety. This discourse mitigates against the protection and welfare of the young women, as adult male workers are constructed as being more at risk of, and in need of protection from, invalid allegations than the young women are from the 'actual' risk of assault. Young women also police and stigmatize their female peers' sexual behaviour if their behaviour contravenes norms of the sexually passive or innocent women (Showalter, 1987).

The fallacious public/private dichotomy (Parkin, 1989; Pateman, 1989) also contributes to the denial and exclusion of sexuality issues from the public sphere. This is because 'sexuality' is presumed to occur only within the private, not the public sphere: even in situations where an individual's home is located within the public domain.

Policy and practice implications

In terms of policy and practice implications, an analysis of three of the major inquiry reports of maltreatment of children in residential care shows that the major themes were: inadequate and hierarchical line management, inadequate staff training and recruitment, social isolation, a 'macho' culture and inappropriate practice methods (Berridge and Brodie,1996). This research has shown that these features are common in many homes – and that they are related to the vulnerability to, and actual sexual exploitation of, young women 'in care' from both inside and outside of the home setting. This research highlights other pertinent features which contribute to young women residents' sexual vulnerability. These include: the institutionalized nature of the settings which lead to divisive staff/resident cultures – hence only prohibitive, rather than educational and preventative, discourses around sexuality are being enacted. Sexuality issues tend to be interpreted by staff in terms of an essentialist, hierarchical heterosexuality, located within a moralistic framework, where women's sexuality is highlighted and problematized and men's sexuality is left unquestioned.

To improve the situation the themes outlined by the major inquiries need to be acted on, in addition to full recognition of the validity and actuality of young people's sexuality. Staff not only need to receive improved general training but also specific training on how to work proactively and sensitively with sexuality and sexual assault issues. To be effective, this training needs to be located in a framework which looks at and challenges the sexual morals and beliefs of staff, including attitudes around gender and sexuality (see also Karban and Horrocks, this volume). Policies also need to be supportive to staff intervention, providing clear guidelines on how staff should work with children on sexuality issues and outlining in an unambiguous manner how staff should tackle issues such as sex education, making this an obligatory staff responsibility.

It is my contention that if adequate training, policies and support are not available, staff will tend to avoid dealing with sexuality issues through embarrassment, lack of knowledge or fear that what they do or say will judged as unacceptable. Attention also needs to be paid to the 'macho', socially isolating and institutionalized cultures predominating within these homes. Attempts must be made to de-institutionalize such settings, so they are not organized along the lines of control which often parade under fallacious notions of care and protection, but are responsive to the social, psychological and sexual needs of the residents within them.

References

Aymer, C. (1992) 'Woman in residential work: dilemmas and ambiguities' in M. Langan and L. Day (eds) *Women Oppression and Social Work: Issues in Anti-Discriminatory Practice*, London, Routledge.

Berridge, D. and I. Brodie (1996) 'Residential child care in England and Wales: the inquiries and after' in M. Hill and J. Aldgate (eds) *Child Welfare Services: Developments in Law Policy, Practice and Research*, London, Jessica Kingsley.

Bloom, R. (1992) 'When staff members sexually abuse children in their care' *Child Welfare*, 71(2), pp.131–45.

Boseley, S. (1996) 'Scandal of abuse "cover up"' *The Guardian*, 5 September 1996.

Bullock, R., M. Little, and S. Milham (1993) *Residential Care for Children: A Review of the Literature*, London, HMSO.

Carter, K. (1997) *Mascu(iso)lation, Power and Control inside a Local Prison*, paper presented to British Sociological Association Annual Conference, 'Power and Resistance', University of York, 1997.

Choi, P. and P. Nicholson (1994) *Female Sexuality: Psychology, Biology and Social Context*, Hertfordshire, HarvesterWheatsheaf.

Corby, B., A. Doig and V. Roberts (1998) 'Inquiries into child abuse', *Journal of Social Welfare and Family Law*, 20 (4), pp.377–96

Dyer, R. (1985) 'Male sexuality in the media', in A. Metcalf and M. Humphries (eds) *The Sexuality of Men*, London, Pluto Press.

Evans, D. (1993) *Sexual Citizenship: The Material Construction of Sexualities*, London, Routledge.

Foucault, M. (1977) *Discipline and Punish: The Birth of the Prison*, Harmondsworth, Penguin.

Foucault, M. (1981) *The History of Sexuality*, Harmondsworth, Penguin.

Goffman, E. (1961) *Asylums*, Harmondsworth, Penguin.

Goffman, E. (1969) 'The characteristics of total institutions' in A. Etzioni (ed.) *A Sociological Reader on Complex Organisations* (2nd edn). New York, Holt, Rhinehart and Winston.

Green, L. (1995) *Sexuality and Residential Childcare – Oppression Through Repression or Protection?* Paper presented at 'Youth 2000' Conference, University of Teesside, July 1995.

Green, L. and W. Parkin (1997) 'Cultures of abuse within residential child care', *Early Child Development and Care*, July 1997, pp.73–86.

Halson, A. (1991) 'Young women, sexual harassment and heterosexuality: violence, power relations and mixed sex schooling' in P. Abbott and C. Wallace (eds) *Gender, Power and Sexuality*, London, Macmillan.

Hearn, J. and W. Parkin (1995) *Sex At Work: The Power and Paradox of*

Organisation Sexuality, New York, St Martin's Press.

Jackson, S. (1987) *The Education of Children In Care*. Bristol, School of Applied Social Studies, University of Bristol.

Jesson, J. (1993) 'Understanding adolescent female prostitution: a literature review' *British Journal Of Social Work*, 23(4), pp.517–30.

Lees, S. (1986) *Losing Out*, London, Hutchinson.

Lees, S. (1993) *Sugar and Spice: Sexuality and Adolescent Girls*, London, Routledge.

McMillen, C. (1991) 'Sexual identity issues related to homosexuality in the residential treatment of adolescents' *Residential Treatment for Children and Youth*, 9(2), pp.5–21.

Moore, S. and D. Rosenthal (1993) *Sexuality in Adolescence*, London, Routledge.

O' Neill, M. (1994) *Feminising Theory/Theorising Sex: Researching the Needs of Young People In Care* Paper given at British Sociological Association Annual Conference, 'Sexualities in Context', University of Central Lancashire, March, 1994.

O'Neill, M., N. Goode and K. Hopkins (1995) 'Juvenile prostitution: the experience of young women in residential care', *Childright*, January 1995, pp.14–16.

Parkin, W. (1989) 'Private experiences in the public domain: sexuality and residential care organisations' in J. Hearn, D. L. Sheppard, P. Tancred-Sheriff and G. Burrell (eds) *The Sexuality of Organisations*, London, Sage.

Parkin, W. and L. Green (1994) *Sexuality and Residential Care: Research in Progress*. Paper given at British Sociological Association Annual Conference, 'Sexualities in Context' University of Central Lancashire, March 1994.

Pateman, C. (1989) *The Disorder of Women*, Cambridge, Polity Press.

Robson, C. (1993) *Real World Research*, Oxford, Blackwell.

Showalter, E. (1987) *The Female Malady*, London, Virago.

Utting, W. (1991) *Children in the Public Care*, London, HMSO.

Utting, W. (1997) *People Like Us: The Report of the Review of the Safeguards for Children Living away from Home*, London, Department of Health.

Vance, C. (1992) 'Social construction theory: problems in the history of sexuality' in H. Crowley and S. Himmelweit (eds) *Knowing Women: Feminism and Knowledge*, Buckingham, Open University Press.

Warner, N. (1992) *Choosing With Care – The Report of the Select Committee of Inquiry into the Selection, Development and Management of Staff in Children's Homes*, London, HMSO.

Weeks, J. (1986) *Sexuality*, London, Tavistock.

White, K. (1987) 'Residential care for adolescents: residents, carers and sexual issues' in G. Horobin (ed.) *Sex, Gender and Care Work*, London, Jessica Kingsley.

Wynn Davies, P. (1996) 'Insurers tried to halt child abuse inquiry' *The Independent*, 5 April 1996.

9

Child Protection Conferences – 'In the Name of the Family'

Ann Potter

Introduction

I remember once being asked what a feminist perspective on Child Protection Conferences is. The questions were: 'what questions do feminists ask, what things do feminists 'see', that others don't?' This chapter raises some issues I believe are relevant to those questions. They are relevant to all those who participate in Child Protection Conferences. They are particularly relevant to those of us who chair such meetings.

When I began to write this chapter, on what the purpose is, the process is, and what the nature of the conclusions reached by Child Protection Conferences are, my reflections were centrally rooted in my daily professional responsibilities. I had been employed as a Chair for the best part of eight years in two local authorities. Now that I have moved on to do other things, I hope that my reflections have gained in sharpness. While I like to think that I was reasonably skilled at my job, I had always found the chairing role a profoundly difficult task. This is not a view shared by some colleagues, many of whom control resources, shape policies and operate at the strategic management level. Neither is it a view held by others who perhaps exert some influence, if not actual authority, within the Child Protection system. From their perspective the Chair's task is very straightforward – it is to 'manage' the meeting: the chairing role is a functional one. The 'effective' Chair is one who can 'control' a meeting, keep it to task and reasonable time-scales, to 'get the business done'. I continue to reject this analysis, having found no evidence to support the notion that, by virtue of providing an information-sharing forum, a Child Protection Conference will be led inexorably to a basic truth. I have found much evidence that such meetings, while on the surface concerned with safeguarding children, at the level below appearances are often the sites of competing interests, and sites where power, or lack of it, are influential in decisions about next steps.

So how does the Child Protection Conference respond to child sexual assault? Where does the Child Protection Conference fit into the child protection system as a whole? What kinds of meanings might it have for its subject children, their mothers, their fathers, and other family members? (see Nighoskar in this volume). What meaning, or sets of meanings, does it have for professionals invited to attend; those who by that invitation are identified as agents of the state? To make sense of these issues, I locate the Child Protection Conference as one part of a process that involves itself in the micro-politics of 'family life', which is informed by a eurocentric analysis of children and childhood and 'the family': by what constitutes abuse, and how abuse is identified. This process, while sometimes well camouflaged, has its roots in a white, middle-class, male and inherently heterosexual set of ideologies, which marginalize the needs, interests and rights of women and children – in particular, their rights to be safe.

Because of the reality of what some children endure, the information that is shared at conferences is often hard to listen to. There is a critical significance in how information is shared, and on where the emphasis is left to lie. So while the information will be shared and sifted using apparently neutral language, there is no doubt that behind this neutrality lie very clear ideological and political positions. They will be often left unspoken. Conference participants may not even be aware of their immediate importance, but they nevertheless are still there. If the conference is truly to be utilized in the interests of the subject child's short- and long-term safety, its content and process needs to be located in both time and space. And if the analysis is not to remain partial, it needs also to be rooted in an understanding of the distribution of power within both the public and private domains. It needs to be informed by a critical analysis of how power is distributed across gender boundaries and within personal relationships (Millett, 1971). More essentially, it needs to consciously address the disposal and maintenance of power between a particular child, their abuser, and their 'non-abusing', or safe carer (Smith, 1994).

A conference should never compound any abuse that has occurred. Its conclusions should not be delivered to family members in a way that makes them feel further oppressed. Time needs to be spent in explaining how and why conclusions have been reached and in listening to the child and their support network. These are matters that a Chair should see as their responsibility to address, either during conference proceedings, or as part of the recommendations. Such comments may appear obvious, but there is research evidence (Dartington Social Research Unit, 1995) to challenge those who assert that 'we do that already'.

Child protection conferences located in the contemporary landscape

While we know that child sexual assault is not a new phenomenon, its extent and impact, and its root causes continue to be kept hidden from the public consciousness (see Cox, this volume). Its survivors and their supporters own its reality almost exclusively (Armstrong, 1978, 1996; Wilson, 1993). Children who tell us that they have been sexually abused, and whose testimonies are judged to be 'competent', 'credible' and 'reliable' (Home Office, 1992), become not only 'forensic exhibits', but the primary witnesses to their own abuse when they enter the adult theatre of the criminal court. My argument is that within the frame of a child-centred child protection system, the requirements of the criminal and civil justice systems need not be incompatible in rela-tion to children's rights to be safe. I also argue that greater emphasis is placed on 'bringing sex offenders to justice, and on containing them' (Sex Offenders Act, 1997) than on the protection of children. The system places obstacles in the path of those who seek to protect chil-dren, and that is whether or not a criminal prosecution is being pursued, is unsuccessful, or is perceived as not viable (Home Office, 1992). All these issues help to set the parameters of the Child Protection Conference.

That being said, when child sexual assault is identified within fami-lies, the rules that govern the investigative and assessment processes, implicitly and sometimes explicitly, afford greater weight to the voices of abusers than to the voices of survivors. And, wrapped inside the concept of 'parental responsibility' (Children Act, 1989: Section 2, 3) is the civil law's increasing preoccupation with doubt. Herein lies the paradox.

While national government and their related institutions make much of children's rights to be safeguarded, when efforts are made to protect children and to utilize the legal system to strengthen those safeguards, children too often become 'objects of concern' as the legal processes unfold. At the same time, the more serious the 'allegation', the higher the standard of proof will be necessary to convince a court of a child's need for protection. A further contradiction is the major preoccupation with seeking out, punishing and 'containing' the 'sex offender'. The public is being courted to receive the reshaping of the legal framework in this area as progressive. But, lest any of us get too excited, we should remind ourselves that things are often not what they seem. We might consider, for example, that what appears to be a preoccupation with 'bringing to justice' those adults who sexually abuse children, inexorably locates danger outside the family. And, since all available evidence points to 'the family' as being the most dangerous place for women and children to be (Bettison, 1999), we might consider that in taking this route, the needs of children and their protecting parents – usually mothers (Hooper, 1992; Smith, 1994; Nighoskar, and Oko, this volume) – are sidelined.

So, while we know where the most dangerous places for children are, we are simultaneously confronted with a social welfare agenda which is driving forward the notion that child sexual assault is best under- stood and explained by defining sexual abusers as 'mad' or 'bad' (see Hirst, this volume). Such labelling preserves the notion that the heterosexual 'family man' is safe: sexual abusers are 'other'. At the same time, by further labelling those that have been identified as 'mad' or 'bad' as 'paedophiles', we can then completely separate them as a category of men. Paedophiles are therefore 'other' (Kelly, 1996a).

Although it is widely known that men perpetrate the vast majority of all forms of violence (Armstrong, 1996; Hester, Kelly and Radford, 1996), and that this fact raises some very basic questions about male behaviour, men as a class are able to feel comforted that the problem is with 'other' men and can thus rest easy on their laurels. Basic ques- tions about the construction of masculinity are not just left unanswered, but remain unasked (Kelly, 1997/98). The implicit concentration on biological explanations of men's sexuality conve- niently allows for the intellectual separation of sexual behaviour and male violence. Power – how, why, and to whom it is assigned is thus excluded from the analysis (see Feminist Review Collective, 1988). Within this state of affairs women, and often children, become respon- sible for their own safety and are made to feel accountable for male violence as it is played out as sexual assault.

At the same time, while there is a veneer of concern, and sometimes apparent outrage, at the circumstances of some women's and chil- dren's lives, social policy initiatives and priorities do little, if anything, to assist abused women and children to find safe places and to recover from their experiences (Mullender, 1996). The primary agenda still seeks to contain women and children within 'the family' (Faludi, 1992). Within that agenda, marriage is determined as the place where women service men's sexual wants, the two parent heterosexual family is the ideal to be aspired to, and the state of being, or becoming, a lone parent is seen as deviant. Children need two parents: so the two-parent family is either an aspiration, or a state to be maintained. The social welfare agenda is thus developed and delivered as being in children's interests. The idea of patriarchy and how it manifests within a capitalist state is hidden (Oakley, 1972). The politics of personal relationships, the constructions of masculinity and femininity, where and how power is located, and how its unequal distribution is reaffirmed and maintained, are sidelined as merely rhetorical questions (Trotter, in this volume). The places that children, women and men inhabit, or are allowed to inhabit in the public and private domains, continue to be treated as 'the natural order of things'. For example: it is hard to find any mention of power or its distribution in any government guidance or legislation which is concerned with child care, child protection or family life (Radford and Kelly, 1995). Within such an analysis it is not difficult to understand why there is resistance to the messages that feminist theories and critiques have brought to our understanding of women and children's circumstances, to our understanding of power, and how it is distributed and validated in personal relationships (see Cox in this volume). That resistance continues to be maintained.

Judicial inquiries such as those at Cleveland (Butler-Sloss, 1988) and Orkney (Clyde, 1992) successfully challenged and downgraded professional attempts to 'hear' children who were 'telling' that they had been sexually abused (Campbell, 1988; Sorenson and Snow, 1991). The emerging knowledge of the probable scale of incidences of child sexual assault in our society was a message that could not be tolerated if homeostasis was to be maintained – a message that was best kept hidden. Thus the defence and consolidation of 'the family' is a necessary prerequisite for stability. And, consequential to this defence and consolidation, children's testimonies about their circumstances and experiences can be devalued, explained away, and ignored in favour of what is given to us as 'parental responsibilities' (Children Act, 1989, Section 2, 3).

The terrain thus is marked out. Within the last decade those who hold and exercise power have made many consolidations: it has become more difficult for children's accounts of their experiences to be heard and taken seriously. Despite research evidence to the contrary, the rule is that we remain sceptical of the truthfulness of children's testimonies. Abused children continue to be silenced, by their abusers, and by a system that really does not want to hear (National Children's Homes, 1996). Children's 'stories' of their lives can only be given veracity within a forensic framework. Constraints are placed on how and in what circumstance professionals are allowed to listen and intervene (Wattam, 1992). Our professional knowledge base and our professional skills are derided unless they conform to the imperatives of the forensic framework. So that knowledge about children's development, about communicating with children, and about how children communicate with us, has been regularly discredited or devalued. While there remains an acknowledgement that in some form our professional skills and knowledge are necessary in child protection work, we are nevertheless faced with an ongoing offensive to have them repackaged to fit the reality of the rules of both the criminal and civil courts. Deviations from those rules means that good practice is in danger of being labelled as 'contaminated evidence' (Spencer and Flin, 1993).

The information that children may have shared with us will be deemed as unreliable and not capable of withstanding the rigors of the rules of evidence. The notion that the interventions of child protection professionals might be driven by personal or political agendas is flagged up on the basis that some professionals are said to see abuse where abuse does not exist. In other words, the circumstances in which child protection professionals can now legitimately talk with children, or in which they are allowed to 'hear' children, over the last decade have been more and more proscribed. The professional mandate to intervene to safeguard children has been enveloped within a forensic framework.

Ostensibly the Child Protection Conference operates within the civil law. Knowing what we do about how difficult it is for children to speak out (Bass and Davis, 1988), we ought to be able to feel more confident in a framework that treats the child's welfare as the paramount consideration (Children Act, 1989, Section 1). Its standard is the balance of probabilities. Yet the reality is that the needs of the criminal justice process, its attention to 'beyond a reasonable doubt', and therefore its 'need' for uncontaminated evidence, circumscribes child protection work and thus the work of the Child Protection Conference: the 'paramountcy principle' (Children Act, 1989, Section 1) becomes conditional. Although historically the civil court has worked within a framework of whether something is more likely to have happened than not, it now works to a rule that the balance will be set to lie according to the seriousness of the allegation against a parent. Thus the standard of proof is likely to be higher according to the probable consequences for that person should they be found culpable.

The Child Protection Conference ought to be concerned not just with the immediate, but with the long-term safety of the children who become its subjects. It does not operate in a vacuum but within defined legal and procedural parameters (Department of Health *et al.*, 1999) which are explicit. Less explicit are the ideological and political positions that underpin how information is delivered and interpreted, what risks are defined, where risks are seen to be located, and how best to address them. Those of us who work within the child protection system have direct knowledge of these difficulties from our own work with children and from work with adults in emotional and psychological distress. We do well to remember also that the vast majority of children who are being, or have been abused, will not come to the attention of the formal system (Browne and Lynch, 1995). For many different reasons children may choose not to tell, or feel they cannot tell, or they might tell but not be 'heard'. When they do tell and the professionals around them are alert to their telling, it has been shown that the system finds difficulty in responding to their circumstances unless there is a real possibility of a successful prosecution.

These difficulties are not new, neither is the reluctance to locate gender and masculine behaviour in the ongoing discourse about the protection of children. Identification of, and aspirations to achieve, best professional practice, and to work in the interests of children, their safety and their wellbeing, are integral components of these tensions too. Resolving to address them would mean taking forward the lessons learned from survivors and from the feminist critiques of 'mainstream' theory and practice. To do so would be to challenge the reality of patriarchal relations as they are played out, not just within private relationships, but also within the institutions and organizations that support and deliver services within the welfare state.

Moving from the universal to the particular

I have been present at, and also chaired, a great many Child Protection Conferences. It has been clear that on some occasions the Conference's task has threatened to become overwhelmed by the emotional impact of hearing some children's experiences: at these times I have often witnessed a sense of powerlessness surface. Sometimes the need to see 'wrongdoers' punished has been apparent. Often a need to blame the parent who is deemed to have 'failed' to prevent the abuse, or stop it happening, has been palpable. On some occasions it has been noticeable that the Conference is so weighed down by the enormity of its task that it has been in danger of mirroring the very processes that have silenced survivors: processes which have created the conditions for the continued sexual assault of some children. Such Conferences are often characterized by high levels of anxiety, not just from family members who might be present, but also from the professionals who constitute its membership.

But a Child Protection Conference does not and cannot deal with certainty (Department of Health *et al.*, 1999). It is concerned with managing risk. And at some point the meeting will be asked by the Chair to consider what risks there might be to the subject children, and what steps ought to be taken to reduce or remove those risks. At that point there will be some participants who wish to defer that responsibility to those they perceive to be more knowledgeable. The contributions made by some participants will be driven by emotional reactions to the information being shared. In many ways this process, or collection of processes, does seem to mirror in a very real sense the feelings of disempowerment that are felt and experienced by children and their protective carers, both when the abuse had been happening and as they face the consequences of making it public.

What then needs to happen to ensure that a Child Protection Conference utilizes knowledge in the interests of the survivors and their supporters, following disclosure of sexual assault? How can a Conference challenge and refuse to engage in sceptical and mother-blaming analyses? How can a Conference contribute to the effective protection of a child, in the immediate and in the long term? How does a Conference pay attention to the meanings that 'clients' or 'service users' might attach to its professional activity, and attempt to show respect, rather than further oppress? The Chair's role is fundamental in all these respects.

The Child Protection Conference as a site of resistance

It is worth repeating that the overwhelming responsibilities of a Child Protection Conference are: to make decisions about levels of risk presented to the child and therefore whether Child Protection

Registration is necessary, and to construct a Child Protection Plan which is sufficient to address the identified risks (Department of Health *et al.*, 1999). Although Registration serves some important purposes – as an alerting mechanism, or as a signal of the importance of interagency co-operation – there is a strong argument that the construction of a Child Protection Plan carries greatest significance in terms of attending to the child's safety. Without an effective Child Protection Plan, the act of registration becomes empty rhetoric. And, if planning for the child's safety is separated from the reality of the mother's circumstances, protection will be partial. A Conference must address the real possibility that a mother might need protection too (Mullender, 1996; Mullender and Morley, 1994).

How should a Conference work with mothers?

We know from our professional experiences that a child is more likely to begin to recover from their abuse if their mother believes and supports them (Saphira, 1987). And we know that the best place for most children to be is with a protecting family (Smith, 1994). It therefore makes sense that operating child-centred practice is to invest resources in working with mothers. Sometimes a Conference will need to be reminded of these facts.

We have no evidence to support the notion that the vast majority of mothers will have known about the abuse of their child while it was happening. It is almost certain that they will be trying to handle a number of competing emotions when they are confronted with the revelations (Hooper, 1992). They will need assistance to do so. Sometimes a Conference will need to be reminded of these facts.

It is axiomatic that most mothers will wish that the revelations were not true, that people would go away, that they could 'turn the clock back', or that they cannot face the future. Mothers will need assistance to confront what they need to, if they and their children are to begin to recover from the abuse (Smith, 1994). A Conference may need a reminder that this kind of help is crucial.

Given that in some form or other she will have, or have had, an attachment to the abuser, the disclosure will almost certainly generate a multitude of ambivalent feelings. A Conference, while remaining child-focused, can and should validate the presence of such feelings. If the Conference does not do so, given the opportunity, the abuser probably will or almost certainly will, attempt to do so. Having said this, the Conference should not either idealize mothers or the notion of motherhood. Women are people who have learned a collection of different survival strategies according to their experiences. Some of those strategies might be unhelpful to her and her child: some might be destructive. These comments do not invalidate what has already been said: rather they indicate the need to look beyond the appearance of things. In this way a Conference prepares itself to signal in its Plan the need to understand more fully the origins of her behaviour and thus be in a better position to work with her to try to address those issues (see also Oko, this volume).

The child as a person

The 'public' disclosure of sexual assault is by no means the end of the matter for a child. If a decision is made to proceed to prosecute, this will bring to the child the responsibility of being the primary witness in a trial. Prosecution is an adult response to what has happened to a child. Prosecution deals with incidents not relationships.

If she really is to have the best opportunity to survive her experiences, then the impact of the investigation *and* her overall therapeutic needs have to be both acknowledged and addressed. She is not responsible for her own protection. Neither should she be given the primary responsibility for society's need to ensure that her abuser is brought to justice. A Conference might need reminding that its responsibilities, resting within the civil law, are first and foremost to the child whose needs should not be allowed to give way to the perceived needs of the criminal justice system.

She too is likely to be handling a series of mixed emotions, particularly around her decision to tell and its consequences. A Conference may need to be reminded that she is a person and not 'an object of concern' (Butler-Sloss, 1988). Professional workers should treat her accordingly, if her needs are not to be obscured or overshadowed by the needs of the systems she has been caught up in. Child sexual assault is the supreme act of disempowerment. As child protection professionals we should act in ways which do not further disempower either the child or her mother. Rather, empowering strategies ensure we focus totally on the safety and recovery of the child: while immediate protective steps might be necessary a Conference might need to be reminded that longer term safety and recovery are synonymous concepts.

The responsibility always placed with the abuser

In the interests of the mother and the child, the power of the abuser needs to be neutralized. There are, therefore, major reasons why attention should be given to whether an abuser is invited to a Conference. While the Chair will be constrained by the locally agreed exclusion criteria, there is strong argument, even with the existence of legal 'parental responsibility' that adults identified as abusers should only be invited to, at most, part of the Conference. Their presence should be limited to specific purposes. First, they should hear that the disclosures that have been made about their abusive behaviour have been taken seriously: (he) should understand that (he) is perceived as a risk to the child. Second, he should know that the Conference will be formulating a Plan and that all professionals will be working alongside the mother to protect the child. Third, it might be useful if he is allowed to be present to hear formally the final recommendations, specifically as they relate to the parameters of what should and should not happen. He should not be allowed to hear information about the mother or the child, but should be informed what decisions have been taken about contact, and what steps will be taken if breaches are made. He should know that any breaches will be dealt with using the civil and criminal laws as necessary. He should be told that he will receive a copy of the relevant recommendations in writing.

Partial attendance of an abuser should happen in the interests of the child and mother. It should be primarily about giving him information, setting the parameters for the child's safety. It should not be about seeking agreements from him. The Conference Chair ought to set those parameters clearly. In the interests of the child's safety, and in an effort to empower the mother effectively, there should be boldness and clarity to this part of the meeting.

Before any of the above is organized, the Chair should always consult with the mother prior to the meeting, in order to establish with her how she feels about his attendance. Where it is decided that his attendance would be helpful, if necessary the Conference should be divided for her benefit, so that she has no need to face him. If he is to attend in her presence, care should be taken about seating arrangements: for example, she should be seated next to the Chair, or someone she trusts. She should never be asked to sit where the abuser could possibly have eye contact with her. The message for all to observe will be that his attendance has been organized in order to be an empowering, not a silencing process for the mother.

The professional dynamics of the meeting

In any interagency meeting like a Child Protection Conference, the participants will bring with them a number of unspoken agendas.

They might not feel qualified to make decisions about risk to a child because they do not feel they have sufficient child protection knowledge. Conversely, they may feel more qualified than others in the meeting by virtue of their training. There might be tensions between the perceived needs of the criminal and civil processes, that become apparent between those professionals with differing responsibilities. There might be explicit deference shown by some to others, according to status. There will be implicit power imbalances according to gender. And, there is likely to be a high degree of emotion being managed by some according to the information they bring and what they hear at the meeting.

In addition to all these issues, each participant will bring into the meeting their particular ideological and theoretical understanding of child sexual assault. These might be implicit, but their presence will influence both process and outcomes. Participants' views might be tempered or strengthened by many issues: by presence or absence of forensic evidence, by their knowledge of the child, by what they hear at the Conference. They might be influenced by where a mother is perceived to be on the 'belief continuum' (Smith, 1994) – whether she has said she does not believe, has doubts, or believes her child. They might be affected by the presentation of the abuser: whether he appears contrite; whether he asks for help; whether he denies, or blames the child or blames the mother; whether they perceive him to be a 'nice' or 'not very nice' person. And while the Conference has to formulate opinions, make decisions and assign professional responsibilities in planning for the child's safety, it should not get entangled with the agenda of the abuser – or in his seductive grooming process. We need to maintain awareness that the majority of child abusers are neither 'mad' nor suffering from a personality disorder; they are, as stated above, ordinary 'men in the street'.

While the phrase 'the grooming process' is usually used to summarise the methods of entrapment used by an abuser to target the child, set up the conditions for secrecy, and provide for and ensure the child's submission and silencing, the capacity for professionals to be 'groomed' also has resonance. Professionals should be assisted by the Chair to develop resistance to being drawn into an abuser's private logic. His agenda will be one that minimizes, casts doubt, or is characterized by distress at the prospect of: 'being convicted for something [I] did not do'. Anger and threats are also characteristic ploys. Confronted with any or all of such behaviours, the Conference, or individual participants, might need assistance to perceive and understand such reactions for what they are: attempts to discredit and undermine the child's account of abusive experiences and to make the abuser appear 'normal'.

Anti-oppressive language as a prerequisite of child protection responsibilities

In addition to the issues already outlined, the Chair of a Child Protection Conference should assist its membership to resist the use of language which either downgrades a child's experiences of child sexual assault, or distributes responsibility for the assault to anyone but the perpetrator. Language that is used should include, not exclude, the mother (see Nighoskar, this volume). In particular, a Conference should not talk about a mother's 'collusion' or 'failure to protect' (Hooper, 1992). Rather it should be concern itself with seeking ways via its planning to strengthen a mother's ability to protect her child (Smith, 1994).

Finally, feminist analyses and feminist practice in child protection work are about opposition to the status quo; to the 'received wisdom' about child abusers, about mothers, and about child sexual assault. They signal 'zero tolerance' of male violence, and of mother blaming. They are interrogative of the child protection policies and practices that serve as a preservation of a patriarchal 'natural order of things'. We continue to learn from survivors – what they need, what would have made things better, and how we can help to strengthen their capacity to overcome their experiences and to build safe futures (Oko in this volume).

Feminist practice is about siding with the powerless, (Friere, 1972) about placing understandings of power and gender at the centre of our understanding of families and family life. To take a neutral approach in child protection work is not possible. To take a neutral approach in child protection is not an option.

References

Armstrong, L. (1978) *Kiss Daddy Goodnight*, New York, Pocket Books.
Armstrong, L. (1996) *Rocking the Cradle of Sexual Politics: What Happened When Women Said Incest*, London, The Women's Press.
Bass, E. and L. Davis (1988) *The Courage to Heal*, New York, Harper and Row.
Bettison, N. (1999) *Opening Address given at the launch of the Merseyside Zero*

Tolerance Initiative, 9 July 1999, Liverpool.

Browne, K. and M. Lynch (1995) 'Guessing at the extent of child sexual abuse' *Child Abuse Review*, 4(2), pp.79–82.

Butler-Sloss, E. (1988) *Report of the Inquiry into Child Abuse in Cleveland*, London, HMSO.

Campbell, B. (1988) *Unofficial Secrets – Child Sexual Abuse: The Cleveland Case*. London, Virago.

Clyde, Lord (1992) *Report of the Inquiry into the Removal of Children from Orkney*, February 1991, London, HMSO.

Dartington Social Research Unit (1995) *Child Protection: Messages from Research*, London, HMSO.

Department of Health (1989) *An Introduction to the Children Act 1989*, London, HMSO.

Department of Health, Home Office, Department for Education and Employment (1999) *Working Together to Safeguard Children: A Guide to Inter-Agency Working to Safeguard and Promote the Welfare of Children*, London, HMSO.

Department of Health (1994) *The Child, The Court and The Video*, London, HMSO.

Faludi, S. (1992) *Backlash: The Undeclared War Against Women*, London, Chatto and Windus.

Feminist Review Collective (1988), *Feminist Review Special Issue on Child Sexual Abuse*, 28.

Friere, P (1972) *Cultural Action for Freedom*, Harmondsworth, Penguin.

Hester, M., L. Kelly and J. Radford (eds) (1996) *Women, Violence and Male Power*, Buckingham, Open University Press.

Home Office in conjunction with the Department of Health (1992) *Memorandum of Good Practice*, London, HMSO.

Hooper, C. A. (1992) *Mothers Surviving Child Sexual Abuse*, London, Routledge.

Kelly, L. (1996a) 'Weasel words: paedophiles and the cycle of abuse.' *Trouble and Strife*, 33, pp.44–9.

Kelly, L. (1997/8) 'Confronting an atrocity' *Trouble and Strife*, 36, pp.16–22.

Millett, K. (1971) *Sexual Politics*, London, Hart and Davis.

Mullender, A. (1996) *Re-thinking Domestic Violence: The Social Work and Probation Response*, London, Routledge.

Mullender, A. and R. Morley (eds) (1994) *Children Living with Domestic Violence: Putting Men's Abuse of Women on the Child Care Agenda*, London, Whiting and Birch.

National Children's Homes (1996) *Hearing the Truth: the Importance of Listening to Children Who Disclose Sexual Abuse*, London, NCH Action For Children.

Oakley, A. (1972) *Sex, Gender and Society*, London, Temple Smith.

Radford, J. and L. Kelly (1995) 'Self preservation: feminist activism and feminist jurisprudence' in M. Maynard and J. Purvis (eds) *(Hetero)sexual Politics*, London, Taylor and Francis.

Saphira, M. (1987) *For Your Child's Sake*, London, Reed Books.

Smith, G. (1994) 'Parent, partner, protector: conflicting role demands for mothers of sexually abused children' in T. Morrison, M. Erooga and R. Beckett (eds) *Sexual Offending Against Children: Assessment and Treatment of Abusers*. London, Routledge.

Sorenson, T. and B. Snow (1991) 'How children tell: the process of disclosure in child sexual abuse', *Child Welfare League of America*, 70(1) pp.3–15.

Spencer, H. and R. Flin (1993) *The Evidence of Children – The Law and Psychology* (2nd edn) London, Blackstone Press.

Wattam, C. (1992) *Making A Case in Child Protection*, London, Longman/NSPCC.

Wilson, M. (1993) *Crossing the Boundary: Black Women Survive Incest*, London, Virago.

Part III
Into the Future

10
Towards a New Model of Practice

Juliette Oko

The diversification of feminist fields of analyses and resultant theories has resulted in many views and conflicts, to the degree that 'Feminism' may well be better understood now as 'Feminisms' (see Cox, Kershaw and Trotter, Introduction and Conclusion to this volume). Olesen (1994) charts the 'complexities in feminists' research' beginning from the 1970s where feminists fields of analyses centred predominantly on women as 'absent and invisible'. Such fields of analyses were concerned about women's marginal status in society (and claims for greater female equality) as well as exposing the 'invisibility' of women's work and its taken for grantedness as indeed problematic. (Finch and Groves, 1983; Graham 1992; Oakley, 1974) However, it is women as 'absent' that interests me and how this has inadvertently contributed to the demise of feminism as a popular ideology. Popular feminism is often taken as a liberal perspective aimed at ameliorating women's marginal status in society with the promotion of equal opportunities and antidiscriminatory legislation. Within British social work praxis, also, the liberal feminist perspective has been subsumed under the generic banner of antidiscriminatory practice, with its emphasis on promoting non-discriminatory services to all minority oppressed groups, including women.

In this chapter, my concern is whether feminist inspired practice can reassert itself within social work which moves beyond some of the limitations of a generic attempt at non-discriminatory practice which is typified by antidiscriminatory practice. First, however, I want to put forward a critique of anti-discriminatory practice as practised within the U.K.

This chapter questions whether feminist inspired practice can reassert itself within social work, moving beyond some of the limitations of non-discriminatory practice, as typified by anti-discriminatory practice as it is practised within the U.K. A popular author in this field is Thompson (1993) who attempts to contribute a theoretical basis for social work practice in addressing a number of discriminatory behaviours. Other writers (Braye and Preston-Shoot, 1995) have developed this theme by emphasizing an empowering relationship between the worker and service user.

Thompson (1993) defines discrimination as:

> Unfair or unequal treatment of individuals or groups, prejudicial behaviour acting against the interest of those people who characteristically tend to belong to relatively powerless groups within the social structure.... Discrimination is therefore a matter of social formation as well as individual/group behaviour or praxis. (p.31).

Antidiscriminatory practice is therefore:

> ... an approach to social work practice which seeks to reduce, undermine or eliminate discrimination and oppression, specifically in terms of challenging sexism, racism, ageism and disablism ... and other forms of discrimination encountered in social work. (Thompson, 1993, p.32)

A central theme of Thompson's work is, therefore, an analysis of the origins of discrimination which is based predominantly on a structural analysis of inequality. However, I believe this is problematic, and I intend to explore some of the areas of concern before moving on to a New Model of Practice.

Limitations of a generic structural approach

Thompson's analysis can be seen in the light of the requirement for British social workers to develop an awareness of structural inequality and oppression as well as developing strategies to promote antidiscriminatory services and practice. This requirement was initially laid out in 'Paper 30' by the Central Council for Education and Training in Social Work (CCETSW, 1989) as part of the education and practice necessary for the Diploma in Social Work. While CCETSW's requirements were aimed at social work education and practice, the emphasis on antidiscriminatory practice also permeated wider into the social and political field and resulted in widespread criticism. In particular, criticism from the Right centred around the hackneyed use of the term 'political correctness', (Hopton, 1997) but also criticism from those who were sympathetic to the principles of antidiscriminatory practice. Here I am not concerned to illustrate the criticisms of the Right, or those overtly unsympathetic to antidiscriminatory practice. What is more important is the concerns of those who do support the principle of greater equality but are still concerned with the limitations of a generic approach.

One of the major difficulties with a generic structuralist approach has been the over-reliance on 'grand theory' to explain the nature of society and an analysis of the social world through oppositional categories, such as woman/man, black/white, dis-abled/able-bodied, homosexual/heterosexual, rather than an acknowledgement and emphasis on the multi-complexity of identities. Concerns therefore have been around the use of these categories as representing fixed universal explanations of reality. It has also been suggested that there is a danger that the influence of feminist thinking and its richness and diversity: '... could be reduced ... to dogma and orthodoxy' (Graham, 1992, quoted in Featherstone and Lancaster, 1997).

An over-reliance on structural analysis is, I believe, potentially de-humanising. While I acknowledge the 'reality' of social structures as a way of conceptualising the social forces that shape our lives politically, individual accounts within antidiscriminatory practice tend to be neglected. So, for example, as a black woman (if I take my skin colour and gender as representing social divisions), I might recognize and share similar experiences of racism and sexism with other black women, however, we have no understanding of individual experiences. Moreover, traditional approaches to antidiscriminatory practice tend to discount individual accounts unless they detail our inequality. There is almost an inherent tendency in antidiscriminatory practice to present individuals as 'victims of their social difference' rather than celebrating stories of every day lives as well as survival. Gilroy (1992), makes a similar point of concern when he points out that orthodox anti-racism has '... trivialised the rich complexity of black life by reducing it to nothing more than a response to racism.' (quoted in Featherstone and Lancaster 1997, p.57)

Such criticisms can be seen to represent a theoretical shift towards a post-modernist paradigm and from a post-modernist feminist perspective, this: '... challenges the validity of categories and promotes the recognition of differences' (Sands and Nuccio, 1992, p.490). A post-modernist perspective, therefore, provides an alternative analysis of women's experiences which has 'her story' central to any kind of understanding. It moves away from universal and objective criteria of understanding and analysis to a subjective understanding. It incorporates questions of 'difference' (between women themselves and women and men), explorations of subjectivity, deconstruction and multiple discourses (Sands and Nuccio, 1992; Williams, 1996). As Williams (1996) argues, these 'conceptual markers of post-modernist thinking' can be used and seen in relation to '... their modernist precursors – universalism, commonality, truth, pattern, structure, essentialism, determinism – [and become a basis] to understand the spaces for movement in between.' (p.69)

A post modernist feminist perspective does therefore offer a valid critique of the generalist antidiscriminatory practice approach which typifies social work practice. Since this perspective has echoes of early feminist work which concentrated on the 'personal' as the 'political', it provides a basis for reasserting some key feminist ethics in social work practice. It is to the area of social work practice and child sexual assault that I now turn, and consider how feminist analyses have been instrumental in exploding the myths of child sexual assault in four key areas.

Feminist contributions to understanding child sexual assault

First, feminism provided a structural analysis of the phenomenon of child sexual assault by revealing it as 'patriarchy's shameful secret'. (Dominelli, 1986). Second, it sought to expose the myth of child sexual assault as an example of a 'dysfunctional family' or an example of excessive rampant male sexual behaviour. Indeed, child sexual assault is a product of patriarchal culture which '... lies in normal family values, not deviant ones' (Nelson, 1982, p.79, quoted in MacLeod and Saraga, 1988). Thus feminist analyses revealed the dynamics of heterosexuality, gender and power, and insisted that any attempt at understanding child sexual assault had to take into account an analysis of men's sexual violence that went beyond individual psychological explanations (see Kelly and also Potter, this volume). An understanding of child sexual assault must also therefore: '... be viewed within the context of men's sexual violence and the subordination of women and children' (Parton, 1990, p.51).

Third, feminists have deconstructed the term 'motherhood' to reveal it as more than just the personal relationship between women as mothers and their children: it is also revealed as the social institution of motherhood (Rich, 1977): '... the particular child-rearing pattern in a society or social groups' (Parton, 1990, p.45). Thus women are assumed to be the guardians of their children's health (emotional, physical and sexual) and that of their male partners. This analysis takes into account the economic and ideological influences on women's lives that impinge on the personal relationships between women and their children. Finally, following on from the above point, feminists have demonstrated that the prevailing literature in this field is: '... preoccupied with the mother's direct or indirect responsibility for child abuse ...' (Parton 1990, p.43) and that: 'mother blame is a consistent feature of all the non-feminist literature on incest ...' (Waldby *et al.*, 1989, p.90).

This results in the assumption of women's culpability. Feminist analyses of child sexual assault have therefore drawn attention to the androcentrism of orthodox theories of child sexual assault and revealed their male bias and resultant policies of intervention. However, despite the significant contribution of feminist analyses to child sexual assault, the last ten years have seen an exponential growth in publications in the field of Child Protection Studies, with child sexual assault increasingly seen as a professional specialization, being colonized by so-called 'experts' (including social workers). Correspondingly, child sexual assault has become de-politicized (that is, feminist analyses have been marginalized), in favour of 'expert' views and opinions. If children's and women's experiences are included, the primary aim is to provide credence for the 'expert's' theory of the nature of child sexual assault. It is thus within the field of statutory social work in child protection on which I wish to focus, in order to argue for a reassertion of feminist based practice.

Within the field of social work and child sexual assault, issues of protection are dealt with primarily through the process of formal assessment. Here the social worker is concerned to gather data on the nature and extent of the abuse in order to categorize/subcategorize different forms of sexual assault. Regretfully, this marks a shift away from feminist analyses which are less concerned about 'types' of sexual assault, seeing them instead more as expressions of male sexuality and masculinity. The emphasis on types of assault which is characteristic of the assessment process, therefore, perpetuates an individualistic perspective on the assault and reinforces orthodox theories of 'the dysfunctional family', 'the culpable female', 'the deviant male' or even where '... a normal father/daughter relationship slides into a sexual relationship' (Secretary of State for Social Services, 1988, quoted in

Parton, 1990, p.54). Such views explicitly encourage a hierarchy of seriousness of assault, concentrating less on the feelings of betrayal of trust, confusion and guilt which follow from child sexual assault (which feminists have always emphasized). Assessment focused approaches reinforce the tendency to pathologisze and distance the problem of child sexual assault as at worst an evil act, or at least, as an aberration. As Browne (1995) suggests, statutory social work in this field will always be: '... piecemeal and inadequate, since the assessment process lacks a sufficient (feminist?) consideration of the social context' (p.161).

Another cornerstone of the assessment process is 'assessment of risk'. While abusers are often removed from the location of the abuse and dealt with by probation or specialist sex abuse units, the focus of social work attention is on the woman. While the bias within statutory child protection is heavily weighted towards criminal investigation and prosecution, it remains a reality that successful conviction of the abuser is hard to obtain (Browne, 1995). In the majority of known cases therefore, it is probable that the perpetrator will remain in the home or have contact with the child, and as many child witness accounts state, the abuse continues (Driver and Droisen, 1989). Thus the assessment process is heavily biased towards maternal responsibility (Milner, 1994; Trotter, 1997). As Parton (1990) suggests, the restructuring of the welfare state and the emphasis on familial responsibility inevitably entails a focus on women's roles and responsibilities within the home, which has consistently emphasized her nurturing and maternal role. The impact on the assessment process is therefore an emphasis on the woman's ability to protect and support the child (Hooper, 1992).

Parton, Thorpe and Wattam (1997) point out the importance of 'maternal response' as a variable in outcomes in child sexual assault cases; namely whether an incident will result in further action or no further action by social workers. Cases with a positive and acceptable maternal response were more likely to be filtered out, whereas: 'cases where the response was negative or unsatisfactory were much more likely to warrant further actions' (p.204). Thus 'maternal response' (as classified by social workers) was the most influential single factor in determining whether children came into care, rather than the nature of the assault or the existence of corroborative evidence. Where the assessment of the mother was as 'unsupportive', the child was removed from home. What is significant here is the assumption of women's culpability for failing to protect their children, and also that such assumptions are based on moral judgements of women which are made by the social worker and go unquestioned (see also Nighoskar, this volume):

> Concerns about a mother's ability to 'cope' are expressed as justifications in and of themselves, without the need for the behaviour or circumstances by which this judgment is reached to be described (Parton *et al.*, 1997, p.207).

This is a fairly damning indictment of social work practice as structurally biased against women if they do not conform to the social idealization of motherhood and, as a form of woman-blaming, is clearly contrary to feminist principles. I am not saying that judgements should not be made about a woman; clearly, statutory social work is concerned with protecting vulnerable people (including children) and therefore making judgements about degrees of vulnerability or risk. Since women continue to take primary responsibility for childcare, judgements will inevitably be made of their capacity to do so. However, the points I wish to emphasize are first, where a woman's behaviour is judged almost exclusively on the social worker's observations alone and second, where the categorization of her behaviour by the social worker is not substantiated by further information. As Parton and colleagues explain:

> Mothers, unlike alleged perpetrators are assessed and judged outside any legal process with very little recourse for revoking the judgment once made. Their previous behaviour and response to the current allegation act as evidence of their ability to protect (p.209).

Such a position clearly undermines feminist principles (London Rape Crisis Centre, 1984; Morgan, 1978; Roberts, 1981) and from a post modern feminist perspective it ignores subjectivity, that is '... the conscious and unconscious thoughts and emotions of the individual, her sense of herself and her ways of understanding her relation to the world ... (Sands and Nuccio, 1992, p.491). Further, the perspective or discourse of the mother is seldom found in agency records; it is the social worker's view of the mother that is usually relied on (Parton *et al.*, 1997).

Discourse theories offer helpful insights into the maintenance of certain perspectives over others and demonstrate how such discourses are enmeshed in social power relations. In this context, what is not part of the discourse also carries meaning (Sands and Nuccio, 1992). Thus the silencing of children who have been abused will be as signif- icant as the writings of the male 'experts' in this field. Any analysis of social work action must, therefore, involve an awareness of how one subsumes and dominates the discourse of others – in this case, women who care for children and the assessment of risk.

My argument suggests therefore that social work practice in the field of child sexual assault and protection of children, remains structurally biased against women. It rests between an uneasy tension of two opposing realities. On the one hand, in our society it is women who have primary responsibility for child care, and therefore have a respon- sibility to protect their children. However, at the same time, it is overwhelmingly men who sexually assault children. Thus social workers make assessments of individual mothers and judge their ability to protect, ignoring feminist analyses of child sexual assault and their contribution to understanding the complexity of emotions experienced by mothers who learn of their child's assault (Hooper, 1992; Potter, in this volume); while the analyses of men who sexually assault children still remains largely located in individual explanations of deviancy and orthodox theories about male sexuality (Kelly, 1996). The tension therefore results in the assumption of female culpability. It has largely been feminist analyses of male sexuality which have drawn out the relationship between men's violence and sexuality which is rooted in the unequal power relationships between men and women and men and children. The belief that antidiscriminatory prac- tice can somehow counteract this tension through such concepts as 'working in partnership' and 'client empowerment' is misplaced, since social work practice is founded on the assumption of maternal respon- sibility and played out in a discourse which favours the social worker's account and orthodox views of male sexuality. The practice of social work in this field is inherently discriminatory.

At the beginning of the chapter, I posed the question as to whether feminist inspired principles could inform social work practice that went beyond the limitations of a generic approach to antidiscrimin- atory practice. By drawing on some of the key terms in post-modern feminism and adopting a strengths perspective, I believe there is the possibility of practice which can rightly claim to be feminist inspired. Although formal social work assessments often carry a dictum to review clients' strengths, this rarely forms the basis of assessment and is often overshadowed by a focus on the concerns which have warranted intervention. This is despite the fact that guidance stipulates that social workers should: 'respect and value uniqueness and diversity and recognize and build strengths ...' (CCETSW, 1995, p.18).

Social work practitioners should therefore develop skills that encourage and facilitate clients' strengths even though an emphasis on the problem focus runs deep in British social work. This can be traced back to the moralistic overtones of its philanthropic origins, which emphasized human failings ('moral deficiencies') as the source of difficulties and social problems, not wider economic or political strategies (Younghusband, 1981). As social work moved from its original charitable status to a more professional basis, approaches emerged which were influenced by the natural sciences, moving social work to a more disciplined practice based on rational assessment. Although the moralistic overtones lost their place centre stage to more rational explanations for personal difficulties, these approaches still retained the belief that human weakness was: 'the critical variable in understanding human problems' (Weick *et al.*, 1989, p.350).

The focus on individual pathology therefore runs deep in social work education and practice. Such an approach does not favour the client: '... the problem invariably is seen as a lack or inability in the person affected' (Weick *et al.*, 1989, p.352) and the nature of the problem is defined by the professional.

The strengths perspective therefore seeks a paradigm shift away from pathological assumptions in favour of reintegrating practice with social work's core values. This is an important process – a powerful counterforce to the preoccupation with people's deficits and liabilities: as Weick and colleagues state '... the effect of a problem focus is to weaken people's confidence in their ability to develop in self-reflecting ways' (Weick *et al.*, 1989, p.353). Despite this however, the strengths perspective as a practice skill is not well developed within British statutory social work, although within American practice, the strengths perspective dates back over four decades (De Jong and Miller, 1995; Saleebey, 1996; Weick *et al.*, 1989).

The strengths perspective is therefore an ideology based on the belief of the potential of people to develop by drawing on their '... talents, abilities, capacities, skills, resources and aspirations' (Weick *et al.*, 1989, p.352). The development of reflective skills is therefore an important aspect of the strengths perspective which parallels feminist analyses, adopting 'progressive' approaches to social work alongside 'radical' and 'socialist' feminist perspectives (Rojek *et al.*, 1989). So for instance, Survivors' Groups were initiated by feminists during the 1970s and 1980s (see also Kelly, in this volume) to negate the personal feelings of self-blame and shame associated with sexual assault, and which used consciousness-raising techniques to emphasize the social and political nature of men's sexual violence as more than personal assaults (Spender, 1982). As Payne (1997) states, consciousness-raising involves:

> ... the process of reflecting on oppressive social structures to try to understand them and then exploring ways of acting on the understanding. Normalisation is another radical technique which is concerned with helping clients to understand that their situation is not unique but is shared with many others (pp.224–5).

Despite similarities between the strengths based perspective and the work of Survivors' Groups, they do not share the same philosophical underpinning and therefore are different. Radical feminizing, by politicising the experience of child sexual assault and focusing on gender differences and commonality of women's experience, is part of the modernist tradition which undermines diversity of interest and experience. The strengths perspective is humanist and more orientated towards reflexive therapeutic views on the nature of social work, and is therefore less concerned with social objectives.

A post-modernist feminist perspective however could be said to bridge the gap between reflexive–therapeutic views and socialist–collectivist positions on the nature of social work, feminism and child sexual assault. It further counters the concern expressed by Graham (1992) earlier about the richness and diversity of feminist thinking being 'reduced to dogma and orthodoxy' (Graham, 1992, quoted in Featherstone and Lancaster, 1997). By adopting a post-modern feminist position in the process of assessment, social workers can facilitate such diversities in order to encourage subjectivity and give 'voice' to the woman's individual experiences and perceptions. By including an analysis of the 'personal and the political' (that is, the experience of child sexual assault), social workers can achieve two things. First, they can draw out: '... the concurrent discourses that are silenced ... [but] also meaningful ...' (Sands and Nuccio, 1992, p.491). Second, they remove the assumption of maternal culpability from the individual woman and instead highlight a feminist analysis of child sexual assault that reveals male sexual behaviour as rooted in unequal power relationships between men, women and children.

Hearing those discourses that are silenced is part of the tradition of feminist thought as well as part of the strengths perspective. As Saleebey suggests, those who experience discrimination and disadvantage do not have their stories told, much less heard '... one of the characteristics of being oppressed is having one's stories buried under the forces of ignorance and stereotype ...' (Saleebey, 1996, p.301).

The strengths perspective therefore stresses the importance of personal accounts in order for the worker to know and appreciate the person. Such an approach to practice can improve the assessment process significantly for women, since there is an attempt to understand and make sense of the woman's behaviour which is grounded in her perspective rather than the social worker's observation. Thus the woman's perspective '... may be entirely different to that of a social worker used to dealing with such cases on a regular basis, and it can change over time' (Cleaver and Freeman, 1995, quoted in Parton *et al.*, 1997, p.209).

The strengths perspective therefore shares many parallels with feminist inspired practice, particularly the emphasis on subjectivity or personal accounts which give women the opportunity to have their story heard, rather than subsumed within the discourse of the social worker. However, there is a challenge in this proposal for uniting a strengths perspective and feminist inspired statutory social work 'Pursuing a practice based on ideas of resilience, rebound, possibility and transformation is difficult because, oddly enough, it is not natural to the world of helping and service' (Saleebey, 1996, p.297).

This challenge is most acute in statutory social work and child protection, since feminist inspired practice typically takes place in non-statutory settings. However, there is no reason why feminist good practice cannot be reintegrated. As Browne (1995) argues, concerns about workers' lack of time and under-resourced agencies rest uneasily with the work of survivors' organizations and allied groups, who typically: 'have no resources and frequently operate from home and with volunteer help ...' (p.168). Yet testimonies of the support and usefulness of these groups abound as they help to '... both validate[s] the sexually abusive experiences and at the same time release the victim from the burden of keeping the guilty secret forever' (p.169).

However, there is another reason why feminist practice seems to rest uneasily within statutory child protection: the question of power, or 'non-consensual statutory social work' (Wise, 1995). As I stated earlier, child protection assessments are founded on two opposing dichotomies (maternal responsibility and male sexuality) which results in the assumption of maternal culpability, despite the fact that it is men who are overwhelmingly the perpetrators of child sexual assault.

Social workers must acknowledge that if women are the primary carers of children, then they also have a responsibility to protect their children (although conflicts of needs between women and their children are not uncommon), but this acknowledgement is not the same as the assumption of culpability. Knowledge about sex offenders reveals their power to dominate and keep their abuse secret through threats and coercion (Hirst and Cox, 1996). Responsibility for child sexual assault is firmly located with the perpetrator and the social structures which perpetuate male violence. Utilising the strengths perspective and post-modern feminism shows that feminist inspired practice is possible as part of the assessment process within statutory child protection social work. Social work action requires an awareness of how one subsumes and dominates the discourse of others – this provides a framework to begin an analysis of the social work relationship between workers and women clients and ways in which the power imbalance is less favourable towards women clients. To assume that this is only possible within non-statutory agencies is based on a particular view of social workers as simply agents of state control, enhancing oppression. Similarly, feminism is presented simply as the pursuit of political goals and implies unity and commonality of experience.

Conclusion

The discourse of child protection is not particularly concerned with the conditions or experiences of children. Instead the focus of intervention is on parental responsibility, more specifically, maternal responsibility. The result of such a focus is that women's identities are only validated by their maternal role. Such an essentialist position results in a very narrow focus of assessment where social workers judge women as either 'good mothers' or 'bad mothers'. The latter judgement is much more likely to result in further surveillance by social workers, with the ultimate likelihood of the child's removal. Underlying the assessment process of child protection, therefore, is an implicit assumption of maternal culpability.

However, the strengths perspective aligns itself well with postmodern feminist inspired practice. It allows women to define their identity, including that of 'mother' and also considers the 'politics of motherhood'. By focusing on a woman's strengths, the social worker can hear 'her story' and support her primarily in respect of her decisions about her maternal role, as defined by the woman. The outcome of the assessment therefore is less likely to be based on the social worker's moral judgements of the woman as a mother and her 'ability to protect': it is instead an assessment based on the woman's definition of her maternal role. Such an approach does not negate conflict, nor does it mean that there will be no consequences for the mother. To imply that feminist practice cannot exist within statutory social work is to suggest that only non-statutory feminist agencies engage in consensual work with women and that there are no subsequent consequences for the actions which women take. All social life is rooted in conflictual needs, rights and responsibilities. Statutory social work and child protection is simply a contentious example of such conflicts. For many women and their children the consequences of this have been deeply damaging, with the woman being blamed for not being a 'good mother' and 'failing to protect' her children. Feminist analyses of social life reveal some of the dynamics of these conflicts and suggest alternative explanations for theory and practice which are women centred. My proposal for a New Model of Practice is one which I believe can claim to be feminist inspired, which attempts to redress the bias in child protection assessments which favour the social worker's moral judgements of the women as 'mother'.

References

Braye, S. and M. Preston-Shoot (!995) *Empowering Practice in Social Care*, Oxford, Oxford University Press.

Browne, J. (1995) 'Can social work empower? in R. Hugman and D. Smith (eds) *Ethical Issues in Social Work* , London, Routledge.

CCETSW (1989) *Rules and Regulations for the Diploma in Social Work*, CCETSW Paper 30, London, Central Council for Education and Training in Social Work.

CCETSW (1995) *Assuring Quality in the Diploma in Social Work – 1: Rules and Requirements for the Dip.SW.* (revised) London, Central Council for Training and Education in Social Work.

De Jong, P. and S. Miller (1995) 'How to interview for clients' strengths', *Journal of National Association of Social Workers*, 40(6), pp.721–864.

Dominelli, L. (1986) 'Father–daughter incest: patriarchy's painful secret', *Critical Social Policy*, 16(6), pp.8–22.

Driver, A. and E. Droisen (eds) (1989) *Child Sexual Abuse: Feminist Perspectives*, London, Macmillan.

Featherstone, B. and E. Lancaster (1997) 'Contemplating the unthinkable: men who sexually abuse children', *Critical Social Policy*, 17(4), pp.51–71.

Finch, J. and D. Groves (1983) *A Labour of Love: Women, Work and Caring*, London, Routledge and Kegan Paul.

Gilroy, P. (1992) 'The end of anti-racism', in J. Donald and A. Rattansi (eds) *'Race', Culture and Difference*, London, Sage.

Graham, H. (1992) *Women, Health and the Family*, Hemel Hempstead, Harvester Wheatsheaf.

Hirst, G. and P. Cox (1996) 'Hearing all sides of the story: integrating teaching on sexual aggression into social work qualifying training', *Journal of Sexual Aggression*, 2(1), pp.33–48.

Hooper, C.-A. (1992) *Mothers Surviving Child Sexual Abuse*, London, Routledge.

Hopton, J. (1997) 'Anti-discriminatory practice and anti-oppressive practice' *Critical Social Policy*, 17(3) pp.47–61.

Kelly, L. (1996) 'Weasel words: paedophiles and the cycle of abuse', *Trouble and Strife*, 33 pp.44–9.

London Rape Crisis Centre (1984) *Sexual Violence: The Reality for Women*, London, The Women's Press.

MacLeod, M. and E. Saraga (1988) 'Challenging the orthodoxy: towards a feminist professional practice' *Feminist Review Special Issue on Child Sexual Abuse*, 28, pp.16–55.

Milner, J. (1994) 'Men's resistance to social workers' in B. Fawcett, B. Featherstone, J. Hearn and C. Toft (eds) *Violence and Gender Relations*, London, Sage.

Morgan, R. (1978) *Going Too Far: The Personal Chronicle of a Feminist*, New York, Vintage Books.

Nelson, S. (1982) *Incest: Fact and Myth*, Edinburgh, Stramullion Press.

Oakley, A. (1974) *The Sociology of Housework*, Oxford, Martin Robertson.

Olesen, V. (1994) 'Feminisms and models of qualitative research' in N. K. Denzin and Y. S. Lincoln (eds) *Handbook of Qualitative Research*, London, Sage.

Parton, C. (1990) 'Women, gender oppression and child abuse' in The Violence Against Children Study Group (eds) *Taking Child Abuse Seriously*, London, Unwin Hyman.

Parton N., D. Thorpe and C. Wattam (1997) *Child Protection, Risk and the Moral Order*, London, Macmillan.

Payne, M. (1997) *Modern Social Work Theory*, London, Macmillan.

Rich, A. (1977) *Of Woman Born: Motherhood as experience and institution*, London, Virago.

Roberts, H. (1981) *Doing Feminist Research*, London, Routledge and Kegan Paul.

Rojek, C., G. Peacock and S. Collins (1989) *Social Work and Received Ideas*, London, Routledge.

Saleebey, D. (1996) 'The strengths perspective in social work practice: extensions and cautions', *Journal of National Association of Social Workers*, 41(3), pp.241–336.

Sands, R. and K. Nuccio (1992) 'Postmodern feminist theory and social work', *Journal of National Association of Social Workers*, 37 (6), pp.481–576.

Spender, D. (1982) *Man Made Language*, London, Routledge.

Thompson, N. (1993) *Anti-Discriminatory Practice* London, Macmillan.

Trotter, J. (1997) 'The failure of social work researchers, teachers and practitioners to acknowledge or engage non-abusing fathers: a preliminary discussion', *Social Work Education Special Issue on Child Protection*, 16 (2), pp.63–76.

Waldby, C., A. Clancy, J. Emetchi and C. Summerfield (1989) 'Theoretical perspectives on father-daughter incest' in A. Driver and E. Droisen (eds) *Child Sexual Abuse: Feminist Perspectives*, London, Macmillan.

Weick, A., A. Rapp, P. Sullivan and W. Kisthardt (1989) 'A strengths perspective for social work practice', *Journal of National Association of Social Workers*,

34(4), pp.289–384.

Williams, F. (1996) 'Postmodernism, feminism and the question of difference' in N. Parton (ed.) *Social Theory, Social Change and Social Work*, London, Routledge.

Wise, S. (1995) 'Feminist ethics in practice' in R. Hugman and D. Smith (eds) *Ethical Issues in Social Work*, London, Routledge.

Younghusband, E. (1981) *The Newest Profession: A Short History of Social Work*, London, Community Care/IPC Business Press.

Conclusion

Pat Cox, Sheila Kershaw and Joy Trotter

As three older women, editors of this book, who began our working careers in the 1970s, we have spent a great deal of time discussing age, the ageing process and how all this impacts on our experiences of feminisms, feminist activism and writing. In the three years it has taken us to get to this stage, we have had many discussions and debates, which mirror those which have occurred during the last 30 years of feminisms. Reflecting on our individual and collective histories, we realize that our credibility with younger readers may not be strong, as their experiences do not always resonate with our own. Despite training and working in different parts of the country, we share a great deal of common history around the developments of specific social work understandings of, and responses to, child sexual assault. These will not be shared by all workers, particularly those who have trained on Diploma in Social Work courses where feminist theoretical perspectives have not formed a major part of the child protection teaching. Those who have entered statutory child protection social work within the last decade have more experience with risk assessment, quality assurance, and legislative and procedural documentation than with innovative therapies or inspirational individuals.

It is our contention that feminists of our generation find it increasingly difficult to be listened to, and to have our political views taken seriously. Other writers (Hughes and Mtezuka, 1992) have shown that women in their middle and older years are two of the most invisible groups in white, western society. Not only are older women silenced, women's issues and feminist thinking are also negated. For example, in the proposal stages of this book, we found that a number of publishers were nervous about our suggested title and also about the subject matter. On one occasion it was suggested to us that if we dropped 'feminisms' from the (original) title, the book would be more likely to be accepted. In her preface, Liz Kelly talks about 'noticing'. We have noticed how difficult it has become to talk about feminisms and to identify publicly as feminists: we do not believe we are alone in this. All three of us have experienced similar responses of ridicule, insults and even anger in certain situations. As we have pointed out in our Introduction and throughout this book, silencing occurs in all sorts of settings and in all sorts of ways.

Over two decades have passed since feminists first became aware of 'incest in families', the first form of sexual assault to be identified (Armstrong, 1978; Fraser, 1987). We wonder exactly what has been the outcome of all the efforts to raise awareness and prevent further abuse; what is now different? Why, on the one hand, is child sexual assault and its associated activities (pornography, sex tourism and the trafficking of children) still attracting media attention; yet on the other hand, many accounts of sexual assault (which we believe should be front page and headline news also) have been relegated to inside pages, or else receive no coverage at all. (Kitzinger, 1996). Unable to find current books about child sexual assault that included both practice and theoretical feminist dimensions as well as survivor accounts, we decided to do something ourselves. As we identified in the Introduction, this book does not contain explicit survivor accounts. We believe that the climate for survivors to give accounts, and have them accepted, is very different in the late 1990s. It seems to us that unless their important accounts are remembered and reproduced, there will be nothing recorded or published for coming generations of survivors and practitioners to learn from. For example, survivors have much to teach about both the uniqueness and the universality of abusive and surviving experiences: and this should not be either minimised or dismissed. Such rich accounts, when taken together with feminist theories, not only inform practice, but help to fill the theoretical vacuums found so often on social care courses.

In the early days, when a lot of the thinking and analysis took place in women-only spaces, it was possible with support to stay with the pain and hear and value the suffering of survivors and witnesses. This 'bottom up' approach to theory and practice was seen and accepted as the way to develop protective strategies. These emotional and moving experiences provided a lasting and invaluable base for our lives as women, and our practice as social workers and academics. However, as time has moved on, we have relied on our memories to inspire our practice and writing.

The climate has now changed to a 'top down' approach. The influences that younger and newer workers will be aware of have come predominantly from central government via managers and management. The culture and language of management have permeated child protection at all levels, from economic accountability strategies to electronic communication systems. Shifting political policies and local government reorganisations have caused tensions allied to regrouping and 'downsizing' (Craig and Manthorpe, 1998). Despite much of the rhetoric of these reformed organisations about being 'user-friendly' and 'needs-led', most of the efforts and energies of the workers seem to have gone into ever more complex bureaucracies (Miller-Pietroni, 1998). In this climate, professional knowledge and practitioner experiences account for little: the knowledge and experience of clients or service-users – particularly if they are children, young women or young men – account for nothing.

This overlooking or disregarding of workers and clients by most of higher management is clearly gendered. The majority of the 'front-line' workers in child care and child protection are women, most of the managers (particularly at policymaking levels) are men (Lupton, 1992). As child protection policies have become more nationally homogenised and procedure led, the policymakers, and designers of software systems and documents, have come to be regarded as the 'experts'.

We have concluded that there are no general experts and no new truths, but that feminist analyses are the only ones which make sense of the causes, prevalence of and resistances to, child sexual assault. Just because these truths have not been universally accepted and acted upon, does not diminish their importance. They need to be stated, if necessary, over and over again.

We want readers to understand the significance of feminist theories to underpin their work and to expand feminists' power/influence base, in order that their analyses remain crucial and central to the debates. One of the most important elements to maintaining power and influence in this context is what we would describe as 'collective diversity'. The history of feminisms bears witness to separations and splits; social history in Britain has seen the emergence of the individual (particularly in relation to citizenship and responsibility). Women and feminists need to connect and assemble again, to hear, collect and value their own and each others' stories.

Some of the contributors to this book are of our age, have similar experiences, and are re-visiting the ideas and feminist analyses that inspired and still inspire them. Some are women for whom these ideas have been learned from feminist writings, from women-centred practice and discussions with women: women for whom the ideas have not been a major part of their lived experience, but to whom the ideas have immediacy and relevance. In effect, we have begun to create such a 'collective diversity'. We hope that our example will inspire you to do as we have done, and connect or re-connect with feminist analyses of child sexual assault.

We are completing this book as part of a one-sided conversation with readers, in the hope that maybe one – or one million – of you will accept and understand, and will translate these analyses into your thinking and practice.

References

Armstrong, L. (1978) *Kiss Daddy Goodnight*, New York, Pocket Books.

Craig, G. and J. Manthorpe (1998) 'Small is beautiful? Local government reorganisation and the work of social services departments', *Policy and Politics*, 26(2), pp. 189–207.

Fraser, S. (1987) *My Father's House*, London, Virago.

Hudson, A. (1992) 'The child sexual abuse "industry" and gender relations in social work' in M. Langan and L. Day (eds) *Women, Oppression and Social Work: Issues in Anti-Discriminatory Practice*, London, Routledge.

Hughes, B. and M. Mtezuka (1992) 'Social work and older women: where have older women gone?' in M. Langan and L. Day (eds) *Women, Oppression and Social Work: Issues in Anti-discriminatory Practice*, London, Routledge.

Kitzinger, J. (1996) 'Media representations of sexual abuse risks', *Child Abuse Review*, 5(5), pp. 319–33.

Lupton, C. (1992) 'Feminism, managerialism and performance management' in M. Langan and L. Day (eds) *Women, Oppression and Social Work: Issues in Anti-Discriminatory Practice*, London, Routledge.

Miller-Pietroni, M. (1998) 'Beyond the bureauprofessional: observational study as a vehicle for interprofessional learning and user-centred practice in community care' in P. Le Riche and K. Tanner (eds) *Observation and its Application to Social Work*, London, Jessica Kingsley.

Bibliography

Action Against Abuse Newsletters (Orr, M. ed.) are available on subscription from AAA, P.O. Box 3125, London NW3 5QB.

Agana, P. (1990) 'Training for life' in M. Sulter (ed.) *Passion: Discourses on Black Women's Creativity*, Hebden Bridge, West Yorkshire, Urban Fox Press.

Agger, I. (1994) *The Blue Room: Trauma and Testimony Among Refugee Women*, London, Zed Press.

Ahluwalia, K. and R. Gupta (1997) *Circle of Light: The Autobiography of Kiranjit Ahluwalia*, London, Harper Collins.

Ahmed, S. (1986) 'Cultural racism in work with Asian women and girls' in S. Ahmed, J. Cheetham and J. Small (eds), *Social Work with Black Children and their Families*, London, Batsford.

Alanen, L. (1994) 'Gender and generation: feminism and the "child question"' in J. Qvortrup, M. Bardy, G. Sgritta and H. Wintersburger (eds) *Childhood Matters: Social Theory, Practice and Politics*, European Centre, Aldershot, Avebury.

Allen, D. M. (1980) 'Young male prostitutes: a psychosocial study', *Archives of Sexual Behaviour*, 9 (5), pp.399–426.

AMOC (1997) *European Network Male Prostitution First Interim Report*, Amsterdam AMOC.

Angelou, M. (1984) *I Know Why the Caged Bird Sings*, London, Virago.

Archer, J. (ed.) (1994) *Male Violence*, London, Routledge.

Armstrong, L. (1978) *Kiss Daddy Goodnight*, New York, Pocket Books.

Armstrong, L. (1994) *Rocking the Cradle of Sexual Politics: What Happened When Women Said Incest*, New York, Addison Wesley.

Armstrong, L. (1996) *Rocking the Cradle of Sexual Politics: What Happened When Women Said Incest* London, The Women's Press.

Atmore, C. (1996) 'Cross-cultural mediations: media coverage of two child sexual abuse controversies in New Zealand/Aotearoa' *Child Abuse Review*, 5(5), pp.334–45.

Aymer, C. (1992) 'Woman in residential work: dilemmas and ambiguities' in M. Langan and L. Day (eds) *Women Oppression* and *Social Work: Issues in Anti-Discriminatory Practice*, London, Routledge.

Bagley, C. and L. Young (1987) 'Juvenile Prostitution and Child Sexual Abuse – A Controlled Study', *Canadian Journal of Community Mental Health*, 6, pp. 5–25.

Balen, R., P. Cox and M. Preston-Shoot (eds) (1997) 'Editorial comment', *Social Work Education: Special Issue on Child Protection*, 16(2), pp.3–5.

Baker, A. and S. Duncan (1985) 'Child sexual abuse: a study of prevalence in Great Britain', *Child Abuse and Neglect*, 9, pp.457–67.

Bannister, A. (ed.) (1992) *From Hearing to Healing*, London, Longman/NSPCC.

Bannister, A., K. Barret and E. Shearer (eds) (1990) *Listening to Children*, London, Longman.

Banyard, V. L. and L. M. Williams (1999) 'Memories for child sexual abuse and mental health functioning: findings on a sample of women and implications for future research' in L. M. Williams and V. L. Banyard (eds) (1999) *Trauma and Memory*, California, Sage.

Barker, M and R. Morgan (1991) 'Probation practice with sex offenders surveyed' *Probation Journal*, 38(4), pp.171–7.

Barnard, M. and N. McKegany (1990) 'Adolescent sex and injecting drug use: risks for HIV infection' *AIDS Care*, 2(2), pp.103–16.

Barrett, D. (1997) 'Child prostitution' *Highlight: National Children's Bureau*, p.135.

Barringer, C. E. (1992) 'Speaking of incest: it's not enough to say the word', *Feminism and Psychology*, 2(2), pp.183–8.

Barry, K. (1979) *Female Sexual Slavery*, New York, Prentice Hall.

Bass, E. and L. Davis (1988) *The Courage to Heal*, New York, Harper and Row.

Beavet, T. and J. Thompson (1996) 'Parents talking: sex education in secondary schools', *Pastoral Care*, December, pp.11–18.

Bebbington, A. and J. Miles (1989) 'The background of children who enter Local Authority Care' *British Journal of Social Work*, 19(5), pp.349–68.

Begum, N. (1991) 'Setting the context: disability and the Children Act 1989' in S. Macdonald (ed.) *All Equal Under the Act? A Practical Guide to the Children Act 1989 for Social Workers*, London, Race Equality Unit.

Bennello, J. (1994) 'One in three rent boys has HIV', *The Independent on Sunday*, 23 January 1994, 8.

Berg, I. and J. Nursten (eds) (1996) *Unwillingly to School* (4th edn), London, Gaskell.

Berridge, D. and I. Brodie (1996) 'Residential child care in England and Wales: the inquiries and after', in M. Hill and J. Aldgate (eds) *Child Welfare Services: Developments in Law, Policy, Practice and Research*, London, Jessica Kingsley.

Bertoia, C. E. and J. Drakich (1995) 'The fathers' rights movement' in W. Marsiglio (ed.) *Fatherhood: Contemporary Theory, Research, and Social Policy*, London, Sage.

Bettison, N. (1999) *Opening Address given at the launch of the Merseyside Zero Tolerance Initiative*, 9 July 1999, Liverpool.

Biehal, N., J. Clayden, M. Stein and J. Wade (1995) *Moving On. Young People and Leaving Care Schemes*, London, HMSO.

Bigner, J. J. and R. B. Jacobsen (1992) 'Adult responses to child behavior and attitudes towards fathering: gay and nongay fathers' *Journal of Homosexuality*, 23, pp.99–112.

Billington, R., J. Hockey and S. Strawbridge (1998) *Exploring Self and Society*, London, Macmillan.

Binney, V., G. Harkell and J. Nixon (1988) *Leaving Violent Men: A Study of Refuges and Housing for Abused Women*, Bristol, Women's Aid Federation.

Birchall, E. (1989) 'The frequency of child abuse: what do we really know?' in O. Stevenson (ed.) *Child Abuse: Public Policy and Professional Practice*, Hemel Hempstead, HarvesterWheatsheaf.

Blagg, H., J. A. Hughes and C. Wattam (eds) (1989) *Child Sexual Abuse: Listening, Hearing and Validating the Experiences of Children*, Harlow, Longman.

Bloom, R. (1992) 'When staff members sexually abuse children in their care', *Child Welfare*, 71 (2), pp.131–45.

Bloor, M., N. McKegany and M. Barnard (1990) 'An ethnographic study of HIV related risk practices among Glasgow rent boys and their clients: report of a pilot study', *AIDS Care*, 2(1), pp.131–7.

Bogle, M. (1988) 'Brixton black womens' centre: organising on child sexual abuse', *Feminist Review Special Issue on Child Sexual Abuse*, 28, pp.132–5.

Booth, T. and W. Booth (1997) *Exceptional Childhoods, Unexceptional Children: Growing Up with Parents who have Learning Difficulties*, London, Family Policies Study Centre.

Boseley, S. (1996) Scandal of abuse 'cover up', *The Guardian*, 5 September 1996.

Boushel, M. and S. Noakes (1988) 'Islington Social Services: developing a policy on child sexual abuse', *Feminist Review Special Issue on Child Sexual Abuse*, 28, pp.150–7.

Braye, S. and M. Preston-Shoot (1995) *Empowering Practice in Social Care*, Buckingham, Open University Press.

Bremner, J. and A. Hillin (1993) *Sexuality, Young People and Care*, Lyme Regis, Russell House Publishing.

Briere, J. and J. Conte (1993) 'Self-reported amnesia for abuse in adults molested as children', *Journal of Traumatic Stress*, 6(1), pp.21–31.

Browne, J. (1995) 'Can social work empower?' in R. Hugman and D. Smith (eds) *Ethical Issues in Social Work*, London, Routledge.

Browne, K. (1994) 'Child sexual abuse' in J. Archer (ed.) *Male Violence*, London, Routledge.

Browne, K. and M. Lynch (1995) 'Guessing at the extent of child sexual abuse' *Child Abuse Review*, 4(2), pp.79–82.

Buchanan, A. and J. Ten Brinke (1998) *What Happened When they Were Grown Up?* York, York Publishing Service.

Bullock, R., M. Little, and S. Milham (1993) *Residential Care for Children: A Review of the Literature*, HMSO, London.

Bunting, M. (1997) 'Abuse claims shake church'. *The Guardian*, 8 November 1997.

Burke, T. (1991) 'Streetwise on street life', *Journal of Young People Now*, November, pp.23–5.

Burman, E., P. Aldred, K. Bewley, B. Goldberg, C. Heenan, D. Marks, J. Marshall, K. Taylor, R. Ullah and S. Warner (1996) *Challenging Women: Psychology's Exclusions, Feminist Possibilities*, Buckingham, Open University Press.

Burrell, G. (1984) 'Sex and organizational analysis', *Organizational Studies*, 5 (2), pp.97–118.

Butler, I. and H. Williamson (1994) *Children Speak – Children, Trauma and Social Work*, Brighton, Pennant Professional Books.

Butler, I. with H. Williamson (1996) '"Safe?" Involving children in child protection' in I. Butler and I. Shaw (eds) *A Case of Neglect, Children's Experiences and the Sociology of Childhood*, Aldershot, Avebury.

Butler-Sloss, E. (1988) *Report of the Inquiry into Child Abuse in Cleveland*, London, HMSO.

Byerly, C. B. (1985) *The Mother's Book. How to Survive the Incest of Your Child*, London, Kendall/Hunt.

Byrne, S. (1997) 'Single-person adoption', *Adoption and Fostering*, 21(1), p.50.

Cameron, D. (1993) 'Telling it like it wasn't: how radical feminism became history' *Trouble and Strife*, 27, pp.11–15.

Campbell, B. (1988) *Unofficial Secrets – Child Sexual Abuse: The Cleveland Case* London, Virago.

Campbell, B. (1997) *Unofficial Secrets – Child Sexual Abuse: The Cleveland Case.* London, Virago.

Campion, M. J. (1995) *Who's Fit to be a Parent,* London, Routledge.

Canadian Panel on Violence Against Women (1993) *Changing the Landscape: Ending Violence – Achieving Equality,* Canadian Ministry of Supply and Services, Ottowa, Canada.

Carlen, P. (1989) 'Feminist jurisprudence or women-wise penology?' *Probation Journal,* 36(3), pp.110–14.

Carter, K. (1997) *Mascu(iso)lation, Power and Control inside a Local Prison,* paper presented to British Sociological Association Annual Conference, 'Power and Resistance', University of York, 1997.

Carter, P., A. Everitt and A. Hudson (1992) '"Malestream" training? Women, feminism and social work education', in M. Langan and L. Day (eds) *Women, Oppression and Social Work: Issues in Anti-Discriminatory Practice,* London, Routledge.

Cashman, H. (1993) *Christianity and Child Sexual Abuse,* London, SPCK.

Cavanagh, K. and V. E. Cree (1996) *Working with Men: Feminism and Social Work,* London, Routledge.

CCETSW (1989) *Rules and Regulations for the Diploma in Social Work,* CCETSW Paper 30, London, Central Council for Education and Training in Social Work.

CCETSW (1995) *Assuring Quality in the Diploma in Social Work -1: Rules and Requirements for Dip.SW,* London, Central Council for Education and Training in Social Work.

Chaffer, A. and D. Garratt (1997) 'A friend in need' in D. Garratt, J. Roche and S. Tucker (eds) *Changing Experiences of Youth,* Buckingham, Open University Press.

Chandy, J. M. (1998) *Victims of Sexual Abuse: Outcomes and Resilience* paper given at the second 'International Conference on Social Work in Health and Mental Health', Melbourne, Australia.

Chaudhary, V. (1998) *Bullying of gays 'rife in schools' The Guardian,* 13 March 1998, 8.

Chesler, P. (1972) *Women and Madness,* New York, Doubleday.

The Children's Society (1989) *Working With Sexually Abused Children: a Resource Pack for Professionals,* London, The Children's Society.

The Children's Society (1997) *Child Prostitution in Britain: Dilemmas and Practical Responses,* London, The Children's Society.

Choi, P. and P. Nicholson (1994) *Female Sexuality: Psychology, Biology and Social Context,* Hemel Hempstead, HarvesterWheatsheaf.

Clyde, Lord (1992) *Report of the Inquiry into the Removal of Children from Orkney,* February 1991, London, HMSO.

Coleman, J. (1994) 'Satanic cult practices', in V. Sinason (ed.) *Treating Survivors of Satanist Abuse,* London, Routledge.

Collier, R. (1995) *Masculinity, Law and the Family,* London, Routledge.

Committee on Sexual Offences Against Children and Youths (1984) *Sexual Offences Against Children,* Ottowa, Canadian Government Publishing Service.

Cook, K. with 'The A Team' (1995–96) 'Survivors and supporters: working on ritual abuse', *Trouble and Strife,* 32, pp.46–52.

Cook, R. (1998) 'The net closes', *The Guardian,* 1 April 1998.

Coombs, N. R. (1974) 'Male prostitution: a psychosocial view of behaviour', *American Journal of Orthopsychiatry*, 44(5), pp.782–9

Corby, B., A. Doig and V. Roberts (1998) 'Inquiries into child abuse', *Journal of Social Welfare and Family Law*, 20(4) pp.377–96.

Cosis Brown, H. (1991) 'Competent child-focused practice: working with lesbian and gay carers' *Adoption and Fostering*, 15(2), pp.11–17

Cosis Brown, H. (1992) 'Lesbians, the state and social work practice' in M. Langan and L. Day (eds) *Women, Oppression and Social Work: Issues in Anti-Discriminatory Practice*, London, Routledge.

Cosis Brown, H. (1998) *Social Work and Sexuality: Working with Lesbians and Gay Men*, London, Macmillan.

Council of Europe (1993) *Sex, Exploitation, Pornography and Prostitution of and Trafficking of Children and Young Adults*, Strasbourg, Council of Europe.

Council of Europe (1994) *Street Children*, Strasbourg, Council of Europe.

Coward, R. (1983) *Patriarchal Precedents: Sexuality and Social Relations*, London, Routledge and Kegan Paul.

Cox, P. (1993) '"Professional survival": a double jeopardy. Some implications for training, education and practice', in H. Ferguson, R. Gilligan and R. Torode (eds) *Surviving Childhood Adversity: Issues for Policy and Practice*, Dublin, Social Studies Press.

Cox, P. (1997) *Challenges and Opportunities: Protecting Children, Young Women and Young Men in a Changing Europe*, paper presented to conference 'Culture and Identity: Social Work in a Changing Europe', Dublin, August 1997.

Cox, P. and G. Hirst (1996) 'Putting young heads onto older shoulders: social work education for work with children, young women and young men' in S. Jackson and M. Preston-Shoot (eds) *Educating Social Workers in a Changing Policy Context*, London, Whiting and Birch.

Craft, M. (1966) 'Boy prostitutes and their fate'. *British Journal of Psychiatry*, 112, pp.1111–14.

Craig, G. and J. Manthorpe (1998) 'Small is beautiful? Local government reorganisation and the work of social services departments', *Policy & Politics*, 26(2), pp.189–207.

Crolley, T. and J. Paley (1982) 'Sexual problems and the probation service' *Probation Journal*, 29(4), pp.133–7.

Crompton, I. (1992) *Child Sexual Abuse; Politics, Ideology and Social Work Practice*, Warwick, University of Warwick and S.C.A.

Cullen, D. (1997/98) 'Adoption: prospective adopter living in lesbian relationship; whether contrary to public policy', *Adoption and Fostering*, 21(4), p.62.

Darlington, Y. (1996) *Moving On: Women's Experiences of Childhood Sexual Abuse and Beyond*, Sydney, The Federation Press Pty Ltd.

Dartington Social Research Unit (1995) *Child Protection: Messages from Research*, London, HMSO.

Davies, B. and R. Harre (1990) 'Positioning: the discursive production of selves', *Journal for the Theory of Social Behaviour*, 20(1), pp.43–63.

Davies, D. (1996) 'Working with young people', in D. Davies and C. Neal *Pink Therapy: A Guide for Counsellors and Therapists Working with Lesbian, Gay and Bisexual Clients*, Buckingham, Open University Press.

Davies, N. (1994) 'Children of the night', *The Guardian*, 15 March 1994, 6.

Davies, N. (1998) 'The most secret crime', *The Guardian*, 2–5 June 1998.

Davies, N. (1998) 'Is the Church forgiving sin or just turning a blind eye?' *The Guardian*, 4 June 1998, 6–7.

Davies, N. and E. O'Connor (1997) 'Special Investigation' *The Guardian*, 5 April 1997.

Davis, N.J. (1971) 'The prostitute: developing a deviant identity', in J. M. Henslin (ed.) *Studies in the Sociology of Sex*, New York, Appleton-Century-Crofts.

Department of Health (1989) *An Introduction to the Children Act*, London, HMSO.

Department of Health (1990) *Consultation Paper No 16: Foster Placement (Guidance and Regulations)*, London, HMSO.

Department of Health (1991) *The Children Act 1989: Guidance and Regulations Volume 4: Residential Care*, London, HMSO.

Department of Health, Home Office, Department for Education and Employment (1999) *Working Together to Safeguard Children: A Guide to Inter-Agency Working to Safeguard and Promote the Welfare of Children*, London, HMSO.

Department of Health (1993) *Adoption: The Future*, London, HMSO.

Department of Health (1994) *The Child, The Court and The Video*, London, HMSO.

Department of Health, Social Services Inspectorate (1995) *The Challenge of Partnership in Child Protection: Practice* Guide, London, HMSO.

Dews, V. and J. Watt (1995) *Review of Probation Officer Recruitment and Qualifying Training*, London, HMSO.

DeJong, P. and S. Miller (1995) 'How to interview for clients' strengths' *Journal of National Association of Social Workers*, 40(6), pp.721–864.

Dominelli, L. (1986) 'Father–daughter incest: patriarchy's painful secret', *Critical Social Policy*, 16(6), pp.8–22.

Donovan, K. (1991) *Hidden From View: An Exploration of the Little Known World of Young Male Prostitutes in Great Britain and Europe*, London, Home Office and West Midlands Police Publication.

Driver, E. and A. Droisen (eds) (1989) *Child Sexual Abuse: Feminist Perspectives*, London, Macmillan.

Dunkerley, A., F. Graham, P. Doyle, T. Gooch and R. Kennington (1994) 'Learning from perpetrators of child sexual abuse' *Probation Journal*, 41(3), pp.147–51.

Dunne, G. A. (1997) *Lesbian Lifestyles: Women's Work and the Politics of Sexuality*, London, Macmillan.

Dworkin, A. (1981) *Pornography: Men Possessing Women*, London, The Women's Press.

Dyer, R. (1985) 'Male sexuality in the media' in A. Metcalf and M. Humphries (eds) *The Sexuality of Men*, London, Pluto Press.

Elliott, M. (ed.) (1993) *Female Sexual Abuse of Children: The Ultimate Taboo*, London, Longman.

English Collective of Prostitutes (1992) *Prostitute Women and Aids: Resisting the Virus of Repression*, London, Crossroads Books.

Epstein, D. (ed.) (1994) *Challenging Lesbian and Gay Inequalities in Education*, Buckingham, Open University Press.

EUROPAP (1997) *Hustling For Health: Health and Social Services for Sex Workers*,

Draft Report, Ghent, Belgium, Department of Public Health, University of Ghent.

Evans, D. (1993) *Sexual Citizenship: The Material Construction of Sexualities*, London, Routledge.

Fairclough, N. (1989) *Language and Power*, London, Longman.

Faludi, S. (1992) *Backlash: The Undeclared War Against Women*, London, Chatto and Windus.

Featherstone, B. and E. Lancaster (1997) 'Contemplating the unthinkable: men who sexually abuse children' *Critical Social Policy*, 17(4), pp.51–71.

Feminist Review Collective (1988) *Feminist Review Special Issue on Child Sexual Abuse*, 28.

Field, N. (1995) *Over the Rainbow: Money Class and Homophobia*, London, Pluto Press.

Finch, J. and D. Groves (1983) *A Labour of Love: Women, Work and Caring*, London, Routledge and Kegan Paul.

Finkelhor, D. (ed.) (1983) *The Dark Side of Families*, London, Sage.

Finkelhor, D. (1984) *Child Sexual Abuse: New Theory and Research*, New York, Free Press.

Finkelhor, D. (1986) *A Sourcebook on Child Sexual Abuse*, London, Sage.

Finkelhor, D. (1994) 'The "backlash" and the future of child protection advocacy – insights from the study of social issues' in J. Myers (ed.) *The Backlash: Child Protection Under Fire*, California, Sage.

Finkelhor, D., L. Meyer Williams and N. Burns (1988) *Nursery Crimes: Sexual Abuse in Day Care*, California, Sage.

Finkelhor, D., G. Hotaling, I. Lewis and C. Smith (1990) 'Sexual abuse in a national survey of adult men and women: prevalence characteristics and risk factors', *Child Abuse and Neglect*, 14, pp.19–28.

Firestone, S. (1971) *The Dialectic of Sex: A Case for Feminist Revolution*, London, Jonathan Cape.

Firestone, S. (1979) *The Dialectic of Sex: A Case for Feminist Revolution* (2nd edn*)*, London, The Women's Press.

Fisher, D. (1995) 'The Therapeutic Impact of Sex Offender Treatment', *Probation Journal*, 42(1), pp.2–6.

Foster, C. (1993) *Male Prostitution: Perspectives, Policy and Practice*, Norwich, University of East Anglia.

Foucault, M. (1977) *Discipline and Punish: The Birth of the Prison*, Harmondsworth, Penguin.

Foucault, M. (1981) *The History of Sexuality*, Harmondsworth, Penguin.

Fox Harding, L. (1991) *Perspectives in Child Care Policy London*, Longman.

Fraser, S. (1987) *My Father's House*, London, Virago.

Friere, P. (1972) *Cultural Action for Freedom*, Harmondsworth, Penguin.

Fromuth, M. and B. Burkhart (1987) 'Childhood sexual victimisation among college men: definitional and methodological issues' *Violence* and *Victims*, 2(4), pp.241–53.

Frost, N. (1990) 'Official intervention and child protection: the relationship between state and family in contemporary Britain' in Violence Against Children Study Group (eds) *Taking Child Abuse Seriously*, London, Unwin Hyman.

Gagnon, J. H. and R. G. Parker (1995) *Conceiving Sexuality*, London, Routledge.

Galford, E. (1994) 'Out and proud in the Athens of the North' in E. Healey and

A. Mason (eds) *Stonewall 25: The Making of the Lesbian and Gay Community in Britain*, London, Virago.

Gallagher, B. (1998) 'Paedophiles: what's the problem?' *NOTANEWS*, 28, pp.3–7.

Gath, A. (1988) 'Mentally handicapped people as parents: is mental retardation a bar to adequate parenting?' *Journal of Child Psychology and Psychiatry*, 29, pp.739–44.

Gerrard, N. (1996) 'Prostitution isn't just another job', *The Observer*, 4 August 1996, 26.

Ghate, D. and L. Spencer (1995) *The Prevalence of Child Sexual Abuse in Britain*. London, HMSO.

Gibbons, J., S. Conroy and C. Bell (1995) *Operating the Child Protection System, a Study of Child Protection Practice in English Local Authorities*, London, HMSO.

Gibson, B. (1995) *Male Order: Life Stories from Boys Who Sell Sex*, London, Cassell.

Gillespie, T. (1996) 'Rape crisis centres and "male rape": a face of the backlash' in M. Hester, L. Kelly and J. Radford (eds) *Women, Violence and Male Power*, Buckingham, Open University Press.

Gilroy, P. (1992) 'The end of anti-racism' in J. Donald and A. Raffansi (eds) *'Race', Culture and Difference*, London, Sage.

Goffman, E. (1961) *Asylums*, Harmondsworth, Penguin.

Goffman, E. (1969) 'The characteristics of total institutions' in A. Etzioni (ed.) *A Sociological Reader on Complex Organisations* (2nd edn), New York, Holt, Rhinehart and Winston.

Goldstein, P. J., L. J. Ouellet and M. Fendrick (1992) 'From bag brides to skeezers: a historical perspective on sex for drugs behaviour' *Journal of Psychoactive Drugs*, 24(4), pp.349–61.

Golston, J. C. (1992) 'Comparative abuse: shedding light on ritual abuse through the study of torture methods in political repression, sexual sadism and genocide', *Treating Abuse Today*, 2 (6).

Goodwin, J. (1994) 'Sadistic abuse: definition, recognition and treatment', in V. Sinason (ed.) *Treating Survivors of Satanist Abuse*, London, Routledge.

Gordon, L. (1989) *Heroes of their Own Lives: The Politics and History of Family Violence*, London, Virago.

Gould, M. (1998) 'Order apologises for school abuse', *The Observer*, 29 March 1998.

Graham, H. (1992) *Women, Health and the Family*, Hemel Hempstead, HarvesterWheatsheaf.

Green, L. (1995) *Sexuality and Residential Childcare – Oppression Through Repression or Protection?* Paper presented at 'Youth 2000' Conference, University of Teesside, July 1995.

Green, L. and W. Parkin (1997) 'Cultures of abuse within residential child care', *Early Child Development and Care*, July 1997, pp.73–86.

Griffin, G. (1993) 'History with a difference: telling lesbian herstories' in G. Griffin (ed.) *Outwrite: Lesbianism and Popular Culture*, London, Pluto Press.

Griffin, C. and M. Zukas (eds) (1993) 'Coming out in psychology: lesbian psychologists talk', *Feminism and Psychology*, 3(1), pp.111–33.

Hall, S. (1994) 'Prostitution', *The Independent*, 24 May 1994, 16.

Hallett, C. (1995) *Interagency Co-ordination and Child Protection*, London, HMSO.

Halson, A. (1991) 'Young women, sexual harassment and heterosexuality:

violence, power relations and mixed sex schooling' in P. Abbott and C. Wallace (eds) *Gender, Power and Sexuality*, London, Macmillan.

Hanmer, J., J. Radford and E. A. Stanko (eds) (1989) *Women, Policing and Male Violence: International Perspectives*, London, Routledge.

Hanscombe, G. E. and J. Forster (1982) *Rocking the Cradle: Lesbian Mothers: A Challenge in Family Living*, London, Sheba.

Harding, S. (ed.) (1987) *Feminism and Methodology: Social Science Issues*, Milton Keynes, Open University Press.

Harris, M. (1973) *The DillyBoys: male prostitution in Piccadilly*, London, Croom Helm.

Haruhi, T., T. Ymi and L. Naoko (1987) 'For a song: female sexual slavery in Asia' *Trouble and Strife*, 12, pp.10–15.

Haugaard, J. and R. Emery (1989) 'Methodological issues in child sexual abuse research', *Child Abuse and Neglect*, 13, pp.89–100.

Health Education Authority (1997) *Life on the Scene*, London, Health Education Authority.

Hearn, J. (1990) '"Child abuse" and men's violence' in Violence Against Children Study Group (eds) *Taking Child Abuse Seriously*, London, Unwin Hyman.

Hearn, J., D. Sheppard, P. Tancred-Sheriff and G. Burrell (eds) (1989) *The Sexuality of Organization*, London, Sage.

Hearn, J. and W. Parkin. (1995) *Sex at Work: The Power and Paradox of Organisation Sexuality*, New York, St Martin's Press.

Hedley, R. and E. Dorkenoo (1992) *Child Protection and Female Genital Mutilation*, London, Forward Press.

Herman, J. L. (1981) *Father–Daughter Incest*, Cambridge MA, Harvard University Press.

Herman, J. and E. Schatzow (1984) 'Time limited group therapy for women with a history of incest', *International Journal of Group Psychotherapy*, 34, pp.605–16.

Hester, M., L. Kelly and J. Radford (1996) *Women, Violence and Male Power*, Buckingham, Open University Press.

Hester, M. and L. Radford (1996) 'Contradictions and compromises: the impact of the Children Act on women and children's safety' in M. Hester, L. Kelly and J. Radford (eds) *Women, Violence and Male Power*, Buckingham, Open University Press.

Hirst, G. (1996) 'Moving forward: how did we do that?' *Probation Journal*, 43(2), pp.58–63.

Hirst, G. and P. Cox (1996) 'Hearing all sides of the story: the challenge of integrating teaching on sexual aggression into social work qualifying training' *Journal of Sexual Aggression*, 2(1), pp.33–48.

Holmes, P. and V. King (1998/9) 'Giving a damn', Trouble and Strife, 38, pp.28–31.

Home Office in Conjunction with the Department of Health (1992) *Memorandum of Good Practice*, London, HMSO.

Home Office (1995) *Looking After Children: Good Parenting, Good Outcomes*, London, HMSO.

Home Office (1995) *National Standards for the Supervision of Offenders in the Community*, London, HMSO.

Home Office (1996) *Sentencing and Supervision of Sex Offenders: a Consultation Document, CM 3304*, London, HMSO.

Home Office (1997) *The Three Year Plan for the Probation Service 1997–2000*, London, Home Office.

hooks, b. (1982) *Ain't I a Woman? Black Women and Feminism*, London, Pluto Press.

Hooper, C.-A. (1992) *Mothers Surviving Child Sexual Abuse*, London, Routledge.

Hopkins, N. (1996) 'In six months this bright middle class girl sank into the seedy twilight world of teenage prostitution. So where did it all go wrong?' *Daily Mail*, 29 August 1996, 18.

Hopton, J. (1997) 'Anti-discriminatory practice and anti-oppressive practice', *Critical Social Policy*, 17(3) pp.47–61.

Hudson, A. (1989) *Changing Perspectives: Feminism, Gender and Social Work*, London, Unwin Hyman.

Hudson, A. (1992) 'The child sexual abuse "industry" and gender relations in social work', in M. Langan and L. Day (eds) *Women, Oppression and Social Work: Issues in Anti-Discriminatory Practice*, London, Routledge.

Hudson, P. (1991) *Ritual Child Abuse: Discovery Diagnosis and Treatment*, California, R.&E Publishers.

Hughes, B. and M. Mtezuka (1992) 'Social work and older women: where have older women gone?' in M. Langan and L. Day (eds) *Women, Oppression and Social Work: Issues in Anti-discriminatory Practice*, London, Routledge.

Hughes, W. (1986) *Report of the Committee of Inquiry into Children's Homes and Hostels*, Belfast, HMSO.

Humphreys, C. (1997) *Case Planning Issues where Domestic Violence Occurs in the Context of Child Protection. Report to Coventry Social Services Child Protection Unit*, Coventry, Coventry City Council Social Services Department.

Hutchinson, S. (1996) Personal communication.

Jackson, S. (1982) *Childhood and Sexuality*, London, Basil Blackwell.

Jackson, S. (1987) *The Education of Children In Care*, Bristol, School of Applied Social Studies, University of Bristol.

Jackson, S. (1994) 'Educating children in residential and foster care', *Oxford Review of Education*, 20(3), pp.267–9.

Jeffreys, S. (1998) *The Idea of Prostitution*, Melbourne, Spinifex Press.

Jehu, D. (1994) *Patients as Victims: Sexual Abuse in Psychotherapy and Counselling*, West Sussex, Wiley.

Jenkins, P. and D. Maier-Katkin (1991) '"Occult survivors" the making of a myth', in J. T. Richardson, J. Best and D. G. Brarnley (eds) *The Satanism Scare*, New York, Aldine de Gruyter.

Jesson, J. (1993) 'Understanding adolescent female prostitution: a literature review', *British Journal Of Social Work*, 23(4), pp.517–30.

John, M. (ed.) (1997) *A Charge Against Society: The Child's Right to Protection*, London, Jessica Kingsley.

Jones, J. (1993) 'Child abuse: developing a framework for understanding power relationships in practice' in H. Ferguson, R. Gilligan and T. Torode (eds) *Surviving Childhood Adversity: Issues for Policy and Practice*, Dublin, Social Studies Press.

Katchen, M. and D. Sakheim (1992) 'Satanic beliefs and practices' in D. Sakheim and S. Devine (eds) *Out of Darkness*, Concord, Lexington Books.

Kelly, L. (1988) *Surviving Sexual Violence*, Cambridge, Polity Press.

Kelly, L. (1989) 'Bitter ironies' *Trouble and Strife*, 16, pp.14–21.

Kelly, L. (1991) 'Unspeakable acts: abuse by women', *Trouble and Strife*, 21, pp.13–20.

Kelly, L. (1994) 'The interconnectedness of domestic violence and child abuse: challenges for research, policy and practice', in A. Mullender and R. Morley (eds) *Children Living with Domestic Violence: Putting Men's Abuse of Women on the Child Care Agenda*, London, Whiting and Birch.

Kelly, L. (1996a) 'Weasel words: paedophiles and the cycle of abuse' *Trouble and Strife*, 33, pp.44–9.

Kelly, L. (1996b) 'When does the speaking profit us?: reflections on the challenges of developing feminist perspectives on abuse and violence by women', in M. Hester, L. Kelly and J. Radford (eds) *Women, Violence and Male Power*, Buckingham, Open University Press.

Kelly, L. (1997/98) 'Confronting an atrocity' *Trouble and Strife*, 36, pp.16–22.

Kelly, L. (1999) Personal communication.

Kelly, L., L. Regan and S. Burton (1991) *An Exploratory Study of the Prevalence of Sexual Abuse in a Sample of 16–21 Year Olds*, London, Child and Woman Abuse Studies Unit, University of North London.

Kelly, L., R. Wingfield, S. Burton and L. Regan (1995) *Splintered Lives: Sexual Exploitation of Children in the Context of Children's Rights and Child Protection*, England, Barnardos.

Kelly, L., S. Burton and L. Regan (1996) 'Beyond victim or survivor: sexual violence, identity and feminist theory and practice' in L. Adkins and V. Merchant (eds) *Sexualizing the Social: Power and the Organization of Sexuality*, London, Macmillan.

Kelly, R. and M. Scott (1986) in M. Wilson, (1993) *Crossing The Boundary: Black Women Survive Incest*, London, Virago.

Kennedy, M. and L. Kelly (eds) (1992) 'Special issue on abuse and children with disabilities', *Child Abuse Review*, 1(3).

Kennington, R. (1994) 'Northumbria sex offender team' *Probation Journal*, 41(2), pp.81–5.

Kershaw, S. (1999) 'Sex for sale', *Youth and Policy*, 63, pp.27–37.

Kilgallon, W. (1995) *Report of the Independent Review into Allegations of Abuse at Meadowdale Children's Home*, Northumberland, Northumberland Council.

King, M. B. (1995) 'Parents who are gay or lesbian' in P. Reder and C. Lucey (eds) *Assessment of parenting*, London, Routledge.

Kirkwood, A. (1992) *The Leicestershire Inquiry: the report of an inquiry into aspects of the management of children's homes in Leicestershire between 1973 and 1986*, Leicester, Leicestershire County Council.

Kitzinger, J. (1991) 'Child sexual abuse and the trials of motherhood' in S. Wyke and J. Hewison (eds) *Child Health Matters*, Buckingham, Open University Press.

Kitzinger, J. (1996) 'Media representations of sexual abuse risks' *Child Abuse Review*, 5(5), pp.319–33.

Kitzinger, J. (1997) 'Who are you kidding? Children, power and the struggle against sexual abuse', in A. James and A. Prout (eds) *Constructing and Reconstructing Childhood: Contemporary Issues in the Sociological Study of Childhood*, London, Falmer Press.

Knutson, J. F. and P. M. Sullivan (1993) 'Communicative disorders as a risk factor in abuse', *Topics in Language Disorders*, 13(4), pp.1–14.

La Fontaine, J. (1990) *Child Sexual Abuse*, Cambridge, Polity Press.

La Fontaine, J. (1998) *Speak of the Devil: Tales of Satanic Abuse in Contemporary England*, Cambridge, Cambridge University Press.

Laing, L. (1999) 'A different balance altogether? Incest offenders in treatment', in J. Breckenridge and L. Laing (eds) *Challenging Silence: Innovative Responses to Sexual and Domestic Violence*, London, Allen and Unwin.

Lancaster, E. (1995) 'Working with sex offenders: where do we go from here', *Probation Journal* 42(2), pp.79–82.

Langan, M. and L. Day (eds) (1992) *Women, Oppression and Social Work: Issues in Anti-Discriminatory Practice*, London, Routledge.

Lees, S. (1986) *Losing Out*, London, Hutchinson.

Lees, S. (1993) *Sugar and Spice: Sexuality and Adolescent Girls*, London, Routledge.

Lees, S. (1996) 'Unreasonable doubt: the outcomes of rape trials' in M. Hester, L. Kelly and J. Radford (eds) *Women, Violence and Male Power*, Buckingham, Open University Press.

Lees, S. and J. Gregory (1993) *Rape and Sexual Assault: A Study of Attrition*, London, Islington Council.

Levy, A. (1995) 'Police investigate 80 social workers in a child sex enquiry' *Sunday Times*, 12 March 1995, 6.

Lind, C. and C. Butler (1995) 'The legal abuse of homosexual children?' *Journal of Child Law*, 7(1), pp.3–9.

Lishman, J. (1994) *Communication in Social Work*, Basingstoke, Macmillan.

Lloyd, R. (1979) *Playland: A Study of Human Exploitation*, London, Quartet Books.

Logan, J. and S. Kershaw (1994) 'Heterosexism and social work education: the invisible challenge' *Social Work Education* 13(3), pp.61–80.

Logan, J., S. Kershaw, K. Karban, S. Mills, J. Trotter and M. Sinclair (1996) *Confronting Prejudice: Lesbian and Gay Issues in Social Work Education*, Aldershot, Arena.

London Rape Crisis Centre (1984) *Sexual Violence: The Reality for Women*, London, The Women's Press.

Lupton, C. (1992) 'Feminism, managerialism and performance management' in M. Langan and L. Day (eds) *Women, Oppression and Social Work: Issues in Anti-Discriminatory Practice*, London, Routledge.

Lyon, C. (1997) 'Children abused within the care system' in N. Parton (ed.) *Child Protection and Family Support: Tensions, Contradictions and Possibilities*, London, Routledge.

MacLeod, M. and E. Saraga (1988) 'Challenging the orthodoxy; towards a feminist theory and practice' *Feminist Review Special Issue on Child Sexual Abuse*, 28, pp.16–55.

McColl, A. and R. Hargreaves (1993) 'Explaining sex offending in court reports', *Probation Journal*, 40(1), pp.15–21.

McCollum, H. (1998) 'What the papers say', *Trouble and Strife*, 37, pp.31–9.

McCracken, S. and I. Reilly (1998) 'The systemic family approach to foster care assessment: a review and update' *Adoption and Fostering*, 22 (3), p 16.

McFadyen, A., H. Hanks and C. James (1993) 'Ritual abuse; a definition' *Child Abuse Review*, 2(1), pp.35–41.

McIntosh, M. (1988) 'Introduction to an issue: family secrets as public drama', *Feminist Review Special Issue on Child Sexual Abuse*, 28, pp.6–15.

McKegany, N., M. Barnard and M. Bloor (1990) 'A comparison between HIV related risk behaviour and risk reduction between female working prostitutes and male rent boys in Glasgow', *Sociology of Health and Illness*, 12(3) pp.274–92.

McKegany, N. and M. Barnard (1996) *Sex Work on the Streets: Prostitutes and their Clients*, Buckingham, Open University Press.

McKegany, N. and M. Bloor (1990) 'A risky business', *Community Care*, 5 July 1990, pp.26–7.

McMillen, C. (1991) 'Sexual identity issues related to homosexuality in the residential treatment of adolescents', *Residential Treatment for Children* and *Youth*, 9(2), pp.5–21.

McMullan, R. J. (1987) 'Youth prostitution: a balance of power', *Journal of Adolescence*, 10(1), pp.35–43.

McMullan, R. J. (1988) 'Boys involved in prostitution', *Youth and Policy*, 23, pp.39–41.

McMullen, R. J. U. (1990) *Male Rape*, London, Gay Men's Press.

McNaron, T. and Y. Morgan (1982) *Voices in the Night*, New York, Cleis Press.

Makrinioti, D. (1994) 'Conceptualization of childhood in a welfare state: a critical reappraisal' in J. Qvortrup, M. Bardy, G. Sgritta and H. Wintersburger (eds) *Childhood Matters: Social Theory, Practice and Politics* European Centre, Aldershot, Avebury.

Manon, I. G., J. Mcintyre, P. Firestone, M. Liaezinsksa, R. Ensom and G. Wells (1996) 'Secondary traumatization in parents following the disclosure of extrafamilial child sexual abuse; initial effects', *Child Abuse and Neglect*, 20 (11), pp.1095–109.

Mark, P. (1992) 'Training staff to work with sex offenders' *Probation Journal*, 39(1), pp.7–13.

Mark, R. (1996*) Research Made Simple: A Handbook for Social Workers,* Thousand Oaks, California, Sage.

Markham, L. (1997) 'Media Issues', *Notanews*, 22, pp.6–8.

Martinson, F. M. (1994) *The Sexual life of Children*, London, Bergin and Garvey.

Mason-John, V. and A. Okorrowa (1995) 'A minefield in the garden: Black lesbian sexuality' in V. Mason-John (ed.) *Talking Black: Lesbians of African and Asian Descent Speak* Out, London, Casson.

Masson, J. (1984) *The Assault on Truth: Freud's Suppression of the Seduction Theory,* London, Penguin.

Mathews, R., J. Kinder Mathews and K. Speltz (1989) *Female Sexual Offenders: An Exploratory Study,* Vermont, The Safer Society Press.

MESMAC (1990) *Men Who Have Sex With Men: Action in the Community. First Report,* London, MESMAC.

Miles, R. (1989) *The Women's History of the World*, London, Paladin.

Millard, L. (1994) 'Between ourselves: experiences of a women's group on sexuality and sexual abuse' in A. Craft (ed.) *Sexuality and Learning Disabilities,* London, Routledge.

Miller, P., M. L. Plant, M. A. Plant and J. Duffy (1995) 'Alcohol, tobacco, illicit drugs and sex: an analysis of risky behaviours among young adults', *International Journal of Addiction*, 30, pp.239–58.

Miller-Pietroni, M. (1998) 'Beyond the bureauprofessional: observational study as a vehicle for interprofessional learning and user-centred practice in community care' in P. Le Riche and K. Tanner (eds) *Observation and its Application to Social Work*, London, Jessica Kingsley.

Millett, K. (1971) *Sexual Politics*, London, Hart-Davis.

Mills, S. (1995) 'Creating a safe environment in residential child care' in K. Stone and I. Vallender (eds.) *Spinning Plates – Practice Teaching and Learning for the Residential Child Care Initiative*, London, CCETSW.

Mills, S. and K. Karban (1996) *Developing Feminist Practice in Residential Child Care: Swimming Against the Tide?* Paper given at 'Feminism and Social Work in the Year 2000: Conflicts and Controversies' Conference, University of Bradford, October 1996.

Milner, C. and R. Milner (1972) *Black Players*, Boston, Little Brown.

Milner, J. (1996) 'Men's resistance to social workers', in B. Fawcett, B. Featherstone, J. Hearn and C. Toft (eds) *Violence and Gender Relations*, London, Sage.

Mollon, P. (1994) 'The impact of evil' in V. Sinason (ed.) *Treating Survivors of Satanist Abuse*, London, Routledge.

Mollon, P. (1996) *Multiple Selves, Multiple Voices: Working with Trauma, Violence and Dissociation*, Chichester, John Wiley.

Monk-Shepherd, R. (1995) 'Mediation in prison following incest' *Probation Journal*, 42(1), pp.26–30.

Moore, S. and D. Rosenthal (1993) *Sexuality in Adolescence*, London, Routledge.

Moran-Ellis, J. (1996) 'Close to home: the experience of researching child sexual abuse' in M. Hester, L. Kelly and J. Radford (eds) *Women, Violence and Male Power*, Buckingham, Open University Press.

Morgan, R. (1978) *Going Too Far: The Personal Chronicle of a Feminist*, New York, Vintage Books.

Morgan, R. (1989) *'The Demon Lover' On the Sexuality of Terrorism*, London, Methuen.

Morgan-Thomas, R., M. Plant and M. R. Plant (1990) 'Alcohol, AIDS and sex industry clients: results from a Scottish study', *Drug and Alcohol Dependence*, 26, pp.265–9.

Morris, J. (1995) *Gone Missing? A Research and Policy Review of Disabled Children Living Away from their Families*, London, Who Cares? Trust.

Morrison, T. (1992) 'Managing sex offenders: the challenge for managers' *Probation Journal*, 39(3), pp.122–8.

Mrazek, P., M. Lynch and A. Ben-Tovim (1983) 'Sexual abuse of children in the United Kingdom' *Child Abuse and Neglect*, 7, pp.147–53.

Mullender, A. (1996) *Rethinking Domestic Violence: The Social Work and Probation Response*, London, Routledge.

Mullender, A. and R. Morley (eds) (1994) *Children Living with Domestic Violence: Putting Men's Abuse of Women on the Child Care Agenda*, London, Whiting and Birch.

Mullender, A. and C. Humphreys (1999) *Domestic Violence and Child Abuse: Policy and Practice Issues for Local authorities and Other Agencies*, London, LGA Publications.

Myers, J. (1994) *The Backlash: Child Protection Under Fire*, California, Sage.

Nash, C. and D. West *(1985)* 'Sexual molestation of young girls' in D. West (ed.)

Sexual Victimisation, London, Gower.

Nataf, Z. I. (1996) *Lesbians Talk: Transgender*, London, Scarlet Press.

National Children's Homes (1992) *The Report of the Committee of Enquiry into Children and Young People who Sexually Abuse Other Children*, London, NCH.

National Children's Homes (1996) *Hearing the Truth: the Importance of Listening to Children who Disclose Sexual Abuse*, London, NCH Action for Children.

National Curriculum Council (1990) *Curriculum Guidance 5: Health Education*, Department for Education, London, HMSO.

National Youth In Care Project (1987) *Who Cares What I have to Say, Nobody Cares, Nobody Knew*, York, In Care Network.

Nava, M. (1988) 'Cleveland and the press: outrage and anxiety in the reporting of child sexual abuse', *Feminist Review Special Issue on Child Sexual Abuse*, 28, pp.103–21.

Nelson, S. (1982) *Incest: Fact and Myth*, Edinburgh, Stramullion Press.

Nelson, S. (1987) *Incest: Fact and Myth* (2nd edn), Edinburgh, Stramullion Press.

Nelson, S. (1996) *Satanist ritual abuse: challenges to the mental health system.* Paper presented at RAINS conference, 'Better the Devil you Know?' University of Warwick, 13–14 September 1996.

Nelson, S. (1998) 'Time to break professional silences', *Child Abuse Review*, 7 (3), pp.144–53.

Newman, C. (1989) *Young Runaways. Findings from Britain's First Safe House*, London, The Children's Society.

NSPCC (1995) *So Who Are We Meant to Trust Now?* London, NSPCC.

Oakley, A. (1972) *Sex, Gender and Society*, London, Temple Smith.

Oakley, A. (1974) *The Sociology of Housework*, Oxford, Martin Robertson.

O'Connell Davidson, J. (1995) 'British sex tourists in Thailand' in M. Maynard and J. Purvis (eds) *(Hetero) Sexual Politics*, London, Taylor and Francis.

Offshe, R. and E. Waters (1994) *Making Monsters*, New York, Scribner.

O'Hare, T., C. L. Williams and A. Ezoviski (1996) 'Fear of AIDS and homophobia: implications for direct practice and advocacy', *Social Work*, 41(1), pp.51–8.

Olafson, E., D. L. Corwin and R. Summit (1993) 'Modern history of child sexual abuse awareness: cycles of discovery and suppression', *Child Abuse and Neglect*, 17, pp.7–24.

Olesen, V. (1994) 'Feminisms and models of qualitative research' in N. K. Denzin and Y. Lincoln (eds) *Handbook of Qualitative Research*, London, Sage.

O' Neill, M. (1994) *Feminising Theory/Theorising Sex: Researching the Needs of Young People In Care.* Paper given at British Sociological Association Annual Conference, 'Sexualities in Context', University of Central Lancashire, March, 1994.

O'Neill, M., N. Goode and K. Hopkins (1995) 'Juvenile prostitution: the experience of young women in residential care', *Childright*, January 1995, pp.14–16.

Open Learning Foundation, (1994) *Social Work with Children and Families*, Birmingham, BASW.

Orr, M. (1997) 'Response to the Royal College of Psychiatrists' report on recovered memory', *Action Against Child Sexual Abuse*, 27/28, pp.3–4.

Otway, O. (1996) 'Social work with children and families: from child welfare to child protection' in N. Parton (ed.) *Social Theory, Social Change and Social Work;* London, Routledge.

Pahl, J. (1985) 'Refuges for battered women: ideology and action', *Feminist*

Review, 19, pp.25–43.

Parkin, W. (1989) 'Private experiences in the public domain: sexuality and residential care organizations' in J. Hearn, D. L. Sheppard, P. Tancred-Sheriff and G. Burrell (eds) *The Sexuality of Organization*, London, Sage.

Parkin, W. and L. Green (1994) *Sexuality and Residential Care: Research in Progress*, paper given at British Sociological Association Annual Conference, 'Sexualities in Context', University of Central Lancashire, March 1994.

Parton, C. (1990) 'Women, gender oppression and child abuse' in The Violence Against Children Study Group (eds) *Taking Child Abuse Seriously*, London, Unwin Hyman.

Parton, N. (1996) 'Child protection, family support and social work: a critical appraisal of the Department of Health research studies in child protection', *Child and Family Social Work*, 1(i), pp.3–11.

Parton, N. (1996) (ed.) *Social Theory, Social Change and Social Work*, London, Routledge.

Parton, N., D. Thorpe and C. Wattam (1997) *Child Protection, Risk and the Moral Order*, London, Macmillan.

Pateman, C. (1989) *The Disorder of Women*, Cambridge, Polity Press.

Patterson, C. J. (1992) 'Children of lesbian and gay parents', *Child Development*, 63, pp.1025–42.

Patterson, C. J. (1995) 'Lesbian mothers, gay fathers, and their children' in A. R. D'Augelli and C. Patterson (eds) *Lesbian, Gay and Bisexual Identities over the Lifespan*, Oxford, Oxford University Press.

Patton, M. Q. (ed.) (1991) *Family Sexual Abuse*, London, Sage.

Payne, M. (1997) *Modern Social Work Theory*, London, Macmillan.

Pecnik, N. and M. Miskulin (1996) 'Psychosocial assistance to refugee and displaced women in Croatia' *Groupwork*, 9(3), pp.328–51.

Pellegrin, A. and W. O. Wagner (1990) 'Child sexual abuse: factors affecting victims' removal from home' *Child Abuse and Neglect*, 14, pp.53–60.

Perry, T. (1993) 'Congruent behaviour: male worker and sex offender' *Probation Journal*, 40(3), pp.140–2.

Peterson, R. F., S. M. Basta and T. A. Dykstra (1993) 'Mothers of molested children: some comparisons of personality characteristics' *Child Abuse and Neglect*, 17, pp.409–18.

Phillips, M. (1993) 'Oppressive urge to stop oppression'. *The Observer*, 1 August 1993, 3.

Phoenix, A. (1994) 'Research: positioned differently? Issues of 'race', difference and commonality', *Changes*, 12(4), pp.299–305.

Pilkington, B. and J. Kremer (1995) 'A Review of the epidemiological research on child sexual abuse' *Child Abuse Review*, 4(2), pp.84–98.

Pithers, W. D. (1994) *Treatment of Sex Offenders*, Conference Speech, Birmingham, England, September 1994.

Plant, M. (ed.) (1990) *AIDS, Drugs and Prostitution*, London, Routledge.

Plant, M., M. Plant, D. Peck and J. Sellers (1989) The sex industry, alcohol and illicit drugs: implications for the spread of HIV infection, *British Journal of Addiction* 84, pp.53–9.

Plant, M. L., M. A. Plant and R. M. Thomas (1990) 'Alcohol, AIDS risks and commercial sex: some preliminary results from a Scottish study', *Drug, Alcohol* and *Dependency*, 25 February 1990, (1), pp.51–5.

Plant, M. and M. Plant (1992) *Risk Takers: Alcohol Drugs Sex and Youth*, London, Routledge.

Plummer, K. (1996) 'Foreword' to W. Simon, *Postmodern Sexualities*, London, Routledge.

Pringle, K. (1990) *Managing to Survive: Developing a Resource for Sexually Abused Young People*, Newcastle upon Tyne, Barnardos.

Pringle, K. (1997) *Men as Workers in Professional Child Care Settings: An Anti-Oppressive Practice Framework*, paper presented at an international seminar, 'Men as Workers in Services for Young Children: Issues of a Mixed Gender Workforce', London, Thomas Coram Research Institute, May 1997.

Pringle, K. (1998) 'Men and childcare: policy and practice' in J. Popay, J. Hearn and J. Edwards (eds) *Men, Gender Divisions* and *Welfare*, London, Routledge.

Pritchard, C. (1998) 'Matter of life and death' *Community Care*, 14–20 May 1998, pp.20–21.

Proctor E. (1994) 'Sex offender programmes: do they work?' *Probation Journal* 41(1), pp.31–2.

Proctor, E. and F. Flaxington (1996) 'Progressing work with sex offenders', *Probation Journal*, 43(4), pp.216–17.

Qvortrup, J., M. Bardy, O. Sgrifta and H. Wintersburger (1994) (eds) *Childhood Matters, Social Theory, Practice and Politics*, European Centre, Aldershot, Avebury.

Radford, J, (1994) 'History of the Women's Liberation Movement in Britain: A Reflective Personal Account' in G. Griffin, M. Hester, S. Rai and S. Roseneil (eds) *Stirring It: Challenges for Feminism*, London, Taylor and Francis.

Radford, J. and L. Kelly (1995) 'Self preservation: feminist activism and feminist jurisprudence' in M. Maynard and J. Purvis (eds) *(Hetero)sexual Politics*, London, Taylor and Francis.

Radford, J., L. Kelly and M. Hester (1996) 'Introduction' in M. Hester, L. Kelly and J. Radford (1996) *Women, Violence and Male Power*, Buckingham, Open University Press.

Rafferty, J. (1997) 'Ritual denial', *The Guardian*, 22 March 1997, pp.26–35.

Redding, D. (1989) 'Reaching out to the rent scene' *Community Care*, 20 April 1989, pp.24–6.

Rees, G. (1993) *Hidden Truth: Young People's Experience of Running Away*, London, The Children's Society.

Rich, A. (1977) *Of Woman Born: Motherhood as experience and institution*, London, Virago.

Rich, A. (1984) 'Compulsory heterosexuality and lesbian existence' in A. Snitow, C. Stansell and S. Thompson (eds) *Introducing Women's Studies*, London, Macmillan

Richardson, D. (1994) 'Lesbians, HIV and AIDS' in L. Doyal, J. Naidoo and T. Wilton (eds) *AIDS: Setting a Feminist Agenda*, London, Taylor and Francis.

Richardson, D. (1996) '"Misguided, dangerous and wrong": on the maligning of radical feminism', in R. Klein and D. Bell (eds) *Radically Speaking: Feminism Reclaimed*, London, Zed Books.

Richardson, S. and H. Bacon (eds) (1991) *Child Sexual Abuse: Whose Problem?*, Birmingham, Venture Press.

Richardson, S. (1998) *Maintaining Awareness of Unspeakable Truths: Responses to Child Abuse in the Longer-Term*, paper presented at 'Trade in People,

Abductions and Abuse of Children in the European Union: Problems and Solutions Conference', European Parliament, Brussels, 15–16 October 1998.

Rights of Women Lesbian Custody Group (1986) *Lesbian Mothers' Legal Handbook*, London, The Women's Press.

Rivers, I. (1995) 'The victimization of gay teenagers in schools: homophobia in education', *Pastoral Care*, March, pp.35–41.

Roberts, B. (1996) *Deception, Tricks and Lies*, paper presented to RAINS conference, 'Better the Devil You Know?' University of Warwick, 13–14 September 1996.

Roberts, H. (1981) *Doing Feminist Research*. London, Routledge and Kegan Paul.

Roberts, J. (1995) 'Caught up in the whirlpool', *The Guardian*, 11 January 1995, 3.

Robson, C. (1993) *Real World Research*, Oxford, Blackwell.

Robson, R. (1994a) 'Resisting the family: repositioning lesbians in legal theory', *Signs*, Summer, pp.975–96.

Robson, R. (1994b) 'Mother: the legal domestication of lesbian existence' in C. Card (ed.) *Adventures in Lesbian Philosophy*, Indiana, Indiana University.

Rojek, C., G. Peacock and S. Collins (1989) *Social Work and Received Ideas*, London, Routledge.

Rose, J. and C. Jones (1994) 'Working with parents' in A. Craft (ed.) *Sexuality and Learning Disabilities*, London, Routledge.

Rowbotham, S. (1983) *Dreams and Dilemmas*, London, Virago.

Rush, F. (1980) *The Best Kept Secret: Sexual Abuse of Children*, New York, McGraw Hill.

Rush, F. (1990) 'The many faces of backlash' in D. Leidholdt and J. G. Raymond (eds) *The Sexual Liberals* and *the Attack on Feminism*, Oxford, Pergamon Press.

Russell, D. E. H. (1983) 'The incidence and prevalence of intrafamilial and extrafamilial abuse of female children' *Child Abuse and Neglect*, 7, pp.133–46.

Russell, D. E. H. (1996) 'Between a rock and a hard place: the politics of white feminists conducting research on black women in South Africa' in S. Wilkinson and C. Kitzinger (eds) *Representing the Other*, London, Sage.

Russell, D. (1995) *Women, Madness and Medicine:* Cambridge, Polity Press

Ryan, G. (1990) 'Developing integrated treatment programmes' *Audiotapes of ROTA Conference*, NOTA.

Sabor, M. (1992) 'The sex offender treatment programme in prisons' *Probation Journal*, 39(1), pp.14–18.

SAFE 'Safe Contact: Newsletter supporting survivors of ritual abuse', available quarterly from SAFE, PO Box 1557, Salisbury, Wilts SP1 2TP.

Saleebey, D. (1996) 'The strengths perspective in social work practice: extensions and cautions' *Journal of National Association of Social Workers*, 41(3), pp.241–336.

Sanderson, T. *(1995) Mediawatch*, London, Cassell.

Sandford, J. (1977) *Prostitutes*, London, Abacus.

Sandfort, T. (1987) 'Paedophilia and the gay movement', *Journal of Homosexuality*, 13, pp.89–110.

Sands, R. and K. Nuccio (1992) 'Postmodern feminist theory and social work', *Journal of National Association of Social Workers*, 37(6), pp.481–576.

Sanford, L. T. (1991) *Strong at the Broken Places*, London, Virago.

Sangster, J. (1998) *Representing and Understanding Violence Against Children in Ontario, 1916–1926*, paper given at 'Child Welfare and Social Action'

Conference, University of Liverpool, July 1998.

Saphira, M. (1987) *For Your Child's Sake*, London, Reed Books.

Saradjian, J. (1996) *Women Who Sexually Abuse Children*, West Sussex, John Wiley.

Savin-Williams, R. C. (1995) 'Lesbian, gay male, and bisexual adolescents' in A. R. D'Augelli and C. J. Patterson. (eds) *Lesbian, Gay and Bisexual Identities Over the Lifespan*, Oxford, Oxford University.

Scambler, G. and A. Scambler (eds) *Rethinking Prostitution: Purchasing Sex in the 1990s*, London, Routledge.

Sereny, G. (1986) *The Invisible Children: Child Prostitution in America, West Germany and Britain*, London, Pan Books.

Shaw, I. and I. Butler (1998) 'Understanding young people and prostitution: a foundation for practice', *British Journal of Social Work*, 28, pp.177–96.

Sheath, M. (1990) '"Confrontative" work with sex offenders. legitimised nonce bashing?' *Probation Journal*, 37(3), pp.159–62.

Sheik, S. (1986) 'An Asian Mothers' Self-Help Group' in S. Ahmed, J. Cheetham and J. Small (eds) *Social Work with Black Children and Their Families*, London, Batsford.

Showalter, E. (1987) *The Female Malady*, London, Virago.

Sigma Research (1996) *Behaviourally Bisexual Men in the UK: Identifying Needs for HIV Prevention*, London, Health Education Authority.

Silbert, M. H. and A. M. Pines (1981) 'Sexual abuse as an antecedent to prostitution', *Child Abuse and Neglect*, 5, pp.407–11.

Silbert, M. H. and A. M. Pines (1983) 'Early sexual exploitation as an influence in prostitution', *Social Work* , July/August, pp.285–9.

Skeates, J. and D. Jabri (eds) (1988) *Fostering and Adoption by Lesbians and Gay Men*, London, Strategic Policy Unit.

Smart, C. (1989) *Feminism and the Power of Law*, London, Routledge.

Smith, G. (1994) 'Parent, partner, protector: conflicting role demands for mothers of sexually abused children' in T. Morrison, M. Erooga and R. Beckett (eds) *Sexual Offending Against Children: Assessment and Treatment of Abusers*, London, Routledge.

Social Services Inspectorate (1998) *Partners in Planning: Approaches to Planning Services for Children and their Families*, London, Department of Health.

Sone, K. (1993) 'Coming out at work', *Community Care*, 7 October 1993, pp.18–19.

Sorensen, T. and B. Snow (1991) 'How children tell: the process of disclosure in child sexual abuse', *Child Welfare*, 70(1), pp.3–15.

Southall Black Sisters (1990) *Against the Grain: a Celebration of Survival and Struggle, 1979–1989*, London, Southall Black Sisters.

Sparks, I. (1997) 'Brutal game of life', *The Guardian*, 8 October 1997.

Spencer, A. (1997) 'Putting one's head above the parapet: professionally speaking', *Notanews*, 24, pp.10–18.

Spencer, H. and R. Flin (1993) *The Evidence of Children – The Law and Psychology* (2nd edn), London, Blackstone Press.

Spender, D. (1982) *Man Made Language*, London, Routledge.

Spring, J. (1987) *Cry Hard and Swim*, London, Virago.

Stardancer, C. (1996) *Ritual Abuse: The Exploitation of Myth*, Paper presented to the RAINS conference, 'Better the Devil You Know?' University of Warwick,

13–14 September 1996.

Stein, M. (1992) *The Abuses and Uses of Residential Child Care*, Paper presented to 'Surviving Childhood Adversity' Conference, Dublin, 2–5 July, 1992.

Stein, M., N. Frost and G. Rees (1994) *Running the Risk: Young people on the Streets of Britain Today*, London, The Children's Society.

Strathdee, R. and M. Johnson (1994) *Out of Care and On the Streets Young People – Care Leavers and Homelessness*, London, Centrepoint.

Streetwise Youth Project (1991) *Streetwise Youth Annual Report*, London, Streetwise Youth Project.

Stone, M. (1990) *Young People Leaving Care*, Redhill, The Royal Philanthropic Society.

Sullivan, T. R. (1994) 'Obstacles to effective child welfare service with gay and lesbian youths', *Child Welfare*, LXXIII (4), pp.291–304.

Summit, R. (1983) 'The child sexual abuse accommodation syndrome' *Child Abuse and Neglect*, 17, pp.177–93.

Summit, R. C. (1988) 'Hidden victims, hidden pain; societal avoidance of child sexual abuse' in G. E. Wyaff and G. J. Powell (eds) *Lasting Effects of Child Sexual Abuse*, California, Sage.

Suriyaprakasam, S. (1995) 'Some of us are younger' in Mason-John, V. (ed.) *Talking Black: Lesbians of African and Asian Descent Speak* Out, London, Casson.

Swann, S. (1997) *Barnardos Street and Lanes Project Report*, Ilford, Barnardos.

Swann, S. (1998) 'Barnardo's Streets and Lanes Project' in *Whose Daughter Next? Children Abused through Prostitution*, Ilford, Barnardos.

Swannell, J. (ed.) (1986) *The Little Oxford Dictionary*, Oxford, Oxford University.

Tasker, F. L. and S. Golombok (1991) 'Children raised by lesbian mothers: the empirical evidence', *Family Law*, May, pp.184–7.

Tate, T. (1991) *Children for the Devil*, London, Methuen.

Taylor-Browne, J. (1997) 'Obfuscating child sexual abuse 1: the identification of social problems' *Child Abuse Review*, 6(1), pp.4–10.

Thompson, N. (1993) *Anti-Discriminatory Practice*, London, Macmillan.

Tomlinson, D. R., R. J. Hiliman and J. R. Harris (1989) 'Setting up a support service for male prostitutes in London' *International Journal of Sexually Transmitted Diseases and AIDS*, 1 September 1989, (5), pp.360–1.

Trenchard, L. and H. Warren (1984) *Something to Tell You: The Experiences* and *Needs of Young Lesbians and Gay Men in London*, London, London Gay Teenage Group.

Trotter, J. (1996) 'Illusive Partnerships: Gender and Sexuality Issues Relating to Child Sexual Abuse and Child Protection Practices', Paper given at ISPCAN Conference, Dublin, August 1996.

Trotter, J. (1997) 'The failure of social work researchers, teachers and practitioners to acknowledge or engage non-abusing fathers: a preliminary discussion', *Social Work Education Special Issue on Child Protection*, 16(2), pp.63–76.

Trotter, J. (1998a) *No One's Listening: Mothers, Fathers and Child Sexual Abuse*, London, Whiting and Birch.

Trotter, J. (1998b) 'Learning and practising, or just saying the words?' *Journal of Practice Teaching in Health* and *Social Work*, 1(2), pp.31–47.

Trotter, J. (1998c) *Pass, Fail or Bypass: Avoiding and Assuming Children's Sexuality in Schools*, paper presented at 'Child Welfare and Social Action' Conference,

University of Liverpool, July 1998.

Trotter, J. and J. Gilchrist (1996) 'Assessing DipSW students: anti-discriminatory practice in relation to lesbian and gay issues' *Social Work Education*, 15(1), pp.75–82.

Trowell, J., I. Kolvin, M. Berelowitz, T.Weeramanthri, H. Sadowski, A. Rushton, G. Miles, D. Glaser, A. Elton, M. Rustin and M. Hunter (1998) 'Psychotherapy Outcome Study for Sexually Abused Girls' in Jones, D. and P. Ramchandani (eds) *Child Sexual Abuse: Informing Practice from Research*, Abingdon, Radcliffe Medical Press.

Trudell, B. N. (1993) *Doing Sex Education*, London, Routledge.

Tymchuk, A. (1992) 'Predicting adequacy of parenting by parents with mental retardation' *Child Abuse and Neglect* 16, pp.165–178.

Tymchuk, A. and L. Andron (1992) 'Project parenting: child interactional training with mothers who are mentally handicapped' *Mental Handicap Research*, 5(1), pp.4–32.

Utting, W (1991) *Children in the Public Care, A Review of Residential Child Care*, London, HMSO.

Utting, W. (1997) *People Like Us: The Report of the Review of the Safeguards for Children Living Away from Home*, London, HMSO.

Vance, C. (1992) 'Social construction theory: problems in the history of sexuality' in H. Crowley and S. Himmelweit (eds) *Knowing Women: Feminism and Knowledge*, Buckingham, Open University Press.

Vine, S. (1996) 'Abusers jailed in paedophile crackdown', *The Independent*, 31 July 1996, 15.

Waldby, C., A. Clancy, J. Emetchi and C. Summerfeld (1989) 'Theoretical perspectives on father–daughter incest' in E. Driver and A. Droisen (eds) *Child Sexual Abuse, Feminist Perspectives*, London, Macmillan.

Walkerdine, V. (1997) *Daddy's Girl: Young Girls and Popular Culture*, Basingstoke, Macmillan

Ward, E. (1984) *Father–Daughter Rape*, London, The Women's Press.

Warner, N. (1992) *Choosing With Care – The Report of the Select Committee of Inquiry into the Selection, Development and Management of Staff in Children's Homes*, London, HMSO.

Warner, S. (1996) 'Constructing femininity: models of child sexual abuse and the production of "women"' in, E. Burman, P. Aldered, K. Bewley, B. Goldberg, C. Heenan, D. Marks, J. Marshall, K. Taylor, R. Ullah and S. Warner (eds) *Challenging Women, Pschology's Exclusions; Feminist Possibilities*, Buckingham, Open University Press.

Wattam, C. (1992) *Making A Case in Child Protection*, London, Longman/NSPCC.

Weeks, J. (1986) *Sexuality*, London, Routledge.

Weick, A., A. Rapp, P. Sullivan and W. Kisthardt (1989) 'A strengths perspective for social work practice', *Journal of National Association of Social Workers*, 34(4), pp.289–384.

Westcott, H. (1991) *Institutional Abuse of Children – From Research to Policy*, London, NSPCC.

Westcott, H. (1993) *Abuse of Children and Adults with Disability*, London, NSPCC.

Westcott, H. (1995) 'Perceptions of child protection casework: views from children, parents and practitioners' in C. Cloke and M. Davies (eds) *Participation and Empowerment in Child Protection*, London, Pitman.

Westcott, H. and C. Merry (1996) *This Far and No Further: Towards Ending the Abuse of Disabled Children*, Birmingham, Venture Press.

White, C. (1992) 'A T.A. approach to child sex abusers' *Probation Journal*, 39(1), pp.36–40.

White, K. (1987) 'Residential care for adolescents: residents, carers and sexual issues' in G. Horobin (ed.) *Sex; Gender* and *Care Work*, London, Jessica Kingsley.

Williams, F. (1992) 'Women with learning difficulties are women too' in M. Langan and L. Day (eds) *Women, Oppression and Social Work: Issues in Anti-Discriminatory Practice*, London, Routledge.

Williams, F. (1996) 'Postmodernism, feminism and the question of difference' in N. Parton (ed.) *Social Theory, Social Change and Social Work*, London, Routledge.

Williams, F. (1997) 'Presentation of 'Work in Progress', *Seminar Series*, University of Liverpool, 11 June 1997.

Williams, P. J. (1997) *Seeing a Colour-Blind Future: The Paradox of Race*, London, Virago.

Wilson, M. (1993) *Crossing The Boundary: Black Women Survive Incest*, London, Virago.

Winn, S., D. Roker and J. Coleman (1995) 'Knowledge about puberty and sexual development in 11–16 year-olds: implications for health and sex education in schools', *Educational Studies*, 21(2), pp.187–201.

Wise, S. (1995) 'Feminist ethics in practice' in R. Hugman and D. Smith (eds) *Ethical Issues in Social Work*, London, Routledge.

Wyatt, G. E. (1985) ' The sexual abuse of Afro-American and white women in childhood' in D. Finkelhor (ed.) (1986) *A Sourcebook on Child Sexual Abuse*, California, Sage.

Wykes, M. (1995) 'Passion, marriage and murder analysing the press discourse' in R. E. Dobash, R. Dobash and L. Noakes (eds) *Gender and Crime*, Cardiff, University of Wales Press.

Wynn Davies, P. (1996) 'Insurers tried to halt child abuse inquiry' *The Independent*, 5 April 1996.

Young, W., R. Sachs, B. Braun and R. Watkins (1991) 'Patients reporting ritual abuse in childhood: a clinical syndrome: Report of 37 Cases', *Child Abuse and Neglect*, 15(3), pp.181–9.

Younghusband, E. (1981) *The Newest Profession A Short History of Social Work*, London, Community Care/IPC Business Press.

Youngson, S. (1994) 'Ritual abuse: the personal and professional cost for workers' in V. Sinason (ed.) *Treating Survivors of Satanist Abuse*, London, Routledge.

Index